THE DYNAMICS OF RACE RELATIONS

A SOCIOLOGICAL ANALYSIS

Graham C. Kinloch

Florida State University

McGraw-Hill Book Company

*New York   St. Louis   San Francisco   Düsseldorf
Johannesburg   Kuala Lumpur   London   Mexico
Montreal   New Delhi   Panama   Paris   São Paulo
Singapore   Sydney   Tokyo   Toronto*

The Dynamics of Race Relations
A Sociological Analysis

1 2 3 4 5 6 7 8 9 0 M U M U 7 9 8 7 6 5 4

This book was set in Times Roman by Black Dot, Inc. The editors were
David Edwards and John M. Morriss; the designer was Joseph Gillians; and
the production supervisor was Thomas J. LoPinto. The drawings were
done by ANCO Technical Services.
The Murray Printing Company was printer and binder.

Library of Congress Cataloging in Publication Data

Kinloch, Graham Charles.
    The dynamics of race relations.

    Includes bibliographies.
    1. Race problems. I. Title.
HT1521.K48   301.45'1042   73-18184
ISBN 0-07-034735-2

To Umtali,
my one and
only home

Contents

SECTION THREE   AN ANALYTICAL FRAMEWORK

SECTION FOUR   THE FRAMEWORK APPLIED

SECTION FIVE   CONCLUSIONS

Preface

Race relations have been a central focus of sociology for many decades. Implicitly, from early discussions of power and stratification to contemporary analyses dealing explicitly with the societal operation of discrimination, racial data have provided sociologists with an important index of the relative flexibility of a social structure and the social processes at work within it.

However, discussion in this field has been and, in my opinion, continues to be hampered by a number of distinct problems: (1) ideologically it has reflected the values of America's white elite and has served their interests rather than attempting objective analysis; (2) its focus has been primarily on attitudes rather than on the social structure behind them, i.e., an emphasis on prejudice rather than on the structure of discrimination; (3) rather than attempting to be theoretical and explanatory, it has concentrated on descriptive accounts of attitudes and discrimination in particular settings; in the past, at least, this field has tended toward the atheoretical; (4) when theory has developed, a trichotomy of perspectives (i.e., psychological, social-psychological, and sociological) has evolved in relative isolation, rather than the development of a general theory; and (5) a further problem of the theory which has developed is its typological, static qualities, resulting in an ability to describe societies in general terms but not in terms of the ongoing dynamics of race relations within them.

Perceiving the above problems as well as the field's potential development, this book represents a modest attempt to develop a general theory of race relations applicable intra- and intersocietally, based on the colonial model and applied to relations at the individual (i.e., attitudinal), group (i.e., intergroup), and societal (i.e., dominant elite) level. Its major aim is an understanding of the structural factors behind race relations and their ongoing dynamics both within and between societies in the hope that social policy may be based on broader and more realistic foundations than previously.

Our approach, then, attempts to be analytical rather than descriptive, sociological rather than psychological, general rather than specific, and structural rather than attitudinal. The aim of this approach is to reveal the major historical-social factors behind racism on a number of levels within society, drawing inspiration from the colonial model and those theoretical analyses—psychological, social—psychological, and sociological—which already exist in the research literature. It is *not* an exhaustive account of particular societies or the various minorities within them; for such data the reader is directed to other readily available material.

Furthermore, the theory developed at the end of our discussion is *tentative* and *suggestive* only—it would be presumptuous to pretend otherwise. However, it does appear to offer at least the beginnings of a framework which may prove useful in directing the field toward general analysis and explanation and away from descriptive and attitudinal studies. A great deal more research and analysis is required, however, to increase the theory's power to handle race relations at the microscopic level and social change—problems of which this writer is only too well aware. On the other hand, the literature and frameworks already available offer exciting prospects for those interested in theoretical analysis, and they provided much of the inspiration behind this text.

I am indebted to the following, in particular, for their critical insight and useful discussion in my writing:

To Professors Clarence Glick and Andrew Lind for introducing me to the major race relations literature and to the complexity of intergroup relations in Hawaii;

To faculty and students who have expressed an interest in the development of general conceptual frameworks and theories in this area;

To David Edwards of McGraw-Hill for his encouragement, help, and interest;

To Beverley for her interest, encouragement, and help; and

To Betty Sue Kurth for her patient and painstaking typing of the manuscript.

Graham C. Kinloch

THE DYNAMICS
OF RACE RELATIONS
A SOCIOLOGICAL ANALYSIS

Section One

Introduction

Chapter 1

Introduction

Interest in race relations has developed markedly in the past decade. The development of ethnic pride has resulted in an increasing awareness of the extent of racism on a societal level and in the consequent emphasis on the relevance of this field to contemporary social problems.

Perhaps more than any other factor, perceived racial differences have been behind the most bitter social conflict, exploitation, and human suffering. Increasing awareness of this has made for a marked rise in the popularity of race relations as a major topic in colleges and in the mass media. The dominant approach, however, is descriptive and rhetorical. While this is understandable, the result is a narrow focus on people's feelings, with little appreciation of the societal context in which these are defined.

Furthermore, the field of race relations continues to be dominated by an elitist perspective, i.e., the conservative view of a white elite. Such a perspective defines subordinate minorities rather than itself as the major source of the "race problem." Awareness of major societal factors—historical, economic, and sociological—behind this form of oppression is either low or nonexistent.

One of the major contributions sociology may make to this topic is an analysis of the societal context in which race relations have developed historically and have come to operate in contemporary society. Highlighting major societal factors behind race relations—individual as well as group—should serve to increase awareness of the most important factors on a number of levels in the social system, thereby contributing to the delineation of those criteria most relevant to meaningful social change. Consequently, a major focus in this work will be upon the *sociological analysis* of race relations on the *individual, group,* and *societal* level as we attempt to abstract the most relevant factors defining such relations throughout society.

APPROACH

In his discussion of race and ethnic relations, Westie has pointed to the field's wealth of research material but almost complete lack of theoretical development—an inadequacy he explains in terms of the problems of ideology, a "social action" or relevancy orientation, and "theoretical particularism."[1]

Considering the predominance of descriptive approaches to race relations, at least in the past, our own approach will be analytical and theoretical. Despite the paucity of explanatory theory in the area, there are attempts to deal with race relations on at least three levels: psychological, social-psychological, and sociological. Our major focus will be on analyzing race relations on *all* these levels, providing conceptual links where possible, and moving toward a theoretical synthesis and conceptual framework which will allow us to analyze such relations on various levels in a number of different societies. In this manner we shall attempt to be theoretical and analytical.

Social behavior may be viewed as socially organized on two

---

[1] F. R. Westie, "Race and Ethnic Relations," in R. E. L. Faris, (ed.), *Handbook of Modern Sociology*, Rand McNally, Chicago, 1964, p. 576.

major levels: the microscopic (i.e., individual and interpersonal systems) and the macroscopic (i.e., societal, colonial, economic, stratification, and power systems). Some factors overlap these two (e.g., group characteristics, social roles). In any adequate explanation of social relations it is necessary to take all three into account. We shall examine the manner in which individual, group, and societal factors define and affect race relations. Furthermore, social relations are dynamic rather than static, providing feedback into the social system, reinforcing certain factors and modifying others. Therefore, we shall take a systems approach, attempting to delineate feedback patterns that contribute to ongoing social change.[2] Thirdly, major emphasis will be placed on the manner in which race relations are based on the economic system, motivations behind it, and social change within it. Finally, we shall center our approach on three major questions:

1   What are the patterns of race relations?
2   What factors define them, and how?
3   How and why are they changing?

In this approach, strong emphasis will be placed on the extent to which a society's structure (i.e., its political, economic, and social institutions) accounts for the level of racism and patterns of race relations within it, particularly the extent to which the society has experienced the effects of a colonial elite. While this will be our major emphasis, it is important to point out that racism within most societies remains fairly strong even when these structural conditions change. The psychological rewards provided by prejudice and scapegoating, for example, play an important role for dominant elites, and feelings of racial superiority die hard. Racism thus becomes a societal tradition, reinforced by stereotypes and cultural norms.

The student should be warned, then, against assuming a simplistic explanation of racism, thereby underestimating the tenacity of prejudice and discrimination. Nevertheless, societal conditions, in our view, are the major explanatory variables in

---

[2]See W. Buckley, *Sociology and Modern Systems Theory,* Prentice-Hall, Englewood Cliffs, N.J., 1967.

our analysis of race relations, and we turn to the model we shall use in that analysis.

OUR MODEL

As we shall see, "race relations" involve a particular elite which defines certain physical differences as socially significant (e.g., the importance of "whiteness" over "blackness"). This negative social definition is translated into political policy through the subordination and exploitation of certain groups defined as "races." In this manner, a racist social system is developed on an ongoing basis by a colonial elite—i.e., an external group that migrates to another society, conquers the local population, imports other race groups for economic-labor purposes, and develops a racist economic and social structure to ensure its superordinate position. Race relations, it would appear, typically involve a process of "colonization."

Further, this process comprises two major elements: social *structure* and social *attitudes*. The former represents the racist institutional structure based on economic, political, and social inequality, while the latter comprise the racial attitudes of both elite and subordinate groups that operate at both group and individual levels. Such attitudes are defined by the social characteristics of the groups and individuals involved. From this it is evident that race relations, as reflected in a society's social structure and predominant racial attitudes, are defined by three major sets of factors: (1) sociological-societal and elite characteristics (e.g., the white political elite); (2) social-psychological–group characteristics and orientations (e.g., "black power"); and (3) psychological-individual personality factors (e.g., prejudice). We shall view race relations, then, as social interaction on societal, group, and individual levels between groups defined as races within the context of a particular social structure.

Thirdly, race relations are far from static: as we shall see, economic development (e.g., industrialization) within a racist structure leads to change in attitudes and, eventually, a modification of that structure. The social system provides its own feedback, resulting in an ongoing process of social dynamics.

According to our view, then, the dynamics of race relations involve the *ongoing interaction on individual, group, and societal levels between groups defined as races, resulting in a continuous modification of intergroup relations on both the structural and attitudinal level.*

The above model is summarized in Figure 1-1. This, in general, represents the approach we shall take to analyze race relations within a particular society and on the comparative level, with particular emphasis on the colonization process.

PROCEDURE

Our main aim is to analyze major psychological, social-psychological, and sociological factors behind various patterns of race relations on both societal and intersocietal levels of analysis. We shall complete this introductory section by discussing what a study of race relations reveals, along with methodological problems involved in their analysis. Such problems have plagued the

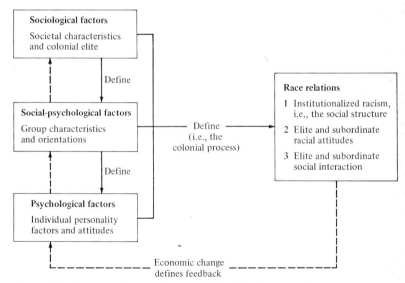

Figure 1-1   A model of major factors defining the dynamics of race relations.

development of the field from its foundation. We shall then review the field's historical development, particularly the debates
over the concept of race. Recent developments will be included.

Section Two deals with basic definitions and approaches to
the analysis of race relations. It represents the working theoretical section of the book in which we shall introduce and draw
together major approaches, working toward a general conceptual
and analytical framework. We shall examine definitions of basic
concepts and three main approaches to the field: the psychological, which identifies personality factors behind racial attitudes;
the social-psychological, examining group dynamics; and the
sociological, which explores societal characteristics, particularly
colonial factors, behind differing patterns of race relations. We
shall attempt to develop general models for each, representing
major variables and interrelationships at each level of analysis.

In Section Three we shall draw together the models we have
developed, moving toward a theoretical synthesis and analytical
framework which will deal with race relations at both microscopic and macroscopic levels. We shall develop the outline provided
in Figure 1-1 in detail before proceeding to analyze specific kinds
of race relations in the second half of the book.

Having completed our theoretical discussion, in Section
Four we shall apply the framework we have developed. In the
first chapter of the section we shall concentrate on the comparative approach, examining differing race relations in South Africa,
the United States, Brazil, and Hawaii, in order to abstract the
major sociological factors that account for highly diverse race
relations in these various societies. We shall conclude by drawing
together the major variables into a typology.

We shall concentrate next on race relations at the intrasocietal level as we examine specific groups and their interrelationships within American society. Whereas in the previous
chapter we concentrated on sociological variables, here we shall
emphasize social-psychological and psychological factors as we
examine whites, blacks, Mexicans, Indians, and Japanese in the
United States, placing particular stress on examining the colonial
position of various minority groups in the racial system. We shall
draw together the major variables into a typology of American
race relations at the conclusion of our discussion.

Section Five will present the conclusions of our analysis. Having examined various theories of race relations, developed an analytical framework and applied it on national as well as international levels, we shall attempt to move toward a broad sociological theory of race relations, incorporating the results of our analysis. Major emphasis in this section will be placed on assessing the implications of this analysis for the reduction of prejudice and discrimination and the use of race as a "role sign"[3] in general. Having initiated our discussion on a practical basis, and moving through the theoretical and analytical, we shall end on the level of sociological relevance, without which our discussion would be merely academic.

TERMINOLOGY

While we shall define basic concepts in some detail later, it is important at this point to introduce the terms we shall be using throughout our discussion to follow.

A number of terms will be used in reference to a society's elite. By "elite" we are referring to the *political* elite which controls a society's subordinate groups economically, politically, and socially. A particular group may also represent a "racial elite" in the context of a particular race relations situation. Thus, whites in the United States constitute an elite insofar as they are part of the dominant majority. We shall also characterize societies as "colonial," i.e., a migrant racial elite that subordinates an indigenous population and imports other race groups for purposes of economic exploitation. Through this process of "colonization" a "colonial social structure" is set up on a racial basis, rationalized on the grounds of superiority-inferiority. Such a social structure represents a racial caste system with the colonial elite in control. While traditionally a colonial elite has constituted a numerical minority, we shall also apply the term to a numerical majority, particularly in the case of American society. Further, with the eventual decline of the caste system, the dominant elite tends to adopt an "assimilationist" orientation toward minority groups; i.e., in order to be accepted, they must conform to that

---

[3]See M. Banton, *Race Relations,* Basic Books, New York, 1967, chap. 4.

elite culturally, politically, and socially, assimilating into the social system on the elite's own terms rather than stipulating their own criteria or asserting their independence.

A second major set of concepts refers to the term "race." By *race* we shall refer to a group which is defined as different from the elite and other minorities on the basis of perceived physical criteria. The consequences of such a social definition include awareness of subordinate group differences by the race group itself and their utilization by the elite to rationalize prejudice and discrimination. It is important to emphasize here that a race is not a physical group, but one which is perceived and defined as different on the basis of physical criteria (i.e., skin color, hair type, etc.) "Race relations," then, refer to interaction between groups socially defined as races at all levels of the social system, i.e., economic, political, and social. "Racism" refers to the acceptance and utilization of racial criteria in social action, while a "racist social structure" is one which is founded on racial criteria (i.e., perceived physical differences). "Racial prejudice" represents acceptance of racial criteria on the attitudinal level, while "racial discrimination" reflects the translation of these attitudes into behavior and political policy. Finally, "minority groups" in general are groups defined as real and different on the basis of perceived cultural and/or physical differences, with race, ethnicity, and sex being the main criteria.

We turn now to a discussion of some of the major sociological factors which a study of race relations reveals.

STUDY QUESTIONS

1 Consider the most negative examples of racism in the history of American society. What historical features do they have in common?
2 Discuss some of the most negative consequences of racism. What do you feel is behind them?
3 What factors do you feel explain why some groups have experienced more racism than others?
4 Why do you think some individuals are more racist in their attitudes than others?
5 Why do you think some societies are more racist in structure and attitudes than others (e.g., South African compared with Brazilian race relations)?

Chapter 2

The Sociological Importance of Race Relations

Before studying race relations in depth, it is important to understand what they reveal about society, i.e., their sociological significance. The first question we turn to, then, is "What do race relations reveal about society and social behavior?" Such a question is central to our discussion throughout this work. In general, race relations reveal the *shape of the social structure and the forces behind social behavior within it,* particularly the degree to which it is colonial in structure—i.e., dominated by a migrant elite for purposes of economic exploitation.

Some of the major sociological insights provided by the study of race relations relate to the society's social structure, its internal social flexibility and change. More specifically, race relations represent a number of indices as follows:

1 An Index of Social Tension Exploration of race relations within any society provides useful insight into its level and sources of social tension.[1] Often such tension is controlled and obscured by the governing elite; subordinate groups inhibit their feelings of dissatisfaction on an everyday basis. In this way, potential conflict is hidden and controlled. Examination of a minority's perception of the social structure and the legitimacy of its elite provides important information on race relations at psychological (individual) and social-psychological (group) levels of analysis. As a group's feelings of deprivation increase with economic change, so tension increases and patterns of race relations begin to change accordingly.

As Benedict has emphasized, we need to appreciate the nature of conflict and social inequality behind race relations rather than race per se, since racial conflict is but a reflection of the societal inequality behind it.[2]

Race relations, then, reflect a society's level of social tension, particularly as subordinate minorities become aware of an oppressive, colonial elite whose control of the society is based upon domination rather than legitimacy.

2 An Index of the Social Structure Race relations also provide insight into a society's social order and the nature of social bonds within it. Such relations reflect the society's social and cultural pluralism (i.e., general level of cultural and socioeconomic heterogeneity) as they are defined and controlled by a particular elite,[3] the resultant sources of conflict, and the general level of social flexibility. The degree to which a society is colonial in structure is of particular relevance to the understanding of rigid intergroup relations.

Race relations at any point in a society's development also reflect the historical and socioeconomic development of that society as reflected in the processes of economic and political domination. In regard to a society's system of stratification, they reveal the complex and changing relationship between racial caste and social class, often reflecting a "plural" stratification

---

[1]See, for example, R. M. Williams, *The Reduction of Intergroup Tensions: A Survey of Research on Problems of Ethnic, Racial, and Religious Group Relations,* Social Science Research Council, New York, 1947.

[2]R. Benedict, *Science and Politics,* Viking, New York, 1940.

[3]For a discussion of social and cultural pluralism, see P. L. van den Berghe, *Race and Racism,* Wiley, New York, 1967, chap. 7.

system (i.e., a separate stratification system for each race group in the society). Resultant reactions such as cross-cutting bonds,[4] antagonism, conflict, and intergroup competition are all related to this caste/class ratio. Race relations thus reflect the type of social structure inherent in a society, particularly the kind of stratification system representing its social foundation.

3 An Index of Social Flexibility The topic of race relations is directly related to a basic question in the social sciences: the relationship between *physical* variables (e.g., genetics) and *social* characteristics (e.g., intelligence), a point of controversy over which bitter arguments continue.[5] More sociologically relevant is the manner in which social variables are *assumed* to have physical origins and are used to rationalize the subordination of groups defined as ethnically or racially different. Relevant, too, is the degree to which racial criteria are part of each group's social identity. The extent to which such an identity can be lowered, made less threatening, and possibly removed entirely becomes an important factor in any discussion of the possibility of social change and the reduction of racial prejudice. In this way, man's social flexibility and related variables is a central question.

4 An Index of Social Conformity The study of race relations also provides information on individual and group conformity. What reinforces such conformity, and how is the individual affected by "definitions of the situation" (i.e., group definitions or norms), particularly in racial terms, provided by the various groups of which he is a member? How does he adjust to inconsistent definitions or situations to which such definitions are lacking? Does his level of conformity change with social mobility, and how is his level of relative deprivation important here? What causes particular groups to change definitions of their societal situation—coming to view the power structure as illegitimate? Individual as well as situational factors are behind such conformity,

---

[4]For a discussion of this, see M. Gluckman, *Custom and Conflict in Africa,* Blackwell, Oxford, 1955.

[5]See A. R. Jensen, "How Much Can We Boost I.Q. and Scholastic Achievment?" *Harvard Educational Review,* **39**, 1969. Critiques of this argument and the author's rejoinder appear in the same journal, Spring and Summer, 1969, issues.

In general, then, the field of race relations reflects the development of the social sciences as they have moved from a physiological to a social conceptualization of "race"—from races and racial attitudes to the process of race relations.

9   Race Relations and Sociological Theory   Theories of race relations typify the traditional split in sociology between two main theoretical approaches—consensus and conflict theory. The organismic model of societal unity was the main concern until quite recently,[7] while in opposition to this perspective, conflict theory has emphasized that conflict rather than consensus is endemic to social life at levels throughout the social system.[8] Attempting to bridge this gap, van den Berghe has pointed out that in both views societies are looked at as systems of interrelated parts; different societal elements may coexist without being significantly complementary, interdependent, or in opposition; both share an evolutionary notion of social change; and both are fundamentally based on an equilibrium model.[9] Gluckman has further emphasized the interrelatedness of a society, without suggesting that such a condition implies social consensus,[10] and in a recent work on *Comparative Ethnic Relations,* Schermerhorn bemoans this theoretical split and discusses some interesting "unexplored types of integration."[11]

In race relations, the trend has moved from consensus and integrationist notions to an emphasis on social conflict as a dominant element. Such differing orientations reflect a change in ideology and increasing awareness of institutional racism (i.e., the manner in which "race" represents the basis of a society's political, economic, and social institutions). All of these perspec-

[7]See, for example, A. Comte, *The Positive Philosophy of Auguste Comte,* trans. H. Martineau, Blanchard, New York, 1855; E. Durkheim, *Elementary Forms of Religious Life,* trans. J. Swain, Macmillan, New York, 1926; T. Parsons, *The Social System,* Free Press, Glencoe, Ill., 1951.

[8]See L. Coser, *The Functions of Social Conflict,* Free Press, Glencoe, Ill., 1956; R. Dahrendorf, *Class and Class Conflict in Industrial Society,* Stanford University Press, Stanford, Calif., 1959.

[9]P. L. van den Berghe, "Dialectic and Functionalism: Toward A Theoretical Synthesis," *American Sociological Review,* 1963, pp. 695–705.

[10]Gluckman, *op. cit.*

[11]R. A. Schermerhorn, *Comparative Ethnic Relations: A Framework for Theory and Research,* Random House, New York, 1970.

tives underline the relevance of race relations to the question of social bonds in society, whether cross-cutting or in opposition, and challenge the social sciences to develop theory that is sophisticated enough to take account of their complexity and changing nature.

Race relations, in general, raise the question of how a heterogeneous society is socially organized, i.e., what kinds of social norms and bonds tie various groups and individuals together. The question of social order as well as change is central to this field.

10   Race Relations and Social Policy   All the above points illustrate the relevance of race relations to questions of social policy. Matters of social policy should become clearer as the field provides increasing insight into sources of social tension; the nature of the social structure; social flexibility and conformity; attitudes, needs, and behavior; the effects of industrialization; and varieties of social bonds. The far-reaching social relevance of the field is thus clear.

Insight on its own, however, may influence the societal power structure little as it controls and protects its vested interests. Discussion of race relations inevitably turns to the power structure in which they are defined. In general, however, the policy implications of this field are vital: *the need to highlight racial oppression and develop techniques for its reduction.*

CONCLUSIONS

In general, then, the study of race relations highlights a society's social structure, particularly the degree to which it is rigid and colonial; behavior within it; and the effects of ongoing social change. Of particular relevance is the manner in which race relations reveal the extent to which a society is *colonial,* for it is this structure that defines the operation of "race" in the intergroup relations that occur within it. This, in turn, defines the relationship between individuals and their reference groups, as well as their racial attitudes. Such a relationship is summarized in Figure 2-1. Broadly speaking, then, the study of race relations

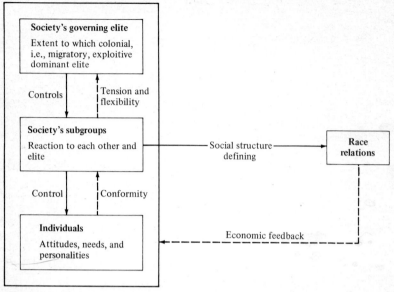

Figure 2-1 Race relations as an index of the social structure.

reveals a society's *social structure* and the *processes* at work within it. It is this structural question that concerns us in this work as we examine the operation of race on the individual, group, and societal levels. We turn first, however, to the problems associated with that task.

STUDY QUESTIONS

1 What aspects of American society do you feel an analysis of race relations would reveal?
2 What aspects of race relations does political rhetoric highlight?
3 Consider the varied and interactive relationships between psychological (personality), social-psychological (group), and sociological (societal) factors that define patterns of race relations.
4 What kind of social tensions do you see reflected in racial conflict (i.e., political, social, and economic)?
5 What changes in race relations would you attribute to the effects of industrialization (e.g., conformity to radicalism)?

READINGS

Banton, M. P., *Race Relations,* Basic Books, New York, 1967, chap. 1.

Berry, B., *Race and Ethnic Relations,* 3rd ed., Houghton Mifflin, Boston, Mass., 1965.

Blalock, H. M., *Toward a Theory of Minority-Group Relations,* Wiley, New York, 1967.

Hunter, G., *Industrialization and Race Relations: A Symposium,* Oxford University Press, New York, 1965.

Mack, R. W. *Race, Class, and Power,* American Book, New York, 1963.

Mason, P., *Race Relations,* Oxford University Press, New York, 1970.

Mead, M., and J. Baldwin, *A Rap on Race,* Lippincott, Philadelphia, Penn., 1971.

Schermerhorn, R. A., *Comparative Ethnic Relations: A Framework for Theory and Research,* Random House, New York, 1970.

Simpson, G. E., and J. M. Yinger, *Racial and Cultural Minorities: An Analysis of Prejudice and Discrimination,* 3rd ed., Harper & Row, New York, 1965.

Tumin, M. M., (ed.), *Comparative Perspectives on Race Relations,* Little, Brown, Boston, Mass., 1969.

Van den Berghe, P. L., *Race and Racism: A Comparative Perspective,* Wiley, New York, 1967.

Westie, F. R., "Race and Ethnic Relations," in R. E. L. Faris (ed.), *Handbook of Modern Sociology,* Rand McNally, Chicago, Ill., 1964.

Chapter 3

Problems Involved in the Analysis of Race Relations

Race relations are among the most complex and subjective phenomena, creating severe difficulties for those attempting to analyze them objectively. Furthermore, the study of race relations usually involves a member of the society's dominant racial elite examining his relationship to minority groups in historical, economic, and psychological perspective. Since the positions of these minorities and the stereotypes describing them have already been defined and institutionalized for many preceding decades, perhaps centuries, it is impossible for the student to be completely objective in his perspective.

Any elite, particularly in a colonial setting, has certain vested interests, psychological as well as economic, in its stereotyping of minorities; these are pervasive throughout the social structure. The prevailing view of minorities has also been delineated by the social sciences, whose perspective is far from completely objective, and has been subjected to the societal distortions outlined above. Terms such as "culturally deprived," "reverse racism," "remedial programs," "institutional deterioration," and "criminal tendencies" as applied to minorities, for example, reflect analyses of race relations by dominant group members on that elite's *own terms,* with major emphasis placed on the assimilation of minorities rather than on their development.

This process of "blaming the victim," as it has been termed,[1] reflects the elite's perspective of race groups on its own terms of domination. Minority students, in turn, tend to overreact to such an imposed view, and this results in problems of objectivity, withdrawal, and lack of communication. The result is a multiplicity of views on society and race relations within it, each view dependent on the analyzer's racial position. Problems of ideology and objectivity for the student are crucial and need to be appreciated at the outset.

It is with these difficulties in mind, then, that we turn to some major problems of analysis—in particular the difficulties of objectivity, theoretical development, and empirical research.

The Question of Objectivity

Since racial perceptions are ultimately subjective, the most perplexing problem is objective analysis. Racial stereotypes are absorbed from the beginning of childhood socialization and on through adulthood. To deny that racial differences are, in fact, real, appears foreign to an individual who has learned the opposite and is socially rewarded on this basis. Since society is organized and controlled on the basis of race, "institutionalized racism"[2] maintains the notion that race is "real" for both dominant and subordinate groups. Under such circumstances, the ability to view race relations on a completely objective basis is impossible. Statements on race, whether political or academic, always have ideological implications, making this field inevitably controversial.

[1]See W. Ryan, *Blaming the Victim,* Pantheon, New York, 1971.
[2]For a useful analysis of institutional racism, see S. Carmichael and C. V. Hamilton, *Black Power: The Politics of Liberation in America,* Vintage Books, New York, 1967, chap. 1.

The objectivity problem delineated above may be broadly divided into two areas: subjectivity and group perspectives. The former refers to individual perspectives, while the latter applies to definitions of race relations on the intergroup level. On the subjective level, racial attitudes, particularly prejudice, tend to reflect personality types and the individual's attitudes generally. Formed in competitive situations and reinforced by society's norms, individual attitudes represent one of the most inflexible elements in intergroup relations. Such views, particularly among dominant group members, are further reinforced by the elite's conservative perspective on race as well as similar orientations within the social sciences. In this manner, the analysis of race relations is basically a subjective problem, structured by the surrounding social environment.

On the group level, perspectives on race relations, particularly in the American case, have been distorted by an assimilationist orientation, which overlooks racial inequality and the colonial aspects of the social structure in general.[3] The "race relations problem" is defined predominantly as the minority groups' lack of conformity to white American culture with its white emphasis on moralism, thrift, and hard work. The perceived solution of this problem is the integration of minority groups with little, if any, attempt to take their inequality and economic deprivation into account.[4]

Such pressures for increased conformity ignore problems of alienation and the recent development of racial separatism. Colonial elites typically attempt to culturally assimilate minorities on their own terms, resulting often in increased nationalism. In this respect American society is little different, making it difficult for students to objectify race relations, since they tend to assume the dominant group's general perspective of the "problem."

[3]For a discussion of this problem, see P. L. van den Berghe, *Race and Racism*, Wiley, New York, 1967, p. 7. By "assimilationist," we are referring to the dominant elite's attempt to assimilate or absorb minorities *culturally on its own terms, without regard to the minorities own culture and socioeconomic deprivation within the racial caste system.* Within this perspective, a minority group's lack of conformity to elite values, rather than its domination and control by the society's colonial elite, is viewed as the source of racial conflict.

[4]Kovel has used the term "metaracism" to describe this "racially blind" approach. See J. Kovel *White Racism: A Psychohistory*, Vintage Books, New York, 1970, pp. 211–230.

Minority group members may also unwittingly conform to this orientation, resulting in social blindness[5] and a level of conformity which social scientists and radicals alike find difficult to understand. The result for elite and minority students is a low level of societal awareness. A general inability to explain high degrees of racial tension and violence in terms other than the need to further implement the "American dream" may also be attributed to this problem.

Given the subjective nature of racial attitudes and the conformity-oriented group perspectives reinforcing them, an explanatory analysis of race relations rather than descriptions of people's attitudes becomes a matter of urgency. Such analysis, however, presents theoretical as well as empirical difficulties.

THEORETICAL PROBLEMS

Without adequate theory (i.e., scientific explanations), it is impossible to understand phenomena, whether natural or social. This necessity represents an acute problem in the area of race relations, where the predominant emphasis has been on the description of *attitudes,* particularly racial prejudice, with little attempt to understand the structure of race *relations* within which they are formed and reinforced. This problem, until recently, has resulted in a low level of theoretical development in the field. The use of psychological variables to explain racial attitudes, however, is a major exception.[6] Attempted explanations of differing patterns of race relations, on the other hand, are a comparatively recent phenomenon.

A second problem is the gap between those areas in the social sciences where race relations theory has developed: the psychological approach attempts to explain the psychopathology of prejudice, the social-psychological explores the group context of racial orientations, while the sociological delineates societal factors behind particular patterns of relations. This trichotomy has resulted in attempts to understand various aspects of race on

---

[5]For an analysis of this problem among blacks, see W. H. Grier and P. M. Cobbs, *Black Rage,* Bantam Books, New York, 1968, chap. 6.

[6]See T. W. Adorno et al., *The Authoritarian Personality,* Harper, New York, 1950.

a number of analytical levels but with little synthesis or focus on race relations in general. Such theoretical "particularism"[7] has further contributed to a generally low level of theoretical development in the field—a central problem in the attempt to analyze these relations.

Further, in the attempt to develop theory, particularly at the sociological level, a number of typologies delineating a number of "types" of race relations have emerged.[8] A major limitation of these typologies is the extent to which they represent static descriptions which take little account of economic and social change. While these constructs are useful in abstracting some of the more relevant general factors, they tend to overemphasize the static, neglecting ongoing change, and overestimate the extent to which total societies may be classified according to one particular "type."

A further problem is inherent in the restricted use of the historical dimension in race relations. This has led to the crude typing of historical periods and the generally low sensitivity to change in race relations. Insight into historical factors behind race relations is limited on both academic and popular levels, reinforcing the kind of social blindness discussed at the beginning of this chapter. While useful historical analyses of race relations exist, few sociological studies make adequate use of available data to provide further depth for their conceptual frameworks.

Inadequate conceptualizations of "race relations" represent a problem also. Definitions of race relations are either absent or limited, moving little beyond the static level of groups and attitudes. Since relationships are dynamic rather than static, and structural rather than attitudinal, the need for an adequate structural-dynamic approach is obvious.

Finally, we have referred to the need for a theoretical synthesis of at least three analytic levels. Developing such a synthesis is a complex task, whether in race relations or the social

[7]See F. R. Westie, "Race and Ethnic Relations," in R. E. L. Faris (ed.), *Handbook of Modern Sociology*, Rand McNally, Chicago, 1964, pp. 576–577.
[8]See, in particular, P. L. van den Berghe, *op. cit.,* "A Typology of Race Relations," pp. 25–34; P. Mason, "Disentangling the Causes," *Race Relations,* Oxford, London, 1970, chap. 8. These discussions describe various "types" of race relations situations.

sciences in general. Particularly troublesome is the extent to which any framework may either be too general to take account of a society's internal heterogeneity[9] or too individualistic to cope with the surrounding social system. Group analyses, on the other hand, tend to be inadequate in handling either end of the continuum. The development of general race relations theory is, therefore, a highly necessary but complex task.

To summarize, in our discussion of theoretical problems, we have highlighted the general lack of theory, theoretical particularism, an emphasis on static typologies, low historical awareness, the need for a structural-dynamic conceptualization of "race relations," and problems generated by attempted theoretical syntheses. Given the further difficulty that theories and attitudes are ideologically based, it can be seen that "knowledge" concerning race relations is a subjective phenomenon. Awareness of these limitations prior to research is particularly important.

EMPIRICAL RESEARCH

Research material in the area of race relations, particularly regarding the topic of prejudice,[10] is voluminous. Such material, however, is restricted in methodology and tends to ignore broader empirical issues.

An initial and crucial problem is the definition of "race." The absence in many works of a clear definition of this concept is striking,[11] particularly since it has been confused with ethnicity, nationality, religion, culture, genetics, and skin color.[12] Only recently has it been clearly defined as an artificial social category developed and reinforced by a particular racial elite.[13] The continuing confusion of the term with other factors, particularly among ‧ the general population, makes the need for a clear

[9]This, perhaps, is one of the major limitations of the typologies referred to in fn. 8 in this chapter.

[10]For a useful summary of these see F. R. Westie, op. cit., pp. 586–603.

[11]See, for example, J. Rex, *Race Relations in Sociological Theory,* Weidenfield and Nicolson, London, 1970.

[12]For a useful discussion of definition problems, see P. L. van den Berghe, op. cit., pp. 9–11.

[13]See, for example, A. W. Lind, *Hawaii: The Last of the Magic Isles,* Oxford, University Press, London, 1969, p. 51.

sociological definition an urgent requirement in view of its past ideological bias. Thus, race has been defined by particular elites, both political and academic,[14] in a manner that reflects their economic interests and cultural ethnocentrism. Concepts and theories are problematic in this field to the extent that they reflect such ideology and vested interests. The general colonial environment in which race relations typically develop has made such conceptual difficulties inevitable.

Even assuming that the term "race" is clearly defined, a number of distinct methodological problems remain. Among these stand the selection of the most suitable index of race relations, along with the most powerful *instruments* for studying them. Index selection is particularly crucial. Is it attitudes, preferences, behavior, patterns of discrimination, or a particular combination of these that represent the most significant indicator of race relations? Instrument design is no less a problem, since each has its own severe limitations, aggravated by the controversial nature of this field's subject matter. Thus, what *kinds* of questionnaires, observation procedures, demographic measures of discrimination, or case studies throw the most light on the problem? Given the complexity of the subject matter, these problems are crucial and, unfortunately, tend to be overlooked in the application of conventional measures. The need for more sophisticated techniques to handle problems of restricted responses is important. The clear distinction between attitudes and behavior is also crucial.

A further problem is the difficulty of sample selection. Setting aside problems of resistance and bias, selection of the most relevant group(s) remains. Often the most cooperative groups represent only a restricted portion of the population. It is difficult, for example, to interpret the significance of analyses of various elites without knowledge of the attitudes of the population at large. Inevitably, questions of availability and cooperation tend to determine sample selection, resulting in varied and uneven results. The predominance of college student samples in

---

[14]For a discussion of this, see M. Banton, *Race Relations,* Basic Books, New York, 1967, pp. 33–35.

studies of racial attitudes typifies this problem, resulting in restricted insight and obscure group boundaries.

Examination of the research material available to those interested in race relations raises at least five problems: concentration on feelings and attitudes rather than on relations; the general failure to take social change into account; a predominance of studies carried out during or after racial crisis situations, with nonconflict situations being neglected; problems of data interpretation, given the bias of the dominant elite; and a "blame-the-victim" orientation. Given such limited data, the student is faced with a narrow and limited perspective of subject matter which requires more dynamic conceptualization and broader data.

The study of race *relations,* as pointed out earlier, is a comparatively recent focus. The predominant emphasis has been upon the measurement and explanation of racial attitudes in psychological terms. Furthermore, there is the tendency in contemporary approaches to emphasize the feelings and reactions of these groups rather than their historical situation. The result of these emphases has been a neglect of the *dynamics* of actual *relations* and the controlling factors behind them.

A further problem has been the neglect of social change over time. Once a society has been "typed," it is consequently assumed that little significant change in intergroup relations takes place. However, as this writer has found, race relations change over time, even in colonial societies, as industrialization takes place.[15] Race relations represent a process of dynamic interaction rather than static social structure and need to be viewed as such even in highly colonial societies, particularly as subordinate minorities begin to reject the society's legitimacy.

Studies of race relations also tend to concentrate on crisis situations, highly racist societies, and personality types. This results in the impression that racism is highly deviant and abnormal, thereby neglecting lower levels of prejudice that are inherent, but not as visible, in all societies. More central to the

---

[15]G. C. Kinloch, "Social Types and Race Relations in the Colonial Setting: A Case Study of Rhodesia," *Phylon,* third quarter, 1972, pp. 276–289.

problem of racism, perhaps, is the manner in which prejudice is absorbed "normally" as part of the socialization process. While high levels of prejudice are obviously important, less visible forms of racism are equally relevant and have been neglected.

A major problem with most studies of race relations available to the student is that inherent in them is the majority interpretation of minority groups. Often members of these groups have been viewed as deprived and deviant individuals whose basic problem is their nonconformity to white middle-class values. This view reveals the majority group's racial and cultural ethnocentrism in its definition of minorities in terms of its own values.

Recently black sociologists have begun to reject this perspective as inaccurate, blind, racist, biased, and extremely ignorant of the complexities of black culture.[16] Clearly, most studies of minorities are carried out by members of the society's elite and accordingly reflect its biased viewpoint. Research on minorities has also neglected the more personal and microscopic aspects of their social life, making for a limited view of their members.[17]

Inherent in the majority viewpoint is an orientation that has been termed the "blame-the-victim" mechanism.[18] This process blames minorities for their situations and the reaction to discrimination, when in fact the colonial elite is responsible for producing it in the first place. Such an orientation contributes to a frustration-aggression cycle in race relations, resulting in the reinforcement of racism and the negative reactions to it. Such elite ethnocentrism only serves to aggravate a highly skeptical view of most studies on minorities, particularly those which interpret the minority members' cultures for them.

A final problem exists in the boundaries of race relations as a subfield within the social sciences. Some writers, for example, have questioned the degree to which this field may legitimately be differentiated from the analysis of social relations in general.[19]

---

[16]See D. Davidson, "Black Culture and Liberal Sociology," *Berkeley Journal of Sociology,* **14**, 1969, pp. 165–175.

[17]See H. H. Smythe and L. Chase, "Current Research on the Negro: A Critique," *Sociology and Social Research,* **42**, 1958, pp. 199–202.

[18]See W. Ryan, op. cit.

[19]For discussions of this problem see P. Mason, op. cit., and J. Rex, op. cit.

While we shall attempt to define those parameters as certain sociological, social-psychological, and psychological variables, this viewpoint is not common to the field as a whole. Not only are the field's major concepts variously defined, but so are its boundaries.

SUMMARY AND CONCLUSIONS

In this chapter we have considered three major problem areas in the analysis of race relations: difficulties of objectivity, theoretical development and conceptualization, and empirical research. We underlined specific problems as follows:

1   Subjectivity and socialization
2   Assimilationist orientations among the white elite
3   A predominance of description rather than theory
4   Theoretical particularism
5   Static typologies
6   Low historical awareness
7   Inadequate conceptualization of "race" and "race relations"
8   Problems of theoretical synthesis
9   Difficulties of index, instrument, sample selection, and sample response bias
10   The predominance of psychological, static, and crisis-oriented data
11   Problems of data interpretation from an elitist perspective
12   The field's obscure boundaries

It can be seen that these problems refer mainly to subjectivity, elite orientations and control, minority reaction and sensitivity, and problems of conceptualization and empirical measurement. All these problems occur within a particular social setting, typically colonial and exploitive, which controls and structures intergroup relations within it. The analysis of race relations is defined and influenced by a variety of factors, making it a complex process. This process is outlined in Figure 3-1.

In conclusion, we have discussed these problems to raise

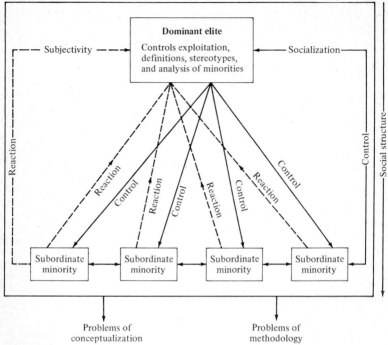

Figure 3-1 Summary of problems of analyzing race relations within the context of the social structure.

the student's sensitivity to major factors controlling perceptions of race relations on both subjective and academic levels. It is hoped that he will thereby gain increased ability to objectively analyze the intergroup relations in which he participates. It is reasonable to assume, at least in some respects, that the analysis of race relations is becoming more scientific and less ideological. As minority nationalism increases and elites are made aware of the extent to which the society is colonial in structure, coupled with more sophisticated theoretical conceptualizations and empirical methodology, this field appears to be moving gradually toward sociological explanations and away from psychological descriptions. Constant care needs to be taken, however, to ensure that ideological biases are recognized and controlled.

STUDY QUESTIONS

1 Consider the major problems, *both* conceptual and methodological, you might have in studying racial attitudes among the following groups:
    a A sample of white college students
    b A sample of black ghetto residents
    c A group of white middle-class suburban residents
    d A sample of black businessmen
    e A group of urban American Indian adolescents
2 Outline similar problems you would have in explaining the racial behavior of the above groups.
3 Discuss the procedures you feel would minimize the problem of subjectivity in the study of white-black relations.
4 How do you feel problems of conceptualization may best be handled?
5 Attempt to put into writing beliefs that you hold or have held about minority groups—negative and positive. Do they affect your perception as you read, or can you tell?

READINGS

Davidson, Douglas, "Black Culture and Liberal Sociology," *Berkeley Journal of Sociology,* 1969, **14**, pp. 165–175.

Jensen, A. R., "How Much Can We Boost I.Q. and Scholastic Achievement?" *Harvard Educational Review,* **39**, 1969.

Ryan, W., *Blaming the Victim,* Pantheon, New York, 1971.

Schneider, Louis, and Arthur J. Brodbeck, "Some Notes on Moral Paradoxes in Race Relations," *Phylon,* 1955, **16**, 2, June, pp. 149–158.

Smythe, Hugh H., and L. Chase, "Current Research on the Negro: A Critique," *Sociology and Social Research,* 1958, **42**, 3, January–February, pp. 199–202.

Chapter 4

The Historical Development of Race Relations as a Field of Study

In our discussion so far we have underlined the influence of society on an individual's perception of race relations. This problem also applies to academic fields, particularly those in the social sciences, where "knowledge" reflects a particular group's position in society as well as its vested interests. As we have pointed out, objectivity in such a situation is impossible: the colonial elite defines intergroup relations on its own exploitive terms, while subordinate minorities eventually reject the legitimacy of these definitions, using various academic fields for purposes of nationalism and politicalization.

The above problem is particularly crucial in the case of race relations: initial definitions of "race" by dominant elites are formed in the context of colonialism, imperialism, and slavery, supported by the attempt to rationalize and elaborate a system of institutionalized exploitation. Subordinate groups submit to such definitions out of physical and economic necessity. Once racism declines, a melioristic orientation becomes evident among sections of the superordinate elite as minorities begin to reject the legitimacy of the social structure as a whole. While former attitudes were paternalistic and assimilationist, the latter continue to be emotional and nationalistic.

The field of race relations thus continues to be closely defined by characteristics of the social system—historical, economic, and sociological—in which it has developed. The field as a whole is inevitably an area of controversy as various group motives influence it at particular points in time. Similarly, the perspectives of social science reflect various group interests, making it particularly difficult to develop race relations as a scientific field. The importance of societal characteristics to any race relations approach at a particular point in time cannot be overestimated, and the student should be particularly aware of them in his study of the subject.[1]

We shall attempt to illustrate the above problems in our discussion of the field's historical background and contemporary state.

HISTORICAL BACKGROUND

In this section we shall discuss early approaches to race developed by natural scientists, the theories of early sociologists, and relevant factors in pre- and postwar America. In all these instances, societal influence is clearly evident.

The Taxonomists

The notion of "race" was injected into science in early attempts by zoologists to classify mankind as a species into a number of subclassifications. Banton divides these theorists into two groups: those holding to the "Doctrine of Mutability," or the development of various groups by environmental influence, and those espousing the "Doctrine of Immutability," a more rigid

---

[1]For a useful discussion of this, see L. Lieberman, "The Debate Over Race: A Study in the Sociology of Knowledge," *Phylon,* **29**, 1968, pp. 127–142.

approach identifying culture with race.[2] The former included Blumenbach and Buffon, the latter Cuvier, Prichard, Knox, Morton, and Nott.[3] The physiological approach was further reinforced by European ethnocentrism, religious dogma, colonialism, and Social Darwinism. The reality of race as a physical category was firmly established in pseudoscientific terms and further elaborated as a rationalization for economic exploitation. Despite the invalidation of this notion by the fields of genetics and comparative anthropology, it is still accepted as valid by elites in South Africa and groups in situations of perceived threat. The genetics of race continues to be controversial in contemporary science, as we shall see. The establishment of race as a physiological category has had far-reaching effects.

Early Sociologists

In previous discussion we emphasized the comparatively recent development of the study of race relations, despite sociology's early foundation as a field in its own right. An important aspect of this neglect is the extent to which men such as Marx, Durkheim, and Weber analyzed intergroup relations in economic and social rather than racial terms. MacRae expresses this well in his view that the field was obscured in the early twentieth century when writers such as Durkheim and Weber analyzed social behavior in social (i.e., power and economic) rather than racial terms.[4] The latter were implicit rather than central.

Neglect of racial criteria was further reinforced, as Rose points out,[5] by sociology's major concern with a structure-functional analysis of society, with its emphasis on functional conformity and problems of adaptation rather than on disruptive conflict. Questions of race were overlooked in the main until violent conflict made the dominant elite aware of the "race problem" in its midst.

[2]For a useful discussion of early definitions of "race," see M. Banton, *Race Relations,* Basic Books, 1967, chap. 2.

[3]For a discussion of other figures in this debate, see P. I. Rose, *The Subject Is Race,* Oxford University Press, New York, 1968, chap. 3.

[4]D. C. MacRae, "Race and Sociology in History and Theory," in P. Mason (ed.), *Man, Race and Darwin,* Oxford University Press, London, 1960, p. 80, quoted in L. Lieberman, op. cit., p. 136.

[5]P. I. Rose, op. cit., p. 57.

Race Relations in the United States

Studies of race relations in the United States followed the dominant perspectives of the day. Early nineteenth-century treatises on the topic, as Frazier points out,[6] were concerned with rationalizing the system of slavery as functional and right. Early sociological analyses by Ward, Sumner, Giddings, and Cooley described racial conflict, the importance of mores, consciousness of kind, racial caste, and intellectual differences.[7]

Behind these perspectives stood a basic element in American culture—the Anglo-Saxon Protestant Ethic emphasizing whiteness, Christianity, cleanliness, and hard work. Such values represented the basis of nonwhite and non-Christian racism. In a well-known work, *Race: The History of an Idea in America,*[8] Gossett traces the influence on highly racist policies of antiheathen values, Social Darwinism, the Social Gospel, immigration restrictions, and American imperialism. American racism can thus be traced back to the society's central value system. Kren also shows how Protestantism has been behind anti-Semitism from the Middle Ages to the present century.[9] The main source of racism should be sought in a society's traditional value system, particularly in the case of America, with its Protestant-oriented culture.

American studies in the early twentieth century, as Frazier points out, underlined the Negro's inferior social heredity, low possibility of assimilation, and the undesirability of physical miscegenation. He sees such views as a function of the society's attempt to solve its racial problems through segregation. Finally, while in the 1930s Park contributed to a more dynamic, social-psychological approach to race, by the prewar period the field remained static and imbued with the rationalization of prejudice.

Early studies of race in the United States were clearly a function of the society's historical development as it moved from

[6]E. F. Frazier, "Sociological Theory and Race Relations," *American Sociological Review*, **12**, 1947, pp. 265–271. This is a useful discussion of early American writing on race.
[7]See E. F. Frazier, ibid.
[8]T. F. Gossett, *Race: The History of an Idea in America,* Southern Methodist University Press, Dallas, 1963. Other useful references include P. Jacobs et al. (eds.), *To Serve the Devil,* vols. 1, 2, Vintage Books, New York, 1971; G. M. Fredrickson, *The Black Image in the White Mind,* Harper & Row, New York, 1971; W. P. Jordon, *White over Black: American Attitudes toward the Negro 1550–1812,* University of North Carolina Press, Chapel Hill, 1968.
[9]G. M. Kren, "Race and Ideology," *Phylon*, **23**, 1962, pp. 167–176.

slavery toward general segregation. Explicit in this literature is acceptance of race as a real physical category with certain "inevitable" problems as a result.

The postwar period through to the 1960s in American race relations research is usefully summarized by Blumer.[10] He sees three major facets: the variety of race groups in the United States, problems presented by these relations, and various approaches taken by the "social and psychological sciences" in studying them.[11] Reaction to these three factors has resulted in differential approaches to the various minorities, "a melioristic interest in the improvement of the relations between racial groups"[12]—an attempt to implement the American ideal—and an emphasis on the study of prejudice and discrimination.

Characteristic of these studies is the historical descriptions of America's major minorities, an applied attempt to reduce racial tension,[13] and the use of prejudice and discrimination as major race relations indices. Such descriptive-attitudinal accounts are limited theoretically as well as ideologically (in conservative terms) in their assimilationist-ameliorative emphasis. Recent writers have bemoaned these limitations. Schermerhorn, for example, criticizes the concentration on prejudice and discrimination, victimology, and updating rather than "rethinking,"[14] while van den Berghe is well known for his critique of applied, noncomparative, and assimilationist tendencies in the field.[15]

In conclusion, the field of race relations in the United States has closely followed social change in the general society: beginning as a rationalization of slavery, it moved to a justification of segregation, then an applied attempt to implement the "American Creed" in the acknowledgment of widespread prejudice and discrimination. From this, it is obvious that the field has been far

[10]H. Blumer, "Recent Research on Race Relations—United States of America," *International Social Science Bulletin*, **10**, 1958, pp. 403–447.

[11]H. Blumer, ibid., p. 403.

[12]H. Blumer, ibid., p. 405.

[13]See, for example, R. M. Williams, *The Reduction of Intergroup Tensions: A Survey of Research on Problems of Ethnic, Racial, and Religious Group Relations,* Social Science Research Council, New York, 1947.

[14]R. A. Schermerhorn, *Comparative Ethnic Relations: A Framework for Theory and Research,* Random House, New York, 1970, pp. 6–12.

[15]P. L. van den Berghe, *Race and Racism,* Wiley, New York, 1967, pp. 2–8.

from objective and, in many respects, exemplifies the utilization of "knowledge" by a colonial elite for its own purposes. We turn, thirdly, to the present scene.

THE CONTEMPORARY SCENE

A number of contemporary trends may be outlined as follows:

1 Increased awareness of the race problem and the manner in which it affects the plurality of America's racial minorities

2 An increase in writing and teaching about these minorities on the descriptive level

3 A gradual movement in the academic literature away from a description of attitudes toward the theoretical analysis of race relations

4 A return to the debate concerning the genetic basis of racial differences

5 Differences in teaching race relations according to a college's racial composition

6 Increased racial awareness and radicalism among minorities, particularly blacks, with the development of specific programs designed to reorient the field toward the perceived political and racial needs of those minorities

Dealing with the above points, in turn, it is evident that awareness of the race problem in American society has increased markedly in the past five years, particularly since the outbreak of widespread violence. Popular literature, as well as college courses on the topic, has proliferated to a remarkable degree, as has appreciation of the problem beyond the traditional white-black confrontation. Accompanying this movement has developed an increase in writing and teaching about these minorities generally.[16] However, the degree to which this material moves beyond the description of various groups in historical perspective to their analysis remains questionable. A danger also exists that

[16]See, for example, L. M. Killian, *White Southerners*, Random House, New York, 1970; J. Lopreato, *Italian Americans*, Random House, New York, 1970; W. Peterson, *Japanese Americans*, Random House, New York, 1971; M. Sklare, *America's Jews*, Random House, New York, 1971.

such descriptive accounts may become substitutes for social action.

In the academic literature, on the other hand, the student may perceive a gradual movement toward theoretical analysis. Typologies such as those developed by van den Berghe,[17] Mason,[18] Lieberson,[19] and Banton,[20] represent the beginnings of theoretical frameworks designed to explain race relations rather than to describe them. On the other hand, a general and deductive theory of these relations is lacking; indeed, some are skeptical that such a theory could ever be developed, given the complexity of the phenomena involved.[21] Whatever the case, there is increasing concern with analysis rather than description.

Recently the issue of genetic differences between race groups has reappeared. In a controversial article entitled "How Much Can We Boost I.Q. and Scholastic Achievement?" Professor A. R. Jensen argues that differences in levels of intelligence are genetically founded, and given that race groups vary markedly in such levels, even controlling for environmental differences, genetic factors appear to be behind these racial differences.[22] In an opening statement, he argues that groups that have been isolated from one another either socially or geographically will differ in "gene pools" and consequent hereditary "phenotypic characteristics." He then proceeds to link variation in intelligence levels to the "genetic component."

Professor Jensen's argument has raised a storm of protest, not only in the United States but in other countries as well.[23] While it is not our purpose here to present a detailed critique of his argument, except to underline the impossibility of adequately

[17]P. L. van den Berghe, op. cit., pp. 25–34.

[18]P. Mason, *Race Relations,* Oxford University Press, New York, 1970, chap. 8.

[19]S. Lieberson, "A Societal Theory of Race and Ethnic Relations," *American Sociological Review,* **26,** 1961, pp. 902–910.

[20]M. Banton, op. cit.

[21]See, for example, A. Lind, "Towards a Theory of Race Relations," paper presented to the Social Science Seminar, University of Singapore, September 23, 1969 (mimeographed).

[22]A. R. Jensen, "How Much Can We Boost I.Q. and Scholastic Achievement?" *Harvard Educational Review,* **39,** 1969. See also related discussion and rebuttal later in the same volume.

[23]See, for example, P. Mason, "Race, Intelligence, and Professor Jensen," *Race Today,* July, 1969, pp. 76–77; Race Today, "Genes and Jensen," *Race Today,* August, 1970, p. 288.

controlling for environmental differences across race groups, his approach has obvious danger in providing credence for the earlier physiological approach to race discussed earlier in this chapter. Given the desirability of such an approach to those wishing to rationalize racial dominance, any suggestion of a genetic basis is given great import, particularly when it comes from scientific sources. Earlier conceptualizations of race have returned, thereby increasing the burden on the social sciences to demonstrate that "race" is a social category defined by particular elites on the basis of perceived rather than actual physical differences.

Approaches to the teaching of race relations are clearly differentiated by the racial composition of the school concerned. In his study of how race relations are taught in American colleges, Rose found that courses in Negro schools tend to concentrate on the cross-cultural approach, while in white schools more emphasis is placed on a theoretical orientation.[24] The former are more descriptive, while the latter are more analytical in approach. The lack of a standardized, analytical approach is striking as is the general absence of an activist orientation in both white and Negro colleges. These data tend to confirm our earlier observations concerning the degree to which the field of race relations study conforms to societal norms. Its past contribution to active social change appears to have been very limited.

In marked contrast to the above courses are, of course, the black studies programs that have developed at various East- and West-coast colleges. In his book *Black Students*,[25] Edwards presents a selection of "curricula outlines" developed for these programs at a number of colleges. It can be seen immediately that these are designed to develop skills for black liberation. Major emphases include attitudinal change, nation building, racial confrontation, and black culture. Such problems are of obvious utility on a number of accounts: politicalization of minorities, rejection of elite dominance, creation of positive identities, and the formulation of minority perspectives as opposed to imposed

[24]P. I. Rose, op. cit., pp. 127–138.
[25]H. Edwards, *Black Students*, Free Press, New York, 1970, pp. 205–227.

majority views. However, insofar as these "new bodies of knowledge" represent weapons rather than scientific analyses, they risk dangers of bias similar to the problems inherent in the traditional elitist perspective, although their level of insight may be higher. Race relations material, whether developed by elite or minority groups, runs similar risks of distortion, and ultimately it requires outside, objective analysis to place it in perspective.

In addition to initiating specific kinds of academic programs, black scholars have begun to reject white viewpoints on black culture, attempting to formulate their own orientations. Alkalimat, for example, sees most analyses of blacks that concentrate on prejudice and discrimination as serving white ideology.[26] He argues, instead, for a perspective focusing on survival, an African identity, and the process of decolonization. Similarly, Jones and Willingham criticize white sociologists for ignoring the perspective of blacks as an oppressed people engaged in a liberation struggle.[27] Instead, they have concentrated on institutional analyses, which ignore the societal context of black oppression. Rejection of the dominant elite's view of minorities has begun to make a significant contribution to the objective study of race relations.

On the contemporary scene, then, we have perceived an increased awareness of the race relations problem, a gradual movement toward theoretical analysis, and increased racial awareness among minorities. On the other hand, we have also seen a revival of the genetic view of race, a lack of activism in race relations courses, and the limitations of special minority group programs. However, the present situation represents a marked contrast to the field's early foundation, when physiological classifications were predominant.

CONCLUSIONS

In this chapter we have attempted to describe the historical development of race relations as a field of study, illustrating the

[26]A. H. I. Alkalimat, "The Ideology of Black Social Science," *Black Scholar,* 1, 2, 1969, pp. 28–36.
[27]M. H. Jones and A. Willingham, "The White Custodians of the Black Experience," *Social Science Quarterly,* 51, 1, 1970, pp. 31–36.

extent to which "knowledge" reflects a group's vested interests. Under the control of a colonial elite, the field was initially established to classify the human species into subgroups and to rationalize forms of exploitation. In the face of widespread prejudice and discrimination, the field turned to the practical problems of implementing the American Creed.

With the development of minority group nationalism and racial violence came awareness of the social structure behind race relations, the development of theoretical analyses, and attempts by minorities to produce their own educational programs and bodies of knowledge. These trends are summarized in Figure 4-1.

From the preceding, it is obvious that the problem of objectivity continues to plague the development of this field. In this situation, no one particular perspective is fully adequate— only out of open interaction and free exchange of ideas between

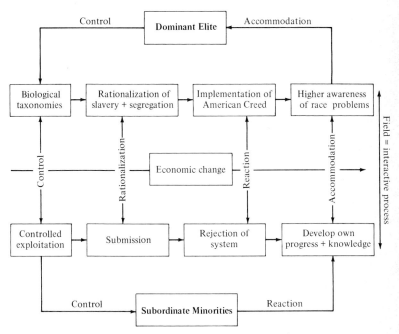

Figure 4-1   Major factors affecting the field of race relations.

majority and minority group members can more objective orientations develop. However, it is only when colonial barriers within academic and societal contexts are overcome that such analysis will develop freely.

STUDY QUESTIONS

1 Outline some of the major problems making it impossible for race relations to be an objective field of analysis.
2 Search out some of the early United States works on race (as referred to by Frazier), and outline their major rationalizations of the race relations structure of the day.
3 Select some recent introductory sociology texts and examine their treatment of race relations as instances of the majority perspective.
4 Examine some recent analyses of the United States race relations situation by minority group authors, and analyze them as instances of the minority perspective.
5 Discuss the implications of Blumer's view that the field of race relations in American society emerged primarily out of the racial conflict and oppression within it.

READINGS

Alkalimat, A. H. I., "The Ideology of Black Social Science," *Black Scholar,* 1969, **1**, 2, pp. 28–36.

Blumer, Herbert, "Recent Research on Racial Relations: United States of America," *International Social Science Bulletin,* 1958 **10**, 3, p. 403.

Campbell, Byram, *American Race Theorists: A Critique of Their Thoughts and Methods,* Chapman and Grimes, Boston, 1952.

Davidson, Douglas, "Black Culture and Liberal Sociology," *Berkeley Journal of Sociology,* 1969, **14**, pp. 165–175.

Deighton, H. S., "History and the Study of Race Relations," *Race,* 1959, **1**, 1, November, pp. 15–25.

Frazier, E. Franklin, "Sociological Theory and Race Relations," *American Sociological Review,* 1947, **12**, 265–271.

———, "Areas of Research in Race Relations," *Sociology and Social Research,* 1948, **42**, 6, July–August, pp. 424–429.

Gossett, Thomas F., *Race: The History of an Idea in America,* Southern Methodist University Press, Dallas, Tex., 1963.

Haller, John S., *Outcasts from Evolution: Scientific Attitudes of Racial Inferiority, 1859–1900,* University of Illinois Press, Urbana, 1971.

Jones, M. H., and A. Willingham, "The White Custodians of the Black Experience," *Social Science Quarterly,* **51**, 1, 1970, pp. 31–36.

Lieberman, L., "The Debate over Race: A Study in the Sociology of Knowledge," *Phylon,* 1968, **29**, pp. 127–142.

MacRae, D. C., "Race and Sociology in History and Theory," in P. Mason (ed.), *Man, Race and Darwin,* Oxford University Press, London, 1960.

Mason, P., "Race, Intelligence and Professor Jensen," *Race Today,* July, 1969, pp. 76–77.

Newby, Idus, A., *Challenge to the Court: Social Scientists and the Defense of Segregation, 1954–1966,* Louisiana State University Press, Baton Rouge, 1967.

Rose, Peter I., *The Subject is Race: Traditional Ideologies and the Teaching of Race Relations,* Oxford University Press, New York, 1968.

Ryan, W., *Blaming the Victim,* Pantheon, New York, 1971.

Smythe, Hugh H., and L. Chase, "Current Research on the Negro: A Critique," *Sociology and Social Research,* 1958, **42**, 3, January–February, pp. 199–202.

Chapter 5

Summary of Section One

In this first section of our discussion we have been primarily concerned with introducing race relations as a topic of analysis, highlighting what these relations reveal about society and social behavior, pointing to the problems involved in their analysis, and delineating the historical development of this field of study.

In Chapter 1 we defined our major focus as the sociological analysis of race relations on the individual, group, and societal level, with particular reference to the dominant colonial elite's control of racial behavior on these levels, the reaction of subordinate minorities, and change in intergroup relations ensuing from economic development in the general society. The colonial model will provide an important foundation to our analysis of the interaction of groups defined as races and of the subsequent social change.

Chapter 2 described race relations as revealing the shape of a society's structure and the forces behind social behavior within it, particularly the degree to which it is colonial in structure. More specifically, we delineated race relations as revealing social tension, the social structure, social flexibility, social conformity, the effects of industrialization, the relationship between attitudes, needs, and behavior, the historical development of the social sciences, the problems of sociological theory, and social policy. In general, then, these relations highlight a society's social structure, behavior within it, and the effects of social change.

Problems involved in the analysis of race relations were discussed in Chapter 3. Three main issues were raised: objectivity, theoretical problems, and empirical research. More specifically, the difficulty of subjectivity and elite assimilationist orientations were discussed. Secondly, the problem of static typologies and the conceptualization of major terms was also underlined. Thirdly, we dealt with empirical issues such as index, instrument, and sample selection; response bias; the predominance of psychological, static, and crisis-oriented data; and the problem of data interpretation.

Section One was completed with a discussion of the field's historical development. We showed how, under the control of a colonial elite, this field was initially established to classify the human species and rationalize racial exploitation. As such oppression lost its legitimacy, race relations turned to the problem of implementing the American Creed of equality in the face of prejudice and discrimination. Recent developments include higher awareness of institutionalized racism, the development of theoretical analysis, and attempts by minorities to produce their own perspectives on the "race problem." However, a colonial environment, even within academia, continues to hamper the development of an objective perspective.

In summary, race relations represent intergroup interaction on the individual, group, and societal level within the context of a colonial society controlled by a particular racial elite. Study of these relations reveals the structure of this colonial society and the processes at work within it. However, the topic is plagued by the problem of subjectivity and social blindness produced by institutionalized racism. Finally, the field of race relations has developed in a manner which, at least in the past, reflects the major needs of white academics and their attempts to handle social change. Race relations operate within a particular societal context, making it difficult for individuals within it to see them objectively. The student should be particularly aware of this problem as we begin our analysis.

Section Two

Definitions
and Approaches

Chapter 6

Defining
Basic Concepts

A fundamental problem in any field is the definition of basic concepts; in this regard race relations is particularly problematic. We have perceived the extent to which conceptualizations of race are ideologically based and time-bound: they have been the prerogative of particular disciplines, beginning with biological criteria in zoology and anthropology, changing to an emphasis on psychological and attitudinal orientations, and then developing into the contemporary awareness of the sociological context of race relations. This trend represents a movement from attempts to classify races in biological terms during an era of colonial expansion and cultural ethnocentrism to contemporary recognition of the problems engendered by prejudice and the utilization of "race" as a social label by particular power elites.

With the notion of genetic races generally being invalidated[1]

[1]For a discussion of this, see M. Banton, *Race Relations,* Basic Books, New York, 1967, pp. 50–54.

and with the movement toward decolonization has come awareness of "race" as an imposed social definition based on motives
of exploitation and social control. However, the continuing
confusion of this term with others relating to religious, national,
and ethnic origins, as well as the latest (and, in some situations,
overt) tendency to assume that there "must be something physically significant about race,"[2] reinforces the general notion that
"race" is a physical category which inevitably serves as the major
criterion of political policy and social behavior. It is crucial,
therefore, that these concepts are clearly defined before proceeding with our analysis of the major factors responsible for their
social utilization.

MINORITY GROUPS

A race is a major example of a minority group. The latter may be
defined as *any group that views itself and/or is defined by a
dominant power elite as unique on the basis of perceived physical,
cultural, economic, and/or behavioral characteristics and is
treated accordingly in a negative manner.* The following are major
types of minority groups:

1   Physical: race, sex, age
2   Cultural: religion, ethnicity
3   Economic: social class
4   Behavioral: deviation

All these minorities have experienced oppression and control in various societies at particular points of historical development. It is reasonable to assume, however, that perceived physical differences are the most viable criteria of minority-group
membership and are the most difficult to erase. Race is, perhaps,
the most persistent and problematic criterion of minority-group
membership. It is also subdifferentiated by cultural, economic,
and behavioral minorities. Generally, then, race represents the
most macroscopic criterion for minority-group membership and
differential treatment.

[2]For a useful example, see A. R. Jensen, "How Much Can We Boost I.Q. and
Scholastic Achievement?" *Harvard Education Review,* **39**, 1969.

THE TERM "RACE"

The concept "race" has been the cause of much controversy in its identification with physical phenomena and with related terms such as physical subpopulation, ethnicity, and human species.[3] Race is none of these, but following the useful definition provided by van den Berghe, it may be viewed as a:

> human group that defines itself and/or is defined by other groups as different from other groups by virtue of innate and immutable physical characteristics. These physical characteristics are in turn believed to be intrinsically related to moral, intellectual, and other nonphysical attributes or abilities.[4]

The emphasis in this definition is upon the *social definition* of race, both by a particular group and others. Race may thus be viewed as a *reciprocal social definition based upon the perception of physical differences as significant.* Races do not exist unless groups are defined as such on the basis of perceived differences; they have to be socially recognized before they exist sociologically. In this connection, Lind provides a dynamic conception of this concept in his analysis of Hawaii. He emphasizes that:

> . . . races come into being and races cease to exist, not because a new breed is born or an old stock dies out, but because the shifting conditions of life have made such groups clearly conscious of their being significantly different from others and have enforced a comparable conviction upon those who do not belong.[5]

Lind's approach is important in its recognition that racial definitions change and are dependent upon the "shifting conditions of life"—the society's historical, political, economic, and demographic development. The social definition of race does not remain static but changes with its societal context.

A number of other writers have taken a similar approach: Banton, for example, sees race as a "role sign"; in other words,

[3]See P. L. van den Berghe, *Race and Racism*, Wiley, New York, 1967. p. 9.

[4]P. L. van den Berghe, ibid., p. 9.

[5]A. W. Lind, *Hawaii: The Last of the Magic Isles*, Oxford University Press, London, 1969, p. 51.

perceived physical differences are used as the basis of assigning people to particular roles or tasks in the social order.[6] According to this view, societies possess well-defined systems of "racial roles" comprising the racial caste structure. Additionally, Blumer sees racial prejudice, not as a "set of feelings," but as a "sense of group position"—an individual's awareness of his race group's economic and power position in society.[7] Prejudice is based on a perceived group threat to this "position." Rex also views race as a "social category," which is defined and utilized in a number of types of situations, ranging from the slave plantation to situations of ethnic pluralism.[8] Montagu, feels that the term "ethnic group" is more appropriate than the biological concept,[9] while an international conference on race relations held in Honolulu emphasized the manner in which various social situations are influenced by the "idea of race"—a social labeling approach.[10]

From these definitions it can be seen that race is not a physical category; rather it is a social label or definition which has evolved out of a society's particular historical development. Because of this, the same race group may be defined differently in various societies. Also, the more colonial the social structure, the more rigid and inflexible will be societal definitions of race. These definitions also change over time, particularly with industrialization, resulting in the redefinition of particular race groups, as perceived threat changes and subordinate minorities redefine their relationship to the dominant elite.

Thus, colonial elites tend to become more accepting of subordinate minorities over time, at least with reference to their social and physical needs, while the latter increasingly question the legitimacy of the elite's power monopoly. In this manner, elites become more accepting and minorities more rejecting over time. In American race relations this trend may be seen in white-black and white-Mexican relations in particular, while a

[6]M. Banton, op cit., pp. 57–62.

[7]H. Blumer, "Race Prejudice as a Sense of Group Position," *Pacific Sociological Review*, **1**, 1958, pp. 3–7.

[8]J. Rex, "Race as a Social Category," *Journal of Biosocial Science*, 1969, pp. 145–152.

[9]A. Montagu, "The Concept of Race," *American Anthropologist*, **64**, 1962, pp. 919–928.

[10]See A. Hourani, "The Concept of Race Relations: Thoughts after a Conference," *International Social Science Bulletin*, **7**, 1955, pp. 335–340.

similar development may be perceived within colonial Africa.[11] Race is thus a dynamic concept rather than a static category and needs to be analyzed within its particular societal context.

"ETHNIC" GROUPS

It is important to differentiate clearly between "races" and "ethnic" groups. These terms are similar insofar as both are social definitions; however, the former is based on perceived physical differences, while the latter utilizes perceived cultural differences, such as religion, dress, and nationality. Both may result in rigid social differentiation, exploitation, and bitter conflict within a colonial context; the present turmoil in Northern Ireland is a relevant example. Both may also contain physical attributes used as a "role sign" (physical characteristics *attributed* to Jews is a case in point), but the former term is broader in application: race groups are internally differentiated by ethnicity rather than the reverse. However a high level intraracial ethnic differentiation contributes to the heterogeneity or "pluralism"[12] of the general social situation, making racial problems more complex and conflict-ridden than they might be otherwise.[13] In general, then, race relations are physically based, while ethnic groups are defined in terms of cultural criteria. However, physical characteristics are attributed to both, and it is important to distinguish analytically between the two concepts.

"RACE RELATIONS"

Race relations refer to the *kind of interaction which occurs between groups and individuals socially defined as "races."* Such interaction occurs on a number of levels, as indicated by the above definition. Blumer distinguishes at least seven types of

---

[11]See, for example, the author's discussion in G. C. Kinloch, "Social Types and Race Relations in the Colonial Setting: A Case Study of Rhodesia," *Phylon,* third quarter, 1972, pp. 276–289.

[12]For a discussion of this term as it relates to race relations, see P. L van den Berghe, op cit., chap 7.

[13]The South African situation, with its high level of white ethnic and black tribal differentiation, is a relevant example.

relations, ranging from "formal economic relations" to "attitudinal or feeling relations."[14] These may be broadly divided into relations on the structural or group level (i.e., the power elite and the racial economic-caste structure) and those on the individual (i.e., attitudinal) level. Further, relations on either level may be what Blumer terms "orderly or discordant."

Whatever the case, such relations are dynamic rather than static and are under the general control of the governing elite. Furthermore, the presence of race relations (based in turn on the presence of social definitions) is dependent on the presence of *colonial characteristics* in the societal environment, i.e., *domination, exploitation, and control by a migrant race group which subjugates the indigeneous population and imports other race groups for purposes of labor and economic development.* Rigid racial definitions function as social control mechanisms in situations of high social, economic, and demographic inequality. Race relations depend on the presence of particular social definitions, reflecting a colonial social structure. Accordingly, the more colonial a society, the more likely rigid race relations will be present.

RACISM, PREJUDICE, AND DISCRIMINATION

"Racism" may be viewed as *uncritical acceptance* (through socialization) *of a negative social definition of a group identified as a race on perceived physical grounds along with the legitimacy of the discriminatory treatment accompanying that definition.* Secondly, "prejudice" is similar *acceptance of negative social definitions without consideration of their validity in reference to ethnic as well as race groups.* Prejudice is also associated with high and overt levels of racism, while the latter may be absorbed normatively without high levels of hostility. Thirdly, "discrimination" may be defined as *applied prejudice in which negative social definitions are translated into action and political policy through the subordination of minorities and deprivation of their political, social, and economic rights.* While racism and prejudice are

---

[14]H. Blumer, "Reflections on Theory of Race Relations," in A. W. Lind (ed.), *Race Relations in World Perspectives,* University of Hawaii Press, Honolulu, 1955, pp. 3–21.

attitudes, discrimination is the institutional expression of these attitudes in the social control of minorities, i.e, institutionalized racism. Furthermore, while prejudice and discrimination are interrelated, they are not necessarily interdependent: one may occur with or without the other, dependent on the predominant norms in the social situation. Situational factors have to be taken into account in any analysis of attitudes and intergroup relations.

It may be useful here to examine the manner in which these concepts are defined by other writers. Banton, for example, views racism as

> . . . the doctrine that a man's behaviour is determined by stable inherited characters deriving from separate racial stocks having distinctive attributes and usually considered to stand to one another in relations of superiority and inferiority.

"Racialism," on the other hand, refers to the practice of racism. "Prejudice" is the attitude, while "discrimination" reflects the manner in which *social relationships* are based upon such attitudes.[15] Similarly, for Simpson and Yinger, prejudice is "an emotional, rigid attitude (a *pre*disposition to respond to a certain stimulus in a certain way) toward a group of people."[16]

In general, then, racial prejudice refers to attitudinal acceptance of racist criteria, while racial discrimination reflects the societal translation of these norms into the form of a racial caste system. In the case of America, whites, blacks, chicanos, Indians, and the Chinese are examples of major race groups. Antiblack or anti-Indian attitudes and associated stereotypes reflect racial prejudice, while residential segregation of and occupational discrimination against these groups are examples of discrimination.

CONCLUSIONS

In this chapter, we outlined types of minorities and changing definitions of "race," moving from the biological through the psychological, to the present awareness of the societal context of

---

[15]M. Banton, *Race Relations,* Basic Books, New York, 1967, p. 8.

[16]G. E. Simpson and J. M. Yinger, *Race and Cultural Minorities: An Analysis of Prejudice and Discrimination,* 4th ed., Harper & Row, New York, 1972, p. 24.

race relations. We viewed race as a reciprocal social definition, rather than a biological category, imposed by a controlling elite in a colonial setting, based upon the perception of physical differences as significant. Racism and prejudice were viewed as the uncritical acceptance of such definitions, while discrimination represents the translation of these definitions into societal action. Furthermore, none of these factors remains static but changes with industrialization. Finally, race relations represent the interaction between race groups on a number of levels in the social system. Factors affecting the definition of the above concepts are summarized in Figure 6-1, highlighting the societal context in which race and intergroup relations are defined.

Having defined our basic concepts, we turn to their analysis in the chapters to follow. We have emphasized that it is factors on all levels of the social system—psychological, social-psychological, and sociological—as they relate to the social definition of race and the manner in which it changes, that constitute the central focus of this field. It is to these "factors" that we turn now, beginning with the psychological.

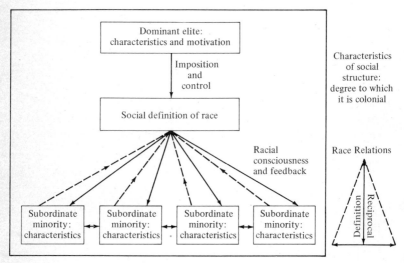

Figure 6-1 Major factors affecting the definition of "race."

STUDY QUESTIONS

1 Develop your *own* definitions of "minority group," "race," "ethnic group," "race relations," "racism," "prejudice," and "discrimination."
2 Delineate clearly between race and ethnic relations, giving specific examples.
3 Show how social definitions of race have changed historically in American society. In what respects have they remained stable?
4 Show how similar race groups have been defined differently in a number of different societies.
5 Consider how ethnicity may increase and/or lower racial conflict.

READINGS

Blumer, H., "Reflections on Theory of Race Relations," in A. W. Lind, *Race Relations in World Perspective,* University of Hawaii Press, Honolulu, 1955.
Mead, Margaret, et al. (eds.), *Science and the Concept of Race,* Columbia University Press, New York, 1968.

Chapter 7

Basic Approaches to the Analysis of Race Relations: I. Psychological

Social behavior may be perceived as the function of at least three elements: the psychological or personality factors; the social-psychological or group context in which that personality operates; and sociological or societal factors, historical and economic, which govern intergroup relations through elite dominance. Approaches to race relations conform to this trichotomy: the psychological attempts to explain the psychopathology of prejudice, the social-psychological explores the group context of racial orientations, while the sociological delineates societal factors behind particular patterns of relations. Thus, an individual's definition of race may be examined in terms of his personality type, the particular race group of which he is a member, and the societal environment in which intergroup relations have developed historically and are presently controlled by a particular power elite. These three levels of analysis are obviously interrelated, which Figure 7-1 attempts to demonstrate in schematic form.

While approaches to race relations in the social sciences concentrate on all of these levels, there is little effort to link them in any general conceptual framework. We shall attempt to develop such a framework by dealing with each set of factors in turn, commencing with the psychological, moving toward the sociological. We shall concentrate in this chapter on psychological analyses of race relations, presenting major theories first, critiquing them next, and finally, attempting to bring them together in a conceptual synthesis.

THE PSYCHOPATHOLOGY OF PREJUDICE

Psychological analyses of race relations see prejudiced attitudes as the function of a particular personality type, supported and reinforced by the social environment in which the individual operates. With its origins in Freudian theory, this analytical approach includes discussion of the "authoritarian" personality, the "prejudiced" personality, and psychiatric analyses of preju-

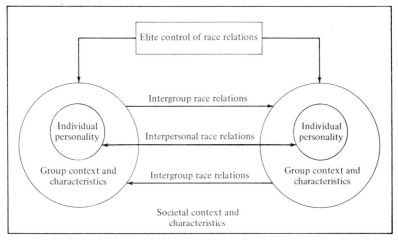

Figure 7-1 Major factors and levels of analysis in race relations.

dice. A central assumption links the frustration of personality need-fulfillment to socially approved forms of adaptation, such as oppression and racism. Personality problems are projected into social behavior in a manner which is reinforced by the dominant elite; *PHYSICAL CHARACTERISTICS* These reactions are defined as "customary," and the frustration-prejudice syndrome becomes a ~~stable~~ *STABLE* part of the social system.

WHAT IS SAID ~~Implicit~~ in much of the ~~above~~ discussion is the notion of a particular personality type. A large body of literature sees racial prejudice as part of a general psychological syndrome, reflecting a negative family environment where rejection and control are dominant. Within such an environment a personality forms which reflects certain features: authoritarianism and prejudice are its central features as the person attempts to ~~compensate~~ *MAKE UP FOR* for his frustrated needs and inferiority complex. Of special interest is the work by Adorno on the "authoritarian personality"[1] and Allport's study of the "prejudiced personality."[2] Characteristics such as "rigidity of outlook," "suggestibility," "moralism," "ambivalence," "authoritarianism," and the "need for definiteness" represent a general psychological syndrome which, according to Allport, represents an "expression of deep-lying trends in the individual's personality—one in which prejudice is "functionally important." According to this work, racial attitudes constitute part of a general personality pattern rather than being isolated and irrational traits. The prejudiced personality represents a particular psychological configuration which has developed within a particular home environment, attempting to compensate for its negativism. According to this approach, then, prejudice is the function of a particular personality type and general syndrome, developed by previous forms of socialization.

The relationship between the family and racial attitudes within it is also discussed by Bloom in his recent work, *The Social Psychology of Race Relations*.[3] He discusses, in some detail, the "ethnocentric child," ~~studied by Frenkel-Brunswick~~, whose per-

[1]T. W. Adorno et al., *The Authoritarian Personality*, Harper, New York, 1950.
[2]G. W. Allport, *The Nature of Prejudice*, Addison-Wesley, Cambridge, Mass., 1954.
[3]L. Bloom, *The Social Psychology of Race Relations*, G. Allen, London, 1971 pp. 60–65.

 FOOT

sonality is similar to the authoritarian type just discussed. An important conclusion of this study is the interpretation of hostile prejudice as the result of "forced submission to authority," suggesting the relevance of the kind of child-rearing methods in a particular home. Bloom also uses a study by Mosher and Scodel to illustrate the close link between the attitudes of mother and child. The relevance of family processes, particularly of socialization, to racial attitudes is evident in this body of work also.

Projection of personality problems in racial prejudice has strong parallels in Freudian explanations of racial attitudes. A recent study of "white racism" epitomizes this approach.[4] Following Freudian theory, the writer assumes that "the whole history of the individual is condensed in the oedipus complex," for it is out of the unsatisfactory resolution of this complex by the ego and the superego, particularly the repression of "unacceptable desires," that cultural institutionalization of dominance and repression develops as compensation. Three types of racism develop in historical order as follows: the "dominant" type, an activity of the id which emphasizes the quality of blackness; the "aversive," an ego activity concentrating on "anal sadism" and characteristics of dirt; and finally "metaracism," or "superego power," consisting of "the pursuit of consciously nonracist behavior in the interests of furthering the destructive work of one's culture."

According to this framework, repression of "instinctual fantasies" finds its outlet in a cultural environment which stresses "anally rooted symbolism"; this allows scapegoating, repression, and racism, based on the assumption that "personality and culture are parallel organisms." Internal personality problems are projected onto the cultural system, which defines their appropriate expression as "dominance" and "repression." In this manner, racism is traced back to fundamental and constant personality problems, particularly the oedipus complex—a problem which can never be fully resolved.

Kovel's work also parallels earlier works which emphasize the psychopathology of prejudice. Frustration-aggression theory,

[4]See J. Kovel, *White Racism: A Psychohistory*, Vintage Books, New York, 1970.

for example, relates "cultural restrictions in childhood" and the "limitations of daily life in adulthood" to social scapegoating within a "permissive social pattern."[5] According to this explanation, prejudice results from reaction to cultural restrictions and resultant frustration. The hostility which results is channeled into visible and convenient "scapegoats," providing a safe and socially sanctioned compensatory mechanism. The process does not end there, however: scapegoating provides only limited satisfaction, frustrating the deprived group, contributing to a feedback cycle in which aggression feeds frustration, leading to increased racism and minority deprivation.

Psychiatrists have also contributed to frustration-aggression theory: in an early study of "Psychodynamic Factors in Racial Relations," McLean sees "myths of racial inferiority" functioning as a source of prestige and feelings of omnipotence among frustrated whites as they enslaved blacks.[6] In an "empty" and "impotent" environment, the dominant group satisfies its needs for a positive ego by subordinating and oppressing other groups. In this manner, repression results in feelings of power and security.

A related topic ~~here~~ is the characteristics of subordinate groups involved in the scapegoating process. Allport delineates these as follows: the scapegoat group should possess high visibility and accessibility, have low power, represent a negative idea, and have functioned as a scapegoat in the past.[7] The more closely a particular group conforms to these characteristics, the more likely it will be involved in the scapegoating process. A minority with little or no power, possessing characteristics defined as negative by the dominant elite,[8] is most often involved.

At the psychological level, then, racial attitudes are viewed as the function of a frustrated personality type that finds its outlet

[5]See, for example, J. Dollard, *Caste and Class in a Southern Town,* Doubleday, Garden City, N.Y., 1957.

[6]H. V. McLean, "Psychodynamic Factors in Racial Relations," *Annals of American Academy of Political and Social Science,* **244**, 1946, pp. 159–166.

[7]G. W. Allport, op cit.

[8]Physical charteristics, such as color, are particularly relevant here; e.g., there are a large number of negative qualities associated with "blackness" and to a lesser extent, "yellowness." For a psychoanalytical discussion of this symbolism, see J. Kovel, op cit.

in socially approved forms of oppression and domination. This type is part of a general psychological syndrome based on the need for power. An equally important, but less analyzed aspect, of this process is the reaction of minorities involved. McLean portrays the marginality of the black who is achievement-oriented in a white-dominated society: he is rejected by whites and resented by blacks.[9] Such ambivalence contributes to frustration among the oppressed minority.

A modern counterpart to this can be found in work done by Grier and Cobbs on *Black Rage*.[10] The authors perceive a variety of reactions to oppression: "blindness to white suppression," self-hatred, and aggression against blacks as the individual "identifies with his oppressor psychologically." Here, then, social blindness and particularly self-scapegoating serve as means of deflecting frustration. Such "models of deflection," however, particularly the latter, contribute to the ongoing cycle of frustration-aggression, which may eventually result in overt violence.

The application of a psychoanalytic approach to blacks in the United States is also emphasized in a recent psychological book by Baughman.[11] Quoting an early study by Powdermaker, published in 1943, this writer delineates a number of ways the black may channel his antiwhite aggression: attacking, substituting, ignoring the problem, identifying with the dominant group, or, to follow the approach of Prange and Vitols, using humor. Such an approach parallels that of Grier and Cobbs in its emphasis on frustration-deflection, resulting in a number of particular personality types.

THE PSYCHOANALYTIC FRAMEWORK

The approach to race relations we have discussed so far, then, sees racial attitudes as projected aggression emanating from frustrated personality needs. This reaction is directed against minorities with particular social characteristics who, in turn, are

---

[9]H. McLean, op cit.

[10]W. H. Grier and P. M. Cobbs, *Black Rage,* Bantam Books, New York, 1968.

[11]E. E. Baughman, *Black Americans: A Psychological Analysis,* Academic Press, New York, 1971.

frustrated and turn aggression upon themselves. The result is an ongoing cycle of frustration and aggression, with little or no intergroup communication and an upward spiral of potential violence. This framework is summarized in Figure 7-2, delineating the major variables and their interrelationships. Such a framework is useful in locating the psychological sources of psychotic levels of prejudice but, as we shall see in the following critique, is highly inadequate on its own, given the complex social environment in which race relations operate.

A crucial problem here, for example, is the extent to which racial prejudice is a function of a particular personality type (i.e., authoritarian) or is learned through social norms, regardless of

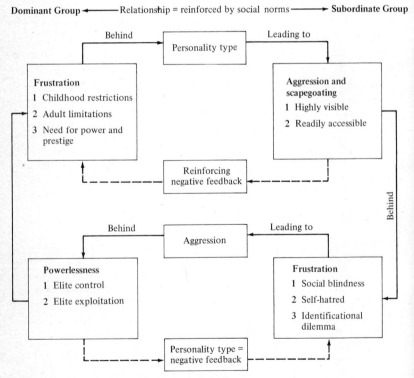

Figure 7-2 The psychopathology of prejudice.

the individual's unique idiosyncracies. Thus, researchers such as Adorno, Hotopf, Schuman, and Harding interpret their data as supporting the former,[12] while Rhyne, McCandless, and Holloway find that their results do not support the personality-type theory with its emphasis on traits such as "intolerance of ambiguity."[13]

On the one hand, then, we have the "personality-type" theory, which explains prejudice in personality and psychoanalytic terms, while the other theory views these attitudes as the function of social norms and different learning experiences. The latter is further reinforced by a cross-cultural study carried out by Pettigrew,[14] who discovered that within samples of South African and United States college students it was *conformity* to societal norms rather than *authoritarianism* which differentiated between high and low prejudice. Van den Berghe also deals with the relationship between personality and prejudice, asserting that in highly racist societies, personality factors bear little relation to normative prejudice, while in less racist situations, the reverse tends to be the case.[15] It is obvious, therefore, that racial attitudes are closely defined by the social context in which they operate—a major point the psychological approach tends to overlook. Personality is not irrelevant to attitudes; rather it interacts with social norms in a particular social context. The relationship between personality, attitudes, and social norms is a complex one which we shall explore in the next chapter. First, however, we turn to a critique of the psychological approach.

CRITIQUE

While the psychological framework is useful in isolating major personality factors commonly used to explain prejudice and

[12]T. W. Adorno, op cit.; W. H. N. Hotopf, "Psychological Studies of Race Prejudice," *Political Quarterly,* **32**, 1961, pp. 328–340; H. Schuman and J. Harding, "Prejudice and the Norm of Rationality," *Sociometry,* **27**, 1964, pp. 353–371.

[13]E. H. Rhyne, "Racial Prejudice and Personality Scales: An Alternative Approach," *Social Forces,* **41**, 1962, pp. 45–53; B. R. McCandless and H. D. Holloway, "Race Prejudice and Intolerance of Ambiguity in Children," *Journal of Abnormal Social Psychology,* **51**, 1955.

[14]T. F. Pettigrew, "Personality and Sociocultural Factors in Intergroup Attitudes: A Cross-National Comparison," *Journal of Conflict Resolution,* **2**, 1958, pp. 29–42.

[15]P. L. van den Berghe, *Race and Racism,* Wiley, New York, 1967, pp. 18–21.

feedback processes, it highlights certain limitations of this kind of approach as follows:

1   It concentrates on very high levels of prejudice, neglecting "average" or "normal" prejudice which is learned, often unconsciously, through in-group socialization. It deals with one end of the scale only.

2   While concentrating in detail on the complexity of a particular personality type, this approach neglects the factors producing such a configuration and how they reflect a particular social situation rather than universal, underlying psychological processes such as "compensation."

3   The distinction between attitudes and actual behavior is neglected, deemphasizing the effects of social constraint and the manner in which such attitudes may be modified or changed by a particular situation. As previously emphasized, van den Berghe points out that in racist societies, most dominant-group individuals reveal both prejudice and discrimination, regardless of personality factors, while in societies which are low on racism, personality characteristics are related to such negative attitudes and behavior.[16] The influence of the social situation on racial attitudes has to be taken into account, particularly in the case of "normal" prejudice.

4   According to this approach, racial attitudes are viewed mainly as individual phenomena, with little regard to group characteristics and identity. However, racial identity may be viewed as part of group identity as well as a set of individual orientations. These links to the group context are important to the development of a fuller analysis of such attitudes.

5   In neglecting these social links, this approach fails to explore factors behind an individual's racial identity, as well as the causes of conformity and deviance. What holds the individual to a particular group orientation, and why may he deviate? Such questions are vital but are not dealt with adequately here.

6   This approach also fails to delineate different kinds of minorities and minority situations. The concentration on white-black relations in the United States is understandable but highly limited from an analytical standpoint. There is usually a plurality of minorities within any industrialized society, resulting in ethnic as well as racial prejudice.

[16]P. L. van den Berghe, op. cit.

Case	Racist society	Authoritarianism	Prejudice	Explanation
1	+	+	+	Racist structure
2	+	−	+	Normative racism
3	−	+	−	Nonracist structure*
4	−	−	−	Nonracist structure
5	−	−	+	Competitive situation
6	−	+	+	Competitive situation*
7	+	+	−	Socioeconomic differences*
8	+	−	−	Socioeconomic differences

*Personality variation in authoritarianism.

Figure 7-3 Possible relationships between social structure, authoritarianism, and racial prejudice.

7   Finally, the manner in which the elite power structure defines and controls race relations is neglected in the concentration upon microscopic variables. Elite control, particularly political domination, is a key variable in any race relations situation.

In general, then, the psychological approach concentrates on personality factors behind extreme racial prejudice, neglecting the social context in which these attitudes have developed, are reinforced, and operate. While valuable in delineating the psychological syndrome behind such views, it is extremely limited as an explanation in the general field of race relations. It has been shown, for example, that the "laws which govern interpersonal relations are not necessarily the same as those which regulate intergroup relations."[17] This may be illustrated by examining the possible relationships between social structure, personality factors, and racial prejudice. There are at least eight possible situations, as illustrated in Figure 7-3. Here it can be seen that attitudes may be defined by a number of social situations: a racist social structure which reinforces authoritarianism and/or racial prejudice; a nonracist social situation in which there is personality variance in authoritarianism; competitive intergroup situations in nonracist societies, resulting in prejudice and the operation of authoritarianism; and racist societies in which prejudice is absent or low among those in positions of socioeconomic security and low threat.

[17]J. Bernard, "The Conceptualization of Intergroup Relations with Special Reference to Conflict," *Social Forces*, **29**, 1951, pp. 243–246.

The importance of such a typology is the relevance of societal and group situations to the operation of personality factors and racial attitudes, making the examination of racial attitudes and intergroup relations in their relevant situational context highly relevant to the development of a sociological approach. Moving toward this level from the psychological requires at least two preliminary steps: (1) the need to specify social links between the individual and his group context; and (2) the relationship between intergroup relations and the societal context in which they operate. The material for both steps is contained within what may be termed the social-psychological approach to race relations; we turn to this next.

CONCLUSIONS

In this chapter, we have examined the psychological approach to race relations, specifically the psychoanalysis of racial prejudice. Explaining such attitudes in terms of specific personality types is conceptually efficient. However, this approach tends to ignore the structure of the social setting in which these attitudes are formed as well as the dynamics of intergroup behavior. The danger of viewing highly prejudiced individuals in terms of particular personality types is the overlooking of "normal" levels of prejudice, which may not be highly visible but nevertheless operate in actual race relations. Such social blindness may be desirable to particular elites but is analytically limited and, in some respects, reflects the perspective of an essentially colonial social system.

STUDY QUESTIONS

1 Outline the major psychological characteristics of prejudice.
2 What aspects of race relations do you feel the psychoanalytic approach may be *most* useful in explaining?
3 Examine the type of explanation (i.e., its theoretical structure) involved in the psychoanalytic approach. What are its obvious weaknesses?
4 Outline the manner in which the social context may control or define the operation of a "prejudiced" personality.

5 Consider the groups that have been used as scapegoats most often. What characteristics do they have in common?

READINGS

Adorno, T. W., et al., *The Authoritarian Personality,* Harper, New York, 1950.

Allport, Gordon W., (ed.), *ABC's of Scapegoating,* Anti-Defamation League of B'nai B'rith, New York, 1948.

———, *The Resolution of Intergroup Tensions: A Critical Appraisal of Methods,* National Conference of Christians and Jews, New York, 1952.

———, *The Nature of Prejudice,* Addison-Wesley, Cambridge, Mass., 1958.

Bettelheim, Bruno, and Barbara Janowitz, *Dynamics of Prejudice: A Psychological and Sociological Study of Veterans,* 1st ed., Harper, New York, 1950.

Dollard, J., *Caste and Class in a Southern Town,* Doubleday, Garden City, N.Y., 1957.

Giddens, Anthony, "The Psychology of Race Riots," *New Society,* 1964, **69**, January 23, pp. 10–11.

Goodman, Mary E., *Race Awareness in Young Children,* Collier Books, New York, 1964.

Gregor, A. J., "Race Relations, Frustration and Aggression," *Revue Internationale de Sociologic,* 1965, **2**, December, pp. 90–112.

Grier, W. H., and P. M. Cobbs, *Black Rage,* Bantam Books, New York, 1968, chap. 6.

Hotopf, W. H. N., "Psychological Studies of Race Prejudice," *Political Quarterly,* 1961, **32**, 4, October–December, pp. 328–340.

Huszar, George B., *Anatomy of Racial Intolerance,* H. W. Wilson, New York, 1946.

Kovel, Joel, *White Racism: A Psychohistory,* Pantheon, New York, 1970.

Lowinger, Paul, "Sex, Selma and Segregation: A Psychiatrist's Reaction," *International Journal of Social Psychiatry,* 1968, **14**, 2, Spring, pp. 119–124.

McCandless, B. R., and H. D. Holloway, "Race Prejudice and Intolerance of Ambiguity in Children," *Journal of Abnormal Social Psychology,* 1955, **51**.

McLean, H. V., "Psychodynamics Factors in Racial Relations," *Annals of American Academy of Political and Social Science,* 1946, **244**.

Marchionne, A. M., and F. L. Marcuse, "Sensitization and Prejudice,"

Journal of Abnormal Social Psychology, 1955, **51**, 3, November, pp. 637–640.

Miller, Herbert A., *Races, Nations and Classes: The Psychology of Domination and Freedom,* Lippincott, Philadelphia, 1924.

Montagu, Ashley, *Man's Most Dangerous Myth: The Fallacy of Race,* 4th ed., World Publishing, Cleveland, 1964.

Schuman, Howard, and John Harding, "Prejudice and the Norm of Rationality," *Sociometry,* 1964, **27**, 3, September, pp. 353–371.

Chapter 8

Basic Approaches
to the Analysis
of Race Relations:
II. Social-Psychological

So far in our discussion we have linked racial attitudes with
personality characteristics. In our critique of this kind of analysis,
we noted a neglect of the social environment in which individual
personalities and attitudes are formed. In this chapter we shall
move toward the group level of analysis in two stages: (1) we
shall specify some of the social links between the individual and
his group context, and (2) we shall delineate the relationship
between intergroup relations and the societal context in which
they exist. Working in this order, we shall discuss theories which
link the individual and the group to racial attitudes and, secondly,
discussions which relate these groups to society.

THEORIES LINKING THE INDIVIDUAL AND THE GROUP

One of the first links required to relate the individual and the
group is one between psychological needs and perceptions of
social norms, i.e., the relationship between norms and the per-

sonalities of those participating in a particular situation. Richmond has discussed such a relationship, arguing for a level of analysis which goes beyond the nature of interaction processes.[1] In establishing this link, he quotes a study by Bott carried out in a working-class area of London. Examining how people define what is the "done thing," she found that in communities which are not closely knit, people had difficulty in defining what others think and feel. Instead, an individual's perception of local group norms reflected his subjective needs rather than the norms themselves. In other words, he projected his psychological needs onto his perception of social reality. Projection thus provides a useful link between norms and personality, as such perceptions are rewarded and find social support.

Richmond concludes that personality and the social structure are interdependent systems through the processes of individual internalization, projection, and institutionalization of norms on the group level. Here, then, are three concepts which link the individual to the group: internalization, projection, and institutionalization, centering on the manner in which subjective needs define an individual's perception of norms and values.

Projection of subjective needs, of course, may neither be socially acceptable nor result in their institutionalization. In such a case the problem of what has been termed "role tension" may arise. In a paper to be discussed in more detail later, Bagley applies theories of status consistency to race relations.[2] This author deals with status inconsistency on the psychological level by examining the concept of role tension—a situation in which role behavior defined as deviant is evaluated negatively and has been found to be correlated with high levels of authoritarianism. He reports a longitudinal study of personality development which revealed that high expressionism in boys resulted in liberal political attitudes, while the reverse was true for girls. Such a difference is interpreted as rank disequilibrium or role tension in

[1] A. H. Richmond, "Sociological and Psychological Explanations of Racial Prejudice: Some Light on the Controversy from Recent Research in Britain," *Pacific Sociological Review*, 4, 1961, pp. 63–68.
[2] C. Bagley, "Race Relationships and Theories of Status Consistency," *Race*, 11, 3, 1970, pp. 267–289. Note that "status consistency" is discussed and defined in Chap. 9, to follow.

which female expressionism is subject to a series of "negative interactions" or sanctions, constituting "disequilibrium between the 'internal' and 'external' aspects of the role, which are in disequilibrium."

According to this approach, racial intolerance may be viewed as the result of role tension—conflict between internal and external situations, resulting in high levels of authoritarianism as a way of dealing with the situation. Rejection of behavior which is deemed socially deviant may reinforce attitudinal negativism. Such frustration-aggression parallels the psychoanalytic theory discussed earlier insofar as it highlights the relationship between frustrated psychological needs and the reinforcement of societal intolerance.

The importance of social reaction to psychological needs brings us to the manner in which race functions at the group level. At this point, Blumer's view of racial prejudice as a "sense of group position" is relevant.[3] He emphasizes that prejudice is based on this "sense" of group identity rather than a particular emotional set. Blumer perceives the source of racial attitudes in a group's racial identity or social definition of themselves and other groups with which they interact. This particular "sense of social position" is based on feelings of superiority, the differentiation of other groups as different or alien, claims to certain privileges and advantages, and suspicion toward subordinate races. Furthermore, the "process of definition" occurs through leadership interaction, is based on an abstract image of the subordinate group, and develops on the remote rather than the immediate level. Race relations are based on social definitions developed by group leaders and are grounded in each group's sense of position in the social system.

According to this approach, race is a social definition provided and modified by leadership elements in response to their social situation, rather than a set of psychological feelings. The relevance of the social context to racial attitudes should be more obvious as we move from the microscopic and psychological to the macroscopic and social-psychological.

Blumer's orientation is echoed in Erikson's discussion of

[3]H. Blumer, "Race Prejudice as a Sense of Group Position," *Pacific Sociological Review*, **1**, 1958, pp. 3–7.

the "The Concept of Identity in Race Relations."[4] As a psycho-analyst, he sees identity as a basic link between the "core" of the individual and the "communal culture." In this manner the individual is integrated with his group setting through the process of identification with it. As applied to race relations, such identities may be negative or positive, the former applying to the subordinate group which is exploited by the oppressor who has vested interests in such negativism since that identity is "a protection of his own unconscious negative identity . . ." Racial identity, then, is an important social-psychological element in group definition and intergroup relations between oppressor and oppressed.

Closely linked to racial identity are the social groups to which an individual refers for his basic values and reinforce-ment—in other words, his reference groups. In a recent work, Pettigrew underlines the importance of "reference-group norms" as they relate to racial behavior.[5] Such racial norms vary by social situation, socioeconomic class, and geographical region in reference to the racial roles of black and white. Not only is an individual's racial identity important, but so is the network of reinforcing social reference groups around him, all of which helps him to maintain a highly stratified and stable system of racial roles.

Other researchers also point to the relevance of reference groups in the relationship between racial attitudes and actual behavior. De Friese and Ford, for example, discover that atti-tudes and reference groups together define overt responses to the open housing issue,[6] while Fendrich finds that perceived refer-ence-group support defines both racial attitudes and behavior.[7] Clearly, then, an individual's perceived social environment af-fects his racial behavior.

[4]E. Erikson, "The Concept of Identity in Race Relations," *Daedalus,* Winter, 1966.
[5]T. F. Pettigrew, *Racially Separate or Together?* McGraw-Hill, New York, 1971, pp. 262–274.
[6]C. H. DeFriese and W. S. Ford, "Verbal Attitudes, Overt Acts, and the Influence of Social Constraint in Interracial Behavior," *Social Problems,* 16, 1969, pp. 439–504.
[7]J. M. Fendrich, "Perceived Reference Group Support: Racial Attitudes and Overt Behavior," *American Sociological Review,* 32, 1967, pp. 960–969. For a study of the relationship between an individual's attitudes toward desegregation, see W. T. Liu, "The Community Reference System, Religiosity, and Race Attitudes," *Social Forces,* 39, 1961, pp. 324–328.

So far we have referred to the concepts of internalization, projection, institutionalization, role tension, racial identity, and reference groups without regard to their interrelationship or social variation. How do these attitudes relate to one another and to the social characteristics of the individuals concerned? Projection is supported by institutionalization, but in what manner? A useful study in this regard is provided by McDill in his analysis of "Anomie, Authoritarianism, Prejudice and Socio-economic Status."[8] Attempting to clarify the relationship between these three scales, he generates a set of four factors interpreted as indicating a general underlying factor. These were as follows: a dim world view; middle-class eunomia (belongingness); antiauthoritarian pessimism; and middle-class marital morality. Together, these factors explained a large degree of people's attitudes. It is reasonable to assume, then, that racial attitudes are related to other negative social orientations.

A crucial aspect, however, is the manner in which such factors relate to an individual's position in the social structure— i.e., his socioeconomic characteristics. Relating the four factors to a respondent's level of social status, McDill found that, generally speaking, his level of education, income, and occupational status was negatively associated with a "dim world view," and positively related to belongingness, antiauthoritarianism, and marital morality. Such data highlight the relationship of an individual's attitudes to his level of reward (i.e., occupational status, income level) and the kind of socialization (i.e., level of education) to which he has been exposed. A person's position within the social structure needs to be taken into account in any appreciation of his social attitudes.

Differences in racial attitudes according to an individual's background characteristics have also been explored by a number of other researchers. Bogardus, for example, finds that "racial distance reactions" are greater among women than men,[9] while Noel and Pinkney reveal the importance of an individual's level of education, the degree of racial contact, authoritarianism; his

[8]E. L. McDill, "Anomie, Authoritarianism, Prejudice, and Socio-economic Status: An Attempt at Clarification," *Social Forces*, **39**, 1961, pp. 239–245.
[9]E. S. Bogardus, "Race Reactions by Sexes," *Sociology and Social Research*, **43**, 1959, pp. 439–441.

sex, marital status; and the extent of his social activity. Thirdly, Selznick and Steinberg find a negative association between an individual's antiblack attitudes and his level of education, income, and urban residence, while age is positively associated with such prejudice. Finally, a recent study of *White Attitudes toward Black People* by Campbell reveals similar trends with respect to age, income, education, and urban residence. Clearly, then, an individual's position in the social structure and his racial experience tend to define his racial perceptions.[10]

Racial socialization is also affected by an individual's previous racial experience, i.e., type and extent of interracial contact. Research shows, for example, that racial contact among children accounts for the development of their racial identity, particularly among whites, while Chadwick-Jones reports that among adults favorable attitudes toward a minority are most dependent on continuous or frequent "face-to-face contact" with minority-group members.[11] A study of integrationist behavior among a group of clergy also revealed a strong relationship between "childhood experiences with nonwhites" and "activist behavior."[12] Furthermore, a recent study of white reactions to the Watts riot found that prior contact with blacks tended to result in less fear or punitive reactions toward them.[13]

From the above literature, then, it appears that racial prejudice is the function of, first, an individual's *position in the social structure* (i.e., his degree of socioeconomic security),

[10]See D. L. Noel and A. Pinkney, "Correlates of Prejudice: Some Racial Differences and Similarities," *American Journal of Sociology,* 6, 1964, pp. 609–622; G. J. Selznick and S. Steinberg, *The Tenacity of Prejudice: Anti-Semitism in Contemporary America,* Harper & Row, 1969; A. Campbell, *White Attitudes toward Black People,* Institute of Social Research, University of Michigan, Ann Arbor, 1971.

[11]See J. K. Morland, "Racial Recognition by Nursery School Children in Lynchburg, Virginia," *Social Forces,* 37, 1958, pp. 132–137; J. K. Morland, "Racial Self-Identification: A Study of Nursery School Children," *American Catholic Sociological Review,* 24, 1963, pp. 231–242; J. K. Chadwick-Jones, "Inter-group Attitudes: A Stage in Attitude Formation," *British Journal of Sociology,* 13, 1962, pp. 57–63.

[12]K. C. Garrison, "The Behavior of Clergy on Racial Integration as Related to a Childhood Socialization Factor," *Sociology and Social Research,* 51, 1967, pp. 208–219.

[13]V. Jeffries and H. E. Ransford, "Interracial Social Contact and Middle-Class White Reactions to the Watts Riot," *Social Problems,* 16, 1969, pp. 312–324. Note that Irish also finds that neighborhood interaction among caucasians and Japanese Americans was significantly related to positive racial attitudes. See D. P. Irish, "Reactions of Caucasian Residents to Japanese-American Neighbors," *Journal of Social Issues,* 8, 1952, pp. 10–17.

secondly, the kind of *racial socialization* to which he has been exposed (i.e., family, peer, and regional pressure), and thirdly, the kind of *racial contact* he has experienced (extent and quality). Background, socialization, and experience appear to be vital factors in the formation of a person's racial views. The next stage of our discussion explores the effects of specific social situations on these attitudes.

The relevance of a particular social situation to race relations is highlighted by Bernard, who points out that the "laws which govern interpersonal relations are not necessarily the same as those which regulate intergroup relations."[14] Illustrating this with a case study of a canning factory, she shows that in this situation intimacy may develop across status and ethnic boundaries, since status within the setting is a "matter of efficiency on the job." However, externally, social distance and even discrimination are reasserted. Such data underline the manner in which intergroup relations are situationally defined rather than generalized, i.e., specific to particular social situations—a concept Kohn and Williams refer to as "situational patterning."[15]

Exploring situations in which a Negro entered a segregated tavern, and the way in which participants in a civil-rights law suit changed their self-concepts and definitions of the situation, the authors discover the degree to which participants seek cues from other individuals' behavior, attempt to resolve role conflict by exemption or compromise, and modify their role definitions to coincide with their changed self-conceptions. Such data reveal the manner in which group definitions of situations control individual behavior in intergroup relations and highlight the effects of "situational patterning" in specific situations, outside of which they may exert little control. Negative attitudes are also situationally defined, as discussed by Raab and Lipset, who emphasize the manner and degree to which prejudice is learned and reinforced within some situations and social communities.[16]

[14]J. Bernard, "The Conceptualization of Intergroup Relations with Special Reference to Conflict," *Social Forces*, **29**, 1951, pp. 243–246.

[15]M. L. Kohn and R. M. Williams, "Situational Patterning in Intergroup Relations," *American Sociological Review*, **21**, 1956, pp. 164–174.

[16]See E. Raab and S. M. Lipset, "The Prejudiced Society," in E. Raab (ed.), *American Race Relations*, Doubleday, Garden City, N.Y., 1962.

Fourthly, Lohman and Reitzes emphasize the manner in which organizational power structures and institutions control racial behavior.[17] Groups such as those in the work situation, in unions, in civic organizations, and in neighborhoods may all be involved in structuring racial attitudes in specific situations— attitudes not necessarily consistent within the same personality system. The relevance of specific group situations to racial attitudes is highlighted in the above work, underlining the need to move from the psychological to a more sociological level of analysis if a fuller and more adequate explanation of race relations is to be developed.

We turn finally in this section to the broad sociocultural context in which racial attitudes operate, in order to ascertain how social factors behind racial attitudes operate differently in various societies. Pettigrew is well known for his cross-cultural study of "Personality and Sociocultural Factors in Intergroup Attitudes."[18] In this, he compares samples of white South African students and American adults. Utilizing scales of authoritarianism, conformity, and prejudice, he discovers that the level of authoritarianism in both societies is highly similar and appears to bear little relationship to prejudice; instead, level of conformity and associated sociocultural factors are more closely associated with racial intolerance. Thus, conformity to societal norms rather than personality accounts for high levels of prejudice.

Relevant sociocultural factors in the South African group proved to be birthplace, political party preference, upward mobility, and ethnic-group membership; the United States sample, on the other hand, revealed the importance of sex, church attendance, social mobility, political party identification, armed service experience, and education. Level of conformity to societal norms, along with associated sociocultural characteristics, is important in differentiating racial prejudice beyond the purely

---

[17]J. Lohman and D. Reitzes, "Note on Race Relations in Mass Society," *American Journal of Sociology*, **58**, 1952, pp. 241–256.
[18]T. F. Pettigrew, "Personality and Sociocultural Factors in Intergroup Attitudes: A Cross-National Comparison," *Journal of Conflict Resolution*, **2**, 1958, pp. 29–42. For a similar lack of results with respect to authoritarianism, see also A. L. Stroup and J. Landis, "Change in Race-Prejudice Attitudes as Related to Changes in Authoritarianism and Conservatism in a College Population," *Southwestern Social Science Quarterly*, **46**, 1965, pp. 255–263.

psychological level. The importance of social norms and situations in conjunction with the characteristics of the individuals involved is well documented by the above discussion and moves us toward the next level of analysis, in which we shall specify some of the major sociological links between racial groups and their societal context. First, however, we pause to summarize our present discussion.

THE INDIVIDUAL AND THE GROUP: TOWARD A MODEL

At this point, it may be useful to draw together the main variables specified by the works to which we have referred and attempt to develop a model of their interrelationships.

We have specified a number of links between the individual and the group context in the following order:

1 Internalization
2 Projection
3 Institutionalization
4 Role tension
5 Sense of group position
6 Racial identity
7 Reference groups
8 Socioeconomic characteristics and racial contact
9 Situational patterning
10 Conformity and sociocultural factors

These factors may be classified into three clusters of variables: (1) those pertaining to the individual (e.g., internalization, projection); (2) those operating at the group level (e.g., institutionalization, situational patterning); and (3) processes which link the above two levels, specifically an individual's racial identity and "sense of group position." This "identity" is viewed as the intervening variable between the individual and his group context, combining both psychological and social-psychological processes simultaneously. These factors may be ordered as shown in Figure 8-1, specifying identity as the intervening variable and the feedback from the group context to the individual. We should emphasize that such a framework is exploratory rather than definitive, representing a theoretical summary of

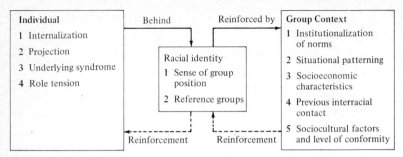

Figure 8-1 Links between the individual and group in race relations.

factors discussed so far in our attempt to develop a broad theory of race relations.

Having specified some of the more microscopic links in race relations, we turn now to explore the manner in which group orientations relate to their societal context.

LINKS BETWEEN GROUPS AND SOCIETY

Major variables in the relationship between groups and their societal context include the varying characteristics of such minorities (e.g., size, visibility, values, level of assimilation) and the policies of the superordinate group toward them, particularly the manner in which the political elite defines these groups (i.e., positively or negatively, exclusively or inclusively). Such "social definitions" are highly relevant to the way in which race relations are controlled by the elite and the degree to which this control is perceived as legitimate by subordinate groups. In this section we shall discuss approaches to race relations which examine the characteristics of elite and subordinate groups and the manner in which these characteristics define intergroup relations.

Delineation of major superordinate and subordinate group characteristics is evident in the work of Blalock[19] and Williams.[20]

---

[19] H. M. Blalock, *Toward a Theory of Minority-Group Relations,* Wiley, New York, 1967.
[20] R. M. Williams, *The Reduction of Intergroup Tensions: A Survey of Research on Problems of Ethnic, Racial, and Religious Group Relations,* Social Science Research Council, New York, 1947.

The former, in attempting to develop a "theory of minority-group relations" provides a detailed set of ninety-seven propositions, relating to topics such as status goals, status consciousness, frontier-contact situations, middleman minorities, power, and discrimination. Attempting to draw together the diversity and detail of all these is clearly impossible and would not do the work justice.

It is, however, relevant here to extract some of the major variables which are seen as defining intergroup relations. Blalock sees the use of discrimination by the dominant group as the function of a number of factors: displaced aggression, limited means to status and economic achievement, the perception of discrimination as important for achievement, the reduction of competition, and the increase of exploitation, low achievement, status consciousness, and threat. Minority-group characteristics relevant to intergroup relations include visibility, the degree to which they constitute a threat to tradition, level of availability, and vulnerability to the dominant elite. Blalock also delineates a number of variables and their relationships within minority groups, which ought, in his opinion, to be examined: parental background, husband-wife interaction within the nuclear family, socialization of offspring, and characteristics of the particular minority group.

Drawing this approach together, the dominant elite perceives racial discrimination as instrumental to its achievement, particularly to its economic development, while various minorities exhibit characteristics which make them especially suited to the scapegoating process. This model is summarized in Figure 8-2.

Williams, in a manner similar to Blalock, outlines the characteristics of the groups involved, attempting to develop a set of propositions to aid the reduction of intergroup tension.[21] This author sees hostility within the dominant group as a function of intragroup loyalty and frustration. The level of this hostility, however, is dependent on the degree of external threat as well as the individual's position in the social structure—i.e., the degree to

[21]Ibid.

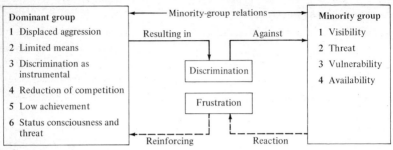

Figure 8-2 A simplified summary of Blalock's approach to minority-group relations.

which he feels threatened. Immigrant groups and the lower-middle class feel particularly vulnerable in this regard. Degree of intergroup tension is also patterned by the nature of group contact, visibility, competition, and the general level of social differentiation, social change, and economic threat within the society at large. Minority-group reactions reflect self-consciousness and sensitivity, while the development of militancy depends on the degree of minority-group improvement. Williams' approach is summarized in Figure 8-3, where its similarity to Blalock is apparent.

Other researchers have also recognized the importance of group characteristics. Dahlke, for example, in a study of anti-Jewish and anti-Negro riots, cites the relevance of religious and color differences, the effect of authority approval of violence, and the function of various societal institutions in the perpetration of racism.[22] Skolnick views white militancy in the case of the Klan as the reaction of a threatened and "insecure class of marginal whites,"[23] while Shibutani and Kwan emphasize the formation of "contrast conceptions" (i.e., highly diverse intergroup definitions) which develop out of such highly varied group characteristics.[24] The relevance of group characteristics to race relations is further evident here.

[22]O. H. Dahlke, "Race and Minority Riots: A Study in the Typology of Violence," *Social Forces,* **30**, 1952, pp. 419–425.

[23]J. Skolnick, *Politics of Protest,* Simon and Schuster, New York, 1969.

[24]T. Shibutani and K. M. Kwan, *Ethnic Stratification,* Macmillan, New York, 1965.

In both of the above approaches, emphasis is placed on characteristics of the groups involved in race relations, in particular the elite's economic goals and the scapegoating characteristics of minorities under its control. Included in this, but not greatly emphasized, is the reaction of minorities to their controlled environment. Relevant at this point is a body of work exploring minority orientations and related variables.

Rinder links the individual to the group through the concept of "identification"—a concept he sees as representing the "typical orientation of the group."[25] This group orientation, in turn, reflects the relationship between its internal and external environments. Factors most relevant to the former include level of group cohesion, which is dependent upon morale—a sense of "cultural superiority," and secondly, the group's level of economic independence from the larger society. The external environment, on the other hand, is represented by the dominant group's level of resistance to and acceptance of the minority groups under its control.

Using the relationship between external and internal environments, Rinder develops a typology of minority orientations ranging from assimilationist and pluralist (including segregated, accommodated, and exotic pluralism), through group self-hatred, to the secessionist and militant. Important here is the emphasis on

[25]I. D. Rinder, "Minority Orientations: An Approach to Intergroup Relations Theory through Social Psychology," *Phylon, 26*, 1965, pp. 5–17.

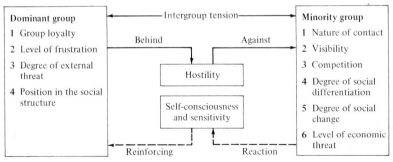

Figure 8-3 A simplified summary of Williams' approach to intergroup tension.

group orientations as reflecting both internal *and* external social environments. resulting in a number of possible *types* of minority groups or "racial roles," depending on their predominant orientations.

Minority orientations are also explored by Rose in reference to two major dimensions: level of acceptance of subordinate status imposed by the majority group and willingness to play an expected "segregated role."[26] Using these two criteria, four types of reaction are delineated: submission (acceptance of both), withdrawal (rejection of segregated role only), avoidance (rejection of subordinate image only), and integration (rejection of both). Rose also makes the important point that all four reactions are possible within the same minority group, depending on the particular circumstances.

We turn, finally, to Wirth's well-known discussion of minority groups. To understand such groups, he emphasizes the importance of their "objective" (i.e., disadvantaged, subordinate position) and their subjective (i.e., attitudinal) positions in society.[27] Furthermore, their length of existence, the social setting in which they find themselves (e.g., caste versus class), and the development of relative deprivation are factors which are related to rejection of their status and attempts to develop political power. Using these criteria, it is possible, according to Wirth, to delineate four main types of minorities: pluralistic, assimilationist, secessionistic, and militant. Once again, the emphasis is clearly on minority *orientations* which are dependent on their internal and external social environments.

So far, then, we have linked groups to their societal context through their social characteristics and the relationship between their internal and external social environments. Basic to our discussion has been the exploitation of minorities by an elite power group. Of relevance at this point is the discussion by Benedict of the persecution behind such exploitation, using racism to legitimize such behavior.[28] Such "racial reasons for

---

[26]P. I. Rose, *They and We*, Random House, New York, 1964.
[27]L. Wirth, "The Problem of Minority Groups," in R. Linton (ed.), *The Science of Man in the World Crisis*, Columbia University Press, New York, 1945.
[28]R. Benedict, *Science and Politics*, Viking, New York, 1940.

persecution" are a function of social inequality, resultant in-group conservatism, and the attempt to exploit others. Behind racial exploitation and racism lies social inequality—the general context in which race relations operate. According to Benedict, therefore, racism is symptomatic of general social problems causing groups to protect themselves and exploit others, using prejudice as the underlying rationale. Such an approach is useful in setting the stage for our analysis of sociological orientations delineating major societal factors behind racism.

GROUPS AND SOCIETY: TOWARD A MODEL

To summarize, minority groups are related to their societal context through characteristics of the groups involved, motivation behind the use of prejudice and discrimination by the elite, the relationship between the internal and external social environments, and the general nature of the social structure, particularly its colonial structure and level of inequality. Drawing these concepts together, it is possible to order them in the framework presented in Figure 8-4. At this level, we are concentrating on the more macroscopic elements of the social-psychological approach in preparation for the next chapter, where we shall place race relations in their total societal setting.

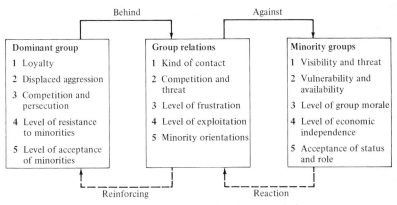

Figure 8-4 Links between groups and society in race relations.

THE SOCIAL-PSYCHOLOGICAL APPROACH:
A SUMMARY MODEL

In this chapter, we have dealt with three main clusters of variables defining race relations: individual factors, the group context in which such factors operate, and the relationship between that context and the controlling elite. All three are related: psychological factors, such as projection, are reinforced by the group context through institutionalization of values and are linked through racial identity, while at the next level group relations are closely defined by the characteristics of the minorities involved, the nature of the elite, and factors governing intergroup relationships.

Furthermore, at each level there is feedback, both positive and negative, reinforcing and changing these relations. It is important to develop a framework which embraces all three sets of factors discussed above. We have attempted to do this in Figure 8-5 which illustrates a synthesis of the major factors discussed in this chapter and their interrelationships, including feedback sources which reinforce as well as lead to change within the system. Such a framework does not pretend to be definitive, but only to specify some of the major psychological and social-psychological factors involved in race relations and the manner in which these provide feedback into the social system leading to reinforcement as well as social change. Our emphasis here is thus *multivariate* and *developmental.*

Having specified some of the major social-psychological factors involved in race relations, we turn next to the sociological perspective in order to place these relations in their societal setting.

CONCLUSIONS

In conclusion, social-psychological theories provide a link between the psychological and sociological levels of analysis by relating (1) the individual to his group context through the processes of projection and social reinforcement, and (2) minorities to the social structure through the characteristics of the groups involved and the relationship between internal and ex-

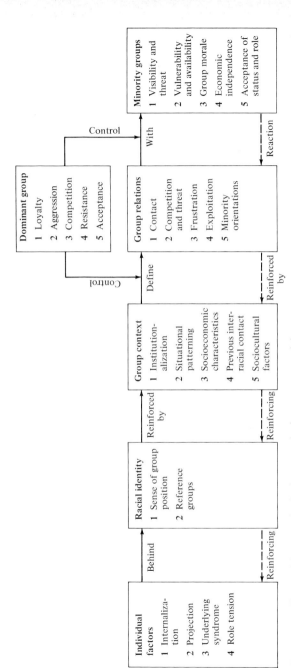

Figure 8-5 The social-psychological approach: A summary model.

ternal social environments. The importance of this kind of analysis lies in its movement away from racial *attitudes*, based upon assumed psychoanalytic constructs, and toward the group context of race *relations*, for it is as we perceive factors behind the social *definition* of race that we become aware of its sociological rather than psychological foundation. Race relations are defined and controlled by particular elites with certain goals, while subordinate minorities react to this structure in a changing manner as their level of societal perception and economic independence rises. Race relations are a matter of group dynamics under particular conditions of social, political, and economic inequality.

STUDY QUESTIONS

1 Analyze in some detail the processes of projection and institutionalization of values, defining a particular race group during a particular period in the history of American society (e.g., frontier whites' racial definitions of Indians).
2 Discuss the manner in which ongoing institutionalization of values is controlled and developed by a society's governing elite.
3 Outline the major characteristics of a variety of minority groups. How have these characteristics operated in the scapegoating process?
4 Delineate some of the major differences in orientation toward the dominant elite among racial minorities in the United States, and attempt to account for them.
5 Discuss what factors you feel may be most important in changing minority group orientations.

READINGS

Bernard, J., "The Conceptualization of Intergroup Relations with Special Reference to Conflict," *Social Forces*, 1951, **29**, pp. 243–246.

Bloom, Leonard, *The Social Psychology of Race Relations*, G. Allen, London, 1971.

Blumer, Herbert, "Race Prejudice as a Sense of Group Position," *Pacific Sociological Review*, 1958, **1**, 1, Spring, pp. 3–7.

Brown, Barry, S., and George W. Albee, "The Effects of Integrated

Hospital Experiences on Racial Attitudes: A Discordant Note," *Social Problems,* 1966, **13**, Winter, pp. 324–333.

Burnstein, Eugene, and Adie V. McRae, "Some Effects of Shared Threat and Prejudice in Racially Mixed Groups," *Journal of Abnormal Social Psychology,* 1962, **64**, 4, April, pp. 257–263.

Chadwick-Jones, J. K., "Intergroup Attitudes: A Stage in Attitude Formation," *British Journal of Sociology,* 1962, **13**, March, pp. 57–63.

DeFleur, Melvin L., and Frank R. Westie, "The Interpretation of Interracial Situations," *Social Forces,* 1959, **38**, 1, October, pp. 17–23.

DeFriese, Gordon H., and W. Scott Ford, "Verbal Attitudes, Overt Acts, and the Influence of Social Constraint in Interracial Behavior," *Social Problems,* 1969, **16**, 4, Spring, pp. 493–504.

Ehrlich, Howard J., "Stereotyping and Negro-Jewish Stereotypes," *Social Forces,* 1962, **41**, 2, pp. 171–176.

Endler, Norman S., and Elizabeth Hoy, "Conformity as Related to Reinforcement and Social Pressure," *Journal of Personality and Social Psychology,* 1967, **7**, 2, October, pp. 197–202.

Erikson, E., "The Concept of Identity in Race Relations," *Daedalus,* Winter, 1966.

Fendrich, James M, "Perceived Reference Group Support: Racial Attitudes and Overt Behavior," *American Sociological Review,* 1967, **32**, 6, December, pp. 960–969.

Glaser, Daniel, "Dynamics of Ethnic Identification," *American Sociological Review,* 1958, **23**, 1, February, pp. 31–40.

Grimshaw, Allen D., "Relationships among Prejudice, Discrimination, Social Tension and Social Violence," *Journal of Intergroup Relations,* 1961, **2**, 4, Autumn, pp. 302–310.

Harris, Edward E., "Family and Student Identities: An Exploratory Study in Self and 'We-Group' Attitudes," *Journal of Negro Education,* 1965, **34**, 1, Winter, pp. 17–22.

——, "Racial and National Identities: An Exploratory Study in Self and 'We-Group' Attitudes," *Journal of Negro Education,* 1965, **34**, 4, Fall, pp. 425–430.

Insko, Chester A., and James E. Robinson, "Belief Similarity versus Race as Determinants of Reactions to Negroes by Southern White Adolescents: A Further Test of Rokeach's Theory," *Journal of Personality and Social Psychology,* 1967, **7**, 2, October, pp. 216–221.

Jacobs, Wilbur, R., *Wilderness Politics and Indian Gifts: The Northern*

   Colonial Frontier, 1748–1763, University of Nebraska Press, Lin-
      coln, 1966.
Jeffries, Vincent, and H. Edward Ransford, "Interracial Social Contact
      and Middle-Class White Reactions to the Watts Riot," *Social
      Problems,* 1969, **16**, 3, Winter, pp. 312–324.
Kidd, J. S., and Donald T. Campbell, "Conformity to Groups as a
      Function of Group Success," *Journal of Abnormal Social Psy-
      chology,* 1955, **51**, 3, November, pp. 390–393.
Kohn, Melvin L., and Robin M. Williams, "Situational Patterning in
      Intergroup Relations," *American Sociological Review,* 1956, **21**, 2,
      April, pp. 164–174.
Laurence, J. E., "White Socialization—Black Reality," *Psychiatry,* 1970,
      33, 2, May, pp. 174–194.
Liu, William T., "The Community Reference System, Religiosity, and
      Race Attitudes," *Social Forces,* 1961, **39**, 4, May, pp. 324–328.
McDill, E. L., "Anomie, Authoritarianism, Prejudice, and Socioeconom-
      ic Status: An Attempt at Clarification," *Social Forces,* 1961, **39**, pp.
      239–245.
Mack, Raymond W., "Riot, Revolt, or Responsible Revolution: Or
      Reference Groups and Racism," *Sociological Quarterly,* 1969, **10**,
      2, Spring, pp. 147–156.
Manheim, Henry L., "Intergroup Interaction as Related to Status and
      Leadership Differences between Groups," *Sociometry,* 1960, **23**, 4,
      December, pp. 415–427.
Martin, James G., "Intergroup Tolerance-Prejudice," *Journal of Human
      Relations,* 1962, **10**, 2, and 3, Winter and Spring, pp. 197–204.
Masuoka, Jitsuichi, "Conflicting Role Obligations and Role Types: With
      Special Reference to Race Relations," *Japanese Sociological
      Review,* 1960, **11**, 1, July, pp. 76–108.
Miyamoto, S. Frank, "The Process of Intergroup Tension and Conflict,"
      in E. W. Burgess and D. J. Bogue (eds.), *Contributions to Urban
      Sociology,* University of Chicago Press, Chicago, 1964, pp. 389–
      403.
Richmond, Anthony H., "Sociological and Psychological Explanations
      of Racial Prejudice: Some Light on the Controversy from Recent
      Researches in Britain," *Pacific Sociological Review,* 1961, **4**, 2,
      Fall, pp. 63–68.
Rinder, I. D., "Minority Orientations: An Approach to Intergroup
      Relations Theory through Social Psychology," *Phylon,* 1965, **26**,
      pp. 5–17.
Rothman, Jack, *Minority Group Identification and Intergroup Relations:*

An Examination of Kurt Lewin's Theory of Jewish Group Identity, Research Institute for Group Work in Jewish Agencies in Cooperation with the American Jewish Committee, New York, 1965.

Selznick, G. J., and S. Steinberg, *The Tenacity of Prejudice: Anti-Semitism in Contemporary America,* Harper & Row, New York, 1969.

Singer, Dorothy G., "Reading, Writing, and Race Relations," *Trans-Action,* 1967, **4**, 7, June, pp. 27–31.

Spilerman, S., "The Causes of Racial Disturbances: Tests of an Explanation," *American Sociological Review,* 1971, **36**, pp. 427–442.

Tajfel, Henri, "Stereotypes," *Race,* 1963, **5**, 2, October, pp. 3–14.

Triandis, Harry C., and Leight M. Triandis, "Race, Social Class, Religion, and Nationality as Determinants of Social Distance," *Journal of Abnormal Social Psychology,* 1960, **61**, 1, July, pp. 110–118.

———, and Vasso Vassiliou, "Frequency of Contact and Stereotyping," *Journal of Personality and Social Psychology,* 1967, **7**, 3, November, pp. 316–328.

Whitman, Frederick L., "Subdimensions of Religiosity and Race Prejudice," *Review of Religious Research,* 1962, **3**, pp. 166–174.

Chapter 9

Basic Approaches to the Analysis of Race Relations: III. Sociological

Analysis of race relations at the sociological level concentrates on the nature of the societal setting in which these relations have developed historically and are presently defined. Its central question is, "What kind of societies or societal characteristics are related to high levels of racism and prejudice?" A major attempt is made to relate various characteristics of the social system in general, particularly its dominant racial power elite (i.e., political, economic, military) and economy, to the kind of race relations predominant within it, in some cases moving toward a model of differing "types" of race relations in particular kinds of societies. Rather than analyzing individual and group dynamics, then, the sociological perspective concentrates upon the societal context in which these dynamics are defined.

The major sociological analyses we shall concentrate on in this chapter deal with societal-characteristics theory, the contact approach, frontier cycle and ecological theories, the demographic approach, the institutional approach, and status-consistency theory focusing on social change. It will be observed throughout these that a major concern is the kind of social *structure* defining relations within it, rather than the latter.

THE SOCIETAL CHARACTERISTICS APPROACH

A traditional concern in sociology is the connection between a particular social structure and relationships within it. This has carried over into the field of race relations in ideal-type or model conceptualizations of race relations which focus on the societal characteristics behind various patterns of race relations. Van den Berghe, for example, characterizes race relations as "paternalistic" or "competitive," according to the nature of the society's economy, division of labor, mobility system, social stratification, population ratios, and value conflict.[1] The former "type" is characteristic of preindustrial settings, such as South Africa, Brazil, and the southern United States, where race has been the major caste element in a rigid, authoritarian, and exploitive situation.

"Competitive" race relations, on the other hand, occur in more industrial and urban settings, where a strict racial caste system is absent and interaction between dominant and subordinate groups is essentially one of negative competition. As examples of this "type," van den Berghe cites modern America, Britain, South Africa, and recently independent colonial societies, such as Kenya and Indonesia. The contrast here is essentially between a static colonial, agricultural regime and an industrialized, urban sphere. Van den Berghe's approach is a useful example of a structural analysis of factors behind intergroup relations, particularly economic and stratification variables, and is summarized in simple form in Figure 9-1.

Mason[2] has recently taken a similar approach. With his intimate knowledge of race relations in a number of colonial societies, this writer underlines factors such as the numerical

---

[1]P. L. van den Berghe, *Race and Racism*, Wiley, New York, 1967, pp. 25–34.
[2]P. L. Mason, *Race Relations*, Oxford University Press, London, 1970, chap. 8.

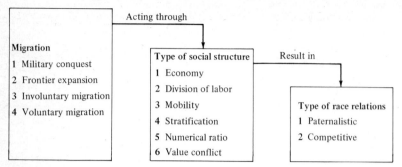

Figure 9-1 A simplified summary of van den Berghe's approach.

proportion of the groups concerned, the purpose behind the
dominant elite's migration, cultural characteristics of the conquered, and the dominant group's norms, stratification system,
power structure, and central values. Of importance here is the
delineation of those factors most closely associated with high
levels of colonial domination: highly disproportionate demographic ratios, colonial migration, heterogeneous indigenous
minorities, and a colonial elite imbued with Protestant Ethic
values of economic development, bureaucratic centralization,
and strict social control. This is illustrated in Figure 9-2. Once
again, emphasis is placed on the abstraction of those societal
factors most clearly related to a racist social system.

A third example of this approach is provided by Lieberson.[3]
In attempting a "societal theory" of race relations, the writer
distinguishes between migrant and indigenous (i.e., local) superordinate elites and ensuing differences in intergroup relations on
the societal level. Migrant elites, on the one hand, result in high
levels of conflict and a low degree of assimilation, while indigenous elites tend toward the opposite. Once again, it is characteristics of the social structure that are seen as defining intergroup
relations within it in a typological manner demonstrated in Figure
9-3.

A similar approach is taken by those who analyze race
relations in terms of stratification: Noel, for example, attempting

[3]S. Lieberson, "A Societal Theory of Race and Ethnic Relations," *American
Sociological Review, 26,* 1961, pp. 902–910.

to explain the origins of slavery in seventeenth-century America, utilizes the factors of "ethnocentrism, competition, and differential power"—clearly a societal-characteristics approach in historical context.[4] According to his view, the presence of these factors made slavery inevitable.

A stratification approach is also taken by Blue. Viewing "European imperialism" and "world capitalism" as major factors behind the evolution of race relations, he delineates an "imperial pattern of racial stratification" containing three subtypes, the "buffer," the "biracial," and "apartheid," depending on the number of groups and the racial policy involved.[5] The importance

[4]S. L. Noel, "A Theory of the Origin of Ethnic Stratification," *Social Problems,* **16,** 1968, pp. 157–172.
[5]J. T. Blue, "Patterns of Racial Stratification: A Categoric Typology," *Phylon,* **20,** 1959, pp. 364–371.

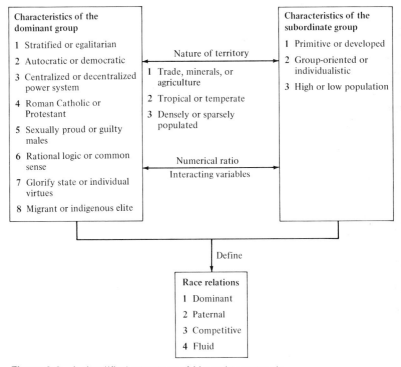

Figure 9-2 A simplified summary of Mason's approach.

| Variable | Kind of superordinate group | |
	Migrant	Indigenous
1 Contact:	Conflict	Accommodation
2 Political-economic control:	Warfare and subdivisions	Low threat and high motivation to conform
3 Ethnic contacts:	Lack of participation by local population	Limited and controlled immigration of minorities
4 Conflict and assimilation:	Increasing consciousness of threat—low assimilation	Low threat and high assimilation

Figure 9-3   A simplified summary table of Lieberson's approach.

of a particular kind of migrant elite is evident here, bringing us to the colonial approach.

It can be seen that the above approaches essentially delineate two types of social structure: (1) the colonial and highly racist; and (2) the more industrialized, indigenous, and less racist. Recent analyses of race relations on the contemporary scene have found this approach useful, particularly in the application of the colonial model. Carmichael and Hamilton, for example, are well known for their use of this approach in analyzing the American scene.[6] They perceive the black-white relationship as essentially colonial in nature, i.e., defined by "institutional racism" This "colonial status" applies to society's major political, economic, and social structure in which blacks are subjugated as colonial subjects who require "liberation."

Blauner has also used the concept to explain "ghetto revolt."[7] According to his analysis, colonization consists of forced entrance into the "colony," a negative impact on the subordinate group's culture, the political control and administration of minorities, and racism. The author applies these conditions to the United States situation to explain black revolt. The

---

[6]S. Carmichael and C. V. Hamilton, *Black Power: The Politics of Liberation in America,* Vintage Books, New York, 1967.

[7]R. Blauner, "Internal Colonization and Ghetto Revolt," *Social Problems,* **16,** 1969, pp. 393–408. For discussion of the implications of Blauner's approach, see J. Prager, "White Racial Privilege and Social Change: An Examination of Theories of Racism," *Berkeley Journal of Sociology,* **17,** 1972–73, pp. 117–150. Prager is particularly concerned with the manner in which "white racial privilege and racism" function as a "mechanism of organization in the economic sphere of American society . . . ," thereby supporting the colonial model.

structural approach has thus been used by a variety of analysts on the theoretical, comparative, national, dominant group, and minority group levels to explain intergroup relations within a particular society. The main structural distinction made by these writers is between the typical colonial situation and those societies less affected by such influence. This distinction, however, is a matter of degree rather than a strict bifurcation, since most, if not all, societies have been exposed to some form of domination during their historical development.

The colonial approach is also implicit in the work of other writers on race relations. In his recent work on *Race Relations in Sociological Theory,* Rex analyzes the "social institutions of colonialism," emphasizing the relevance of social differentiation based upon physical and/or cultural differences and the rationalization of discrimination on the basis of a biological theory of racial differences.[8]

Clearly relevant at this point also is the Marxian approach to race relations developed by Cox.[9] This early writer on race perceives America's ruling class as fostering racial prejudice in order to maintain the exploitation of blacks for economic purposes. Such motivation is identical to that of migrant colonial elites who possess a vested economic interest in the continuous subordination of indigenous and imported racial groups. As stated in Chapter 1, colonization represents the basic sociological process involved in the foundation and development of race relations.

THE CONTACT-THEORY APPROACH

The above view is complemented by what may be termed the "contact-theory" approach. Here, emphasis is placed upon the racial implications of the kind of intergroup contact which initially takes place in a society's interaction with outsiders. Banton, for example, describes "six orders of race relations,"[10] in which he perceives initial domination resulting in racial pluralism,

---

[8]J. Rex, *Race Relations in Sociological Theory,* Weidenfield and Nicolson, London, 1970.

[9]O. C. Cox, *Caste, Class and Race,* Monthly Review Press, New York, 1959.

[10]M. Banton, *Race Relations,* Basic Books, New York, 1967, chap. 4.

Figure 9-4 A simplified summary of Banton's contact approach.

while paternalistic contact leads to eventual integration, as demonstrated in Figure 9-4. This kind of initial contact has far-reaching sociological effects on the kind of intergroup relations which follow. Van den Berghe also delineates particular kinds of contact leading to racism: military conquest, frontier expansion, and voluntary or involuntary migration represent the major forms of contact behind the evolution of racist societies.[11]

A third writer on this topic is Schermerhorn. In his attempt to build a "general theory of minority groups," this sociologist also used the contact approach: initial degree and type of value conflict between groups results in certain patterns of power relations, concomitant beliefs in legitimacy, and resultant social action.[12] Schermerhorn places particular emphasis on what he terms "cumulative directionality"—the manner in which the outcome of conflict occurs in a similar manner throughout a society's development, depending on the factors specified above. According to this analysis, initial contact has far-reaching effects on the intergroup relations which follow in a manner which becomes typical: value conflict results in conflict and a particular pattern of power relations, beliefs in legitimacy, and, ultimately, a pattern of intergroup relations, as demonstrated in Figure 9-5.

The contact approach emphasizes the viability of the initial contact situation for ensuing race relations. Such an approach is useful, but limited on its own: it neglects change in race relations, regardless of initial contact, and is simplistic in its description of race relations systems in typological terms—a common problem with the sociological approach. However, it provides a starting point for the historical analysis of race relations, relating directly

[11]Van den Berghe, op. cit., p. 14.
[12]R. A. Schermerhorn, "Toward a General Theory of Minority Groups," *Phylon,* 25, 1964, pp. 238–246.

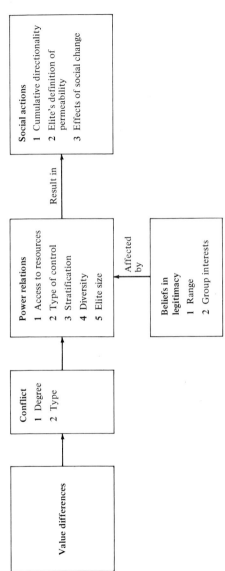

Figure 9-5 A simplified summary of Schermerhorn's approach.

to the frontier-cycle approach developed by the ecological school.

THE ECOLOGICAL FRONTIER APPROACH

A useful conceptualization of race relations has been made in terms of ecological "racial frontiers." Developed by Park, this concept is seen as reflecting the idea of the "zone of transition," which, wherever it occurs, has distinctive features and in which "common controlling factors . . . operate over widely separated areas and conditions of life."[13] Emphasis is placed on the major economic and political "controlling factors" at a society's particular point of historical development. These frontiers represent certain economic demands which result in certain kinds of intergroup relations under the control of the power elites.

Thus, Lind sees the various frontiers on which different groups meet—whether trading, plantation, political, urban, or tourist—as related to differing patterns of race relations in response to varying kinds of contact and economic pressure in a particular social setting.[14] Each frontier represents a particular social situation defined by particular economic needs and elite reaction. In this manner, frontiers differ in their effects on race relations: the plantation frontier, for example, demands the importation of other race groups for economic purposes and controls them in a rigid castelike structure on racial terms. Plantation economics eventually decline, moving toward industrialization and urbanization in which different economic demands and intergroup relations occur. Race relations then move toward the more "competitive" type described by van den Berghe. However, earlier frontiers continue to influence the situation to the degree that various race groups remain in the society under historically determined disadvantageous conditions.

Major advantages of the above approach lie not only in its descriptive power but also the manner in which it may be related to social change. Park, for example, is known for his delineation

---

[13]See A. W. Lind, *Hawaii: The Last of the Magic Isles,* Oxford University Press, London, 1969, chap. 2.
[14]A. W. Lind, ibid.

of a race relations cycle in which he specifies that the "interracial adjustments that follow . . . migration and conquest . . . involve racial competition, conflict, accommodation, and eventually assimilation . . ."[15] According to his approach race relations follow a particular path once contact is established, and intergroup competition for resources inevitably develops.

Other writers have also traced a number of phases in race relations. Glick, for example, perceives four major stages in intergroup contact: (1) the precontact stage; (2) contact and predomination; (3) the domination period; and (4) postdomination.[16] These trends delineate the development of colonial and postcolonial development in which Glick perceives a number of differing racial roles, or "social types" as he calls them. Such types reflect the predominant social definition of race within a particular frontier and change as the frontier changes. The advantage of the approaches developed by Park and Glick are their developmental character and ability to outline broad trends in intergroup relations.

Frazier also follows an ecological approach in his study of "race relations in world perspective."[17] Assuming that race relations did not arise until nineteenth-century European colonial expansion began, he delineates the evolution of three major types of racial frontiers: areas of European dominance in Asia; tropical areas controlled but not settled by Europeans; and multiracial communities produced by European settlement. As with the societal-characteristics approach, the importance of dominance by a particular kind of elite is evident here.

Finally, in a recent study of Rhodesia, this author found a synthesis of Glick, Park, and Lind useful in understanding changing racial attitudes over time: it was found that differing racial social types appear as different frontiers emerge, moving segregation to types with more emphasis on the limited assimilation of minority groups. Such a synthesis emphasizes the devel-

[15]R. E. Park, *Race and Culture*, Free Press, Glencoe, Ill., 1950, p. 104.
[16]C. E. Glick, "Social Roles and Types in Race Relations," in A. W. Lind (ed.), *Race Relations in World Perspective*, Honolulu, University of Hawaii Press, 1955, pp. 239–262.
[17]E. F. Frazier, "Race Relations in World Perspective," *Sociology and Social Research*, **41**, 1957, pp. 331–335.

opmental quality of race relations, even within a colonial setting.[18]

The frontier approach, then, concentrates on those ecological factors, both economic and political, defining a particular social situation and relations within it. As these factors change, the race relations situation also changes in a number of sequential stages.

THE DEMOGRAPHIC APPROACH

Social, physical, and cultural characteristics of the groups involved in race relations have obvious relevance, as discussed in the last chapter. Demographic variables (i.e., population characteristics) are also involved: both Mason and van den Berghe, for example, in their typologies just discussed, include the numerical ratio of elite and subordinate groups as important variables, with the former writer concerned with the manner in which small elites tend to be more rigid in their racial policies.[19] Change in population size among minority groups may also affect their orientation toward the elite and thus other subordinate groups around them. Population ratios have obvious relevance to intergroup definitions and racial policies, particularly in the initial contact situation, but also during periods of social change; they directly affect social definitions of threat and competition—cultural, social, occupational, and economic.

Demographic characteristics beyond population size, however, are also relevant to the explanation of race riots and the social assimilation of black Americans. In exploring the "underlying conditions of race riots," Lieberson and Silverman discovered the importance of "occupational and municipal characteristics"—riots appear most likely to occur in cities containing institutions which are unable to solve or deal with racial problems.[20] Secondly, while other factors were found to contribute little to the occurrence of riots, it was found that in cities where riots tended to occur white-black occupational and income differ-

[18]See G. C. Kinloch, "Social Types and Race Relations in the Colonial Setting: A Case Study of Rhodesia, *Phylon*, third quarter, 1972, pp. 276–289.

[19]P. Mason, op. cit., pp. 143–148.

[20]S. Lieberson and A. R. Silverman, "The Precipitants and Underlying Conditions of Race Riots," *American Sociological Review*, **30**, 1965, pp. 887–898.

ences tended to be lower than in more peaceful communities, suggesting that riots may be attributed to the "relative threat to whites where Negroes are less concentrated in their traditional pursuits."[21] In later work, Spilerman finds that outbreaks of violence are more likely to occur in cities where nonwhites are high in occupational, educational, and income achievement.[22]

However, these factors contribute relatively little to the statistical explanation of riots; instead, size of Negro population is the most important factor—a finding this researcher reinforces with further data.[23] Spilerman's explanation for this is the development of a national rather than community-bound racial identity and the influence of television. Whatever the case, the demographic structure of a society and communities within it is obviously relevant to a fuller understanding of race relations.

Economic and occupational assimilation of blacks in urban areas is dealt with by Jiobu and Marshall.[24] Based on a large-scale analysis of census data, these researchers discover that such assimilation is dependent upon "educational assimilation" but is also primarily due to the percentages of blacks in the urban population and the rate of increase of the black population. Once again the importance of a minority's size and population growth rate is evident.

The demographic approach to race relations, as discussed here, then, highlights the importance of a group's objective characteristics, particularly its size and growth, to the kind of race relations which ensue in the greater society.

INSTITUTIONAL ANALYSES

An important contribution to the study of race relations is provided by Lohman and Reitzes in their "Note on Race Relations in Mass Society."[25] While the frontier approach highlights

[21]S. Lieberson and A. R. Silverman, ibid., p. 894.

[22]S. Spilerman, "The Causes of Racial Disturbances: A Comparison of Alternative Explanations," *American Sociological Review,* **35**, 1970, pp. 627–649.

[23]S. Spilerman, "The Causes of Racial Disturbances: Tests of an Explanation," *American Sociological Review,* **36**, 1971, pp. 427–442.

[24]R. M. Jiobu and H. H. Marshall, "Urban Structure and the Differentiation between Blacks and Whites," *American Sociological Review,* **36**, 1971, pp. 638–649.

[25]J. Lohman and D. Reitzes, "Note on Race Relations in Mass Society," *American Journal of Sociology,* **58**, 1952, pp. 241–256.

the general effects of broad economic situations, these authors discuss the relevance of racial definitions provided by an individual's reference groups. These groups may vary in size from the work situation through to the neighborhood, while their racial definitions may not necessarily be consistent in their effect on the individual's attitudes: the local work setting, for example, may emphasize nondiscrimination, while the person's local club may be highly discriminatory in policy.

The relevance of varying institutional definitions of race to an individual's perspective is underlined here, a process which assumes increasing importance as the traditional structure of society breaks down and moves toward what some have termed a "mass society"—one which is highly differentiated by internal subgroups with industrialization and ongoing institutionalization. The authors further point out that where clear organizational policies are lacking in a tension-filled situation (e.g., the role of the police in a racial ghetto) other conflicting interests may take over and result in violence. Varying organizational definitions of race are involved within any particular frontier, particularly as industrialization proceeds, and these should be taken into account, particularly in the understanding of inconsistent attitudes.

Reitzes supports his approach in a study of white factory workers in which he discovers a relationship between their involvement in neighborhood activities and the degree of neighborhood rejection of Negroes. Conversely, involvement in union activities is related to the level of acceptance of blacks at work.[26] He concludes that individual attitudes in modern mass society are increasingly defined by the "organized collectives" in which they participate—an approach also taken by Williams to Negro social movements, which he sees becoming increasingly national rather than local in orientation.[27] The relevance of organizational definitions of race to individual attitudes is clearly evident in the above work in a manner similar to the reference-group approach discussed in the last chapter.

[26]D. C. Reitzes, "Behavior in Urban Race Contacts," in E. W. Burgess and D. J. Bogue (eds.), *Contributions to Urban Sociology*, University of Chicago Press, Chicago, 1964, pp. 471–486.
[27]R. M. Williams, "Social Change and Social Conflict: Race Relations in the United States, 1944–1964," *Sociological Inquiry*, **35**, 1965, pp. 8–25.

STATUS CONSISTENCY AND SOCIAL CHANGE

Social change in race relations has rarely been discussed adequately. One of the earliest was, of course, Park's cycle notion described already: change is seen as the function of intergroup competition moving through a number of specific stages. Such an approach is useful in its broad application but lacks differentiation of a society's most relevant internal mechanisms.

An important attempt to explain social change in intergroup relations utilizes the notion of status consistency. As applied to race relations and within the context of our discussion here, "status consistency" is viewed as the consistency with which racial status (high and low) is correlated with socioeconomic status in the general society. Thus, in a racial caste system (e.g., a slave, plantation society) black equals low socioeconomic status, while white is equivalent to high status, with little or no exception within the context of this particular setting. When the relationship between race and socioeconomic status is consistent, race relations tend to be stable even within highly racist societies.

However, as we shall perceive, it is as this relationship or correlation is affected by the influence of industrialization that changes in racial orientations, particularly among subordinate minority groups, begin to occur. Status consistency also applies to the status system *within* particular race groups—the relationship, for example, between occupational-educational-income consistency and political attitudes.[28] Our concern here, however, is with the degree of consistency between racial and socioeconomic status.

In his discussion of status-consistency theory, Bagley perceives a state of harmony or nonconflict when race and social class are equivalent.[29] This is typical of the plantation or "paternalistic" frontier in which whites represent the upper class, while nonwhites and/or blacks are exclusively the lower and working class. Such a caste structure is stable insofar as race and

---

[28]For related literature and criticism of the utility of the status consistency concept when used in this manner, see the recent paper by M. E. Olsen and J. C. Tully, "Socioeconomic-Ethnic Status Inconsistency and Preference for Political Change," *American Sociological Review*, **37**, 1972, pp. 560–574.

[29]C. Bagley, "Race Relations and Theories of Status Consistency," *Race*, **11**, 1970, pp. 267–289.

socioeconomic status are equivalent, as are the expectations which relate to them. However, with economic change, the correlation between race and economic status loses its consistency. A situation of "rank disequilibrium" develops, resulting in an increased sense of deprivation, social injustice, and racial hostility. Such structural discontinuity results in rejection of the social system's legitimacy as minorities become aware of its colonial and oppressive structure.

Using this approach, Bagley attempts to explain racial harmony in Brazil as a function of the coincidence between race and social class; in the United States, on the other hand, social mobility experienced by some Negroes has resulted in "rank disequilibrium," an increased sense of deprivation and racial disorder.

Rank disequilibrium is obviously not limited to race and economic status: there are a number of dimensions to social status making for different types of status inconsistency and resultant reactions. In this regard Geschwender makes an important contribution by revealing that high ethnic status and low levels of occupational status or income tend to result in rightist orientations, while high educational status in conjunction with similarly low occupational and economic levels results more often in leftist views.[30] Different kinds of rank disequilibrium may occur within the same race group, resulting in a plurality of reactions and social movements.[31] The effects of economic change on intergroup relations are, therefore, complex, making for a variety of attitudes within any one group in the race relations situation.

Status inconsistency, as can be seen, refers to change within the stratification system. Shibutani and Kwan take such a stratification approach to race, perceiving high racial conflict during periods of "transition" when traditional stratification systems begin to weaken. Any basic change in a society's mode of social organization, then, tends to modify people's definition of the social system and subsequent intergroup relations.[32]

[30]J. A. Geschwender, "Explorations in the Theory of Social Movements and Revolutions," *Social Forces*, **47**, 2, 1968, pp. 127–136.

[31]Bagley makes a similar point in his assumption that status disequilibrium results in conservatism, while racial disequilibrium tends to account for left-wing radicalism.

[32]T. Shibutani and K. M. Kwan, *Ethnic Stratification*, Macmillan, New York, 1965.

According to this approach, then, social change in race relations occurs as a result of the effects of economic change on the society's colonial caste structure. Various types of "rank disequilibrium" or "status inconsistency" between race and socioeconomic characteristics develop, resulting in increasing social awareness, particularly among minorities, and consequent rejection of the elite's legitimacy. Economic change results in a modification of racial orientations, particularly among subordinate minorities. In fact, the colonial system itself contributes to this development by using minorities, both indigenous and imported, to maximize economic development. Change in race relations is inevitable, resulting in a number of social movements within race groups involved in the situation, both dominant and subordinate. This link between economic development and social change is particularly useful, since it can be viewed within the context of Park's cycle concept: it is status inconsistency that results in conflict, thereby contributing to the cycle's ongoing development.[33]

THE SOCIOLOGICAL APPROACH: A SUMMARY MODEL

In this chapter we have seen how sociological analyses of race relations examine a society's characteristics, particularly the degree to which it is colonial, the contact situation in which intergroup relations originate, changing ecological frontiers, demographic factors, racial definitions provided by specific reference groups, and the manner in which economic change may introduce status inconsistency into the social structure, resulting in the heightening of racial tension. Taken together, a society's structural characteristics define the initial contact situation, which in turn is modified by changing racial frontiers through economic development. A basic mechanism in this economic change is the status inconsistency which develops, disrupting the racial-caste equilibrium, and results in racial conflict which moves in the direction of some new form of accommodation.

[33]Note here that we are not assuming that conflict will develop within the minority group(s) as a whole. As previously noted, different kinds of rank disequilibrium occur within the same race group. Thus, the "black bourgeoisie" represents a kind of economic disequilibrium, resulting in conservatism rather than radicalism.

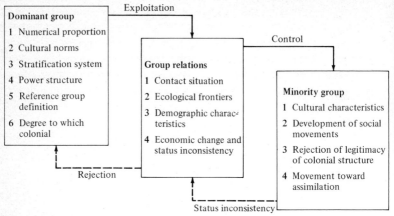

Figure 9-6 The sociological approach: A summary model.

In the sociological context, then, race relations are examined as a function of their societal setting and the manner in which that setting is modified by economic development. We have attempted to summarize this conceptual framework in Figure 9-6—a synthesis of the major factors discussed in this chapter. Once again, this is a summary figure rather than a definitive explanation.

CONCLUSIONS

In conclusion, sociological theories analyze the societal structure in which intergroup relations are controlled and operate. Racism typically occurs in a colonial situation where a migrant elite subordinates local minorities and imports others for economic purposes. Out of an initial situation of negative contact a racial caste system evolves, representing institutionalized racism on the societal level. This system is modified through economic change and changing ecological frontiers. Rank disequilibrium develops, resulting in racial tension and, eventually, new forms of accommodation. If one accepts Park's cycle concept, these forms move in the direction of assimilation rather than segregation. Furthermore, the relevance of reference-group definitions of race increases with economic change.

The above is particularly useful in delineating the societal setting in which the psychological and social-psychological factors discussed in the previous two chapters operate. Having completed our discussion of the major approaches to race relations, we turn in the next section to examine their interrelationships and to develop an analytical framework.

STUDY QUESTIONS

1 What particular historical characteristics of American society do you see accounting for contemporary race relations within it?
2 Describe some of the major features of the initial contact situation between major race groups in the United States.
3 Delineate some of the major ecological frontiers in the history of American race relations and assess their "cumulative directionality."
4 Examine the absence of clear institutional "definitions of the situation" in recent race riots in the United States.
5 Outline how the development of rank disequilibrium has affected white-black relations in the United States. Relate different kinds of disequilibrium to the various social movements which have developed within *both* race groups. In what ways are they similar?

READINGS

Bagley, C., "Race Relations and Theories of Status Consistency," *Race,* 1970, **11**, 3, pp. 267–289.

Banton, Michael P., *Race Relations,* Basic Books, New York, 1967.

————, "Race as A Social Category," *Race,* 1966, **8**, 1, July, pp. 1–16.

Benedict, Ruth F. and Gene Weltfish, *Race: Science and Politics,* Viking, New York, 1959.

Berreman, Gerald D., "Caste as Social Process," *Southwestern Journal of Anthropology,* 1967, **23**, 4, Winter, pp. 351–370.

Berry, Brewton, *Race Relations: The Interaction of Ethnic and Racial Groups,* Houghton Mifflin, Boston, Mass., 1951.

Blalock, Hubert M., "A Power Analysis of Racial Discrimination," *Social Forces,* 1960, **39**, 1, October, pp. 53–59.

————, *Toward a Theory of Minority-group Relations,* Wiley, New York, 1967.

Blauner, Robert, "Internal Colonialism and Ghetto Revolt," *Social Problems,* 1969, **16**, 4, Spring, pp. 393–408.

Blue, John T., "Patterns of Racial Stratification: A Categoric Typology," *Phylon,* 1959, **20**, 4, Winter, pp. 364–371.

Blumer, H., "Reflection on Theory of Race Relations," in A. W. Lind, *Race Relations in World Perspective,* University of Hawaii Press, Honolulu, 1955, pp. 3–21.

Bogardus, Emory S., "Race Reactions by Sexes," *Sociology and Social Research,* 1959, **43**, 6, July–August, pp. 439–441.

Bonilla, Seda E., "Social Structure and Race Relations," *Social Forces,* 1961, **40**, 2, December, pp. 141–148.

Buckley, W., *Sociology and Modern Systems Theory,* Prentice-Hall, Englewood Cliffs, N.J., 1967.

Carmichael, S., and C. V. Hamilton, *Black Power: The Politics of Liberation in America,* Vintage Books, New York, 1967, chap. 1.

Chasteen, Edgar, "Who Favors Public Accommodations: A Demographic Analysis," *Sociological Quarterly,* 1968, **9**, 3, Summer, pp. 309–317.

Dahlke, O. H., "Race and Minority Riots: A Study in the Typology of Violence," *Social Forces,* 1952, **30**, pp. 419–425.

Eitzen, D. S., "Status Inconsistency and Wallace Support," *Social Forces,* 1970, **48**, pp. 493–498.

Frazier, E. F., "Race Relations in World Perspective," *Sociology and Social Research,* 1957, **41**, 5, May–June, pp. 331–335.

————, and F. Edwards, (eds.), *On Race Relations: Selected Writings,* University of Chicago Press, Chicago, 1968.

Garrison, Karl C., "The Behavior of Clergy on Racial Integration as Related to A Childhood Socialization Factor," *Sociology and Social Research,* 1967, **51**, 2, January, pp. 208–219.

Geschwender, J. A., "Explorations in the Theory of Social Movements and Revolutions," *Social Forces,* 1968, **47**, 2, pp. 127–136.

Glazer, Nathan, "Blacks and Ethnic Groups: The Difference and the Political Difference It Makes," *Social Problems,* 1971, **18**, 4, Spring, pp. 441–461.

Guttman, Louis, "A Structural Theory for Intergroup Beliefs and Action," *American Sociological Review,* 1959, **24**, 3, June, pp. 318–328.

Hamblin, Robert L., "The Dynamics of Racial Discrimination," *Social Problems,* 1962, **10**, 2, Fall, pp. 103–121.

Herman, Reg, "Power and Prejudice: A Survey and a Hypothesis," *Journal of Human Relations,* 1969, **17**, 1, pp. 1–11.

Hills, Stuart L., "Are Negroes Just Another Immigrant Group?" *Discourse,* 1968, **11**, 4, Autumn, pp. 450–459.

Hourani, A., "The Concept of Race Relations: Thoughts After a Conference," *International Social Science Bulletin,* 1955, **7**, 2, pp. 335–340.

Hughes, Everett C., and Helen McGill, *Where Peoples Meet: Racial and Ethnic Frontiers,* Free Press, Glencoe, Ill., 1952.

———, "Race Relations and the Sociological Imagination," *American Sociological Review,* 1963, **28**, 6, December, pp. 879–890.

Ireland, Ralph R., "The Role of Economic Motivation in Ethnic Relations," *Sociology and Social Research,* 1958, **43**, 2, November–December, pp. 119–126.

Jiobu, R. M., and H. H. Marshall, "Urban Structure and the Differentiation between Blacks and Whites," *American Sociological Review,* 1971, **36**, pp. 638–649.

Katz, Irwin, and Patricia Gurin, *Race and the Social Sciences,* Basic Books, New York, 1969.

Kinloch, G. C., "Social Types and Race Relations in the Colonial Setting: A Case Study of Rhodesia," *Phylon,* third quarter, 1972, pp. 276–289.

Kuttner, Robert E., (ed.), *Race and Modern Science: A Collection of Essays by Biologists, Anthropologists, Sociologists, and Psychologists,* Social Science Press, New York, 1967.

Lefton, Mark, "Race, Expectations and Anomia," *Social Forces,* 1968, **48**, 3, March, pp. 347–352.

Lieberson, S., "A Societal Theory of Race and Ethnic Relations," *American Sociological Review,* **26**, 1961, pp. 902–910.

Lieberson, S., and A. R. Silverman, "The Precipitants and Underlying Conditions of Race Riots," *American Sociological Review,* 1965, **30**, pp. 887–893.

Lohman, Joseph D., and Dietrich C. Reitzes, "Note on Race Relations in Mass Society," *American Journal of Sociology,* 1952, **58**, pp. 240–246.

Lymann, Stanford M., "The Race Relations Cycle of Robert E. Park," *Pacific Sociological Review,* 1968, **11**, 1, Spring, pp. 16–22.

Martin, James G., "Group Discrimination in Organizational Membership Selection," *Phylon,* 1959, **20**, 2, Summer, pp. 186–192.

Mason, Phillip, "An Approach to Race Relations," *Race,* 1959, **1**, 1, November, pp. 41–52.

———, *Patterns of Dominance,* Oxford University Press, New York, 1970.

———, *Race Relations,* Oxford University Press, New York, 1970.

Masuoka, Jitsuichi, and Preston Valien (eds.), *Race Relations: Problems* and Theory, Essays in Honor of Robert E. Park, University of North Carolina Press, Chapel Hill, 1961.

Mead, Margaret, "The Student of Race Problems Can Say," Race, 1961, 3, 1, November, pp. 3–9.

Molotch, Harvey, "Racial Integration in a Transition Community," American Sociological Review, 1969, 34, 4, December, pp. 878–893.

Montagu, Ashley, "The Concept of Race," American Anthropology, 1962, 64, 5, 1, October, pp. 919–928.

———, "Racial Recognition by Nursery School Children in Lynchburg, Virginia," Social Forces, 1958, 37, 2, December, pp. 132–137.

Morland, J. Kenneth, "Racial Acceptance and Preference of Nursery School Children in a Southern City," Merrill-Palmer Quarterly, 1962, 8, 4, October, pp. 271–280.

———, "The Development of Racial Bias in Young Children," Theory into Practice, 1963, 2, 3, June, pp. 120–127.

———, "Racial Self-Identification: A Study of Nursery School Children," American Catholic Sociological Review, 1963, 24, 3, Fall, pp. 231–242.

———, "A Comparison of Race Awareness in Northern and Southern Children," American Journal of Orthopsychiatry, 1966, 36, 1, January, pp. 22–31.

———, and J. E. Williams, "Cross-Cultural Measurement of Racial and Ethnic Attitudes by the Semantic Differential," Social Forces, 1969, 64, 1, September, 107–112.

Noel, Donald L., and Alphonso Pinkney, "Correlates of Prejudice: Some Racial Differences and Similarities," American Journal of Sociology, 1964, 69, 6, May, pp. 609–622.

Noel, S. L., "A Theory of the Origin of Ethnic Stratification," Social Problems, 1968, 16, pp. 157–172.

Orbell, John, and Eugene K. Sherrill, "Racial Attitudes and the Social Context," Public Opinion Quarterly, 1969, 33, 1, Spring, pp. 46–54.

Park, Robert E., Race and Culture, Free Press, Glencoe, Ill., 1950.

Pettigrew, Thomas F., "Personality and Sociocultural Factors in Intergroup Attitudes: A Cross-National Comparison," Journal of Conflict Resolutions, 1958, 2, 1, March, pp. 29–42.

———, "Regional Differences in Anti-Negro Prejudice," Journal of Abnormal Social Psychology, 1959, 59, 1, July, pp. 28–36.

Pinkney, Alphonso, "The Quantitative Factor in Prejudice," Sociology and Social Research, 1963, 47, 2, January, pp. 161–168.

Pollard, William R., Black Literature, North Carolina State University, Raleigh, 1969.

Raab, E., and S. M. Lipset, "The Prejudiced Society," in E. Raab, (ed.), *American Race Relations,* Doubleday, Garden City, N.Y., 1962.

Reitzes, Dietrich C., "Institutional Structure and Race Relations," *Phylon,* 1959, **20**, 1, Spring, pp. 48–66.

———, "Behavior in Urban Race Contacts," in E. W. Burgess and D. J. Bogue, *Contributions to Urban Sociology,* University of Chicago Press, Chicago, 1964.

Reuter, E. B., (ed.), *Race and Culture Contacts,* 1st ed., McGraw-Hill, New York, 1934.

Rex, John, "Race as a Social Category," *Journal of Biosocial Science,* 1969, Supplement 1, July, pp. 145–152.

———, *Race Relations in Sociological Theory,* Schocken Books, New York, 1970.

Rose, Arnold M., (ed.), *Race Prejudice and Discrimination: Readings in Intergroup Relations in the United States,* 1st ed., Knopf, New York, 1951.

———, "Inconsistencies in Attitudes toward Negro Housing," *Social Problems,* 1961, **8**, 4, Spring, 286–292.

Rose, P. I., *They and We,* Random House, New York, 1964.

Roucek, Joseph S., "The Sociological Aspects of the Progress of Integration of American Minorities," *Sociological Interaction,* 1964, **2**, 2, pp. 143–156.

Schermerhorn, R. A., "Minorities: European and American, *Phylon,* 1959, **20**, 2, Summer, pp. 178–185.

———, "Toward a General Theory of Minority Groups," *Phylon,* 1964, **25**, pp. 238–246.

———, *Comparative Ethnic Relations,* Random House, New York, 1970.

Segal, Bernard, E., (ed.), *Racial and Ethnic Relations: Selected Readings,* Crowell, New York, 1966.

Segal, David R., "Status Inconsistency, Cross Pressures, and American Political Behavior," *American Sociological Review,* 1969, **34**, 3, June, pp. 352–358.

Shepherd, George W., and T. J. LeMelle (eds.), *Race Among Nations,* Heath Lexington Books, Lexington, Mass., 1970.

Shibutani, T., and K. M. Kwan, *Ethnic Stratification,* Macmillan, New York, 1965.

Simpson, George E., and J. Milton Yinger, *Racial and Cultural Minorities: An Analysis of Prejudice and Discrimination,* 3rd ed., Harper & Row, New York, 1965.

Skolnick, J., *Politics of Protest,* Simon and Schuster, New York, 1969.

Spilerman, S., "The Causes of Racial Disturbances: Tests of an Explanation," *American Sociological Review*, 1971, **36**, pp. 427–442.

Stein, David D., Jane A. Hardyck, and M. Brewster Smith, "Race and Belief: An Open and Shut Case," *Journal of Personality and Social Psychology*, 1965, **1**, 4, April, pp. 281–289.

Stryker, Sheldon, "Social Structure and Prejudice," *Social Problems*, 1958–59, **6**, 4, Winter, pp. 340–354.

Van den Berghe, P. L., *Race and Racism: A Comparative Perspective*, Wiley, New York, 1967.

———, *Race and Ethnicity: Essays in Comparative Sociology*, Basic Books, New York, 1970.

Vander Zanden, J. W., *American Minority Relations: The Sociology of Race and Ethnic Groups*, Ronald Press, New York, 1963.

Westie, F. R., "Race and Ethnic Relations," in R. E. L. Faris, (ed.), *Handbook of Modern Sociology*, Rand McNally, Chicago, 1964.

Williams, R. M., *The Reduction of Intergroup Tensions: A Survey of Research on Problems of Ethnic, Racial, and Religious Group Relations*, Social Science Research Council, New York, 1947.

———, *Strangers Next Door: Ethnic Relations in American Communities*, Prentice-Hall, Englewood Cliffs, N.J., 1964.

Wirth, L., "The Problem of Minority Groups," in R. Linton, (ed.), *The Science of Man in the World Crisis*, Columbia University Press, New York, 1945.

Woofter, T. J., *Races and Ethnic Groups in American Life*, McGraw-Hill, New York, 1933.

Young, D. R., *American Minority Peoples: A Study in Racial and Cultural Conflicts in the United States*, Harper & Brothers, New York, 1932.

Chapter 10

Summary
of Section Two

Section Two of our discussion has been concerned with the definition of basic concepts and approaches to the study of race relations. The former focused on the social definition of race, while the latter dealt with the major psychological, social-psychological, and sociological theories of race relations.

In Chapter 6 we raised the general question of developing objective definitions of concepts in the area of race. We attempted to develop sociological definitions of minority groups and the terms "race," "ethnic" groups, "race relations," as well as "racism," "prejudice," and "discrimination." Major emphasis was placed on these terms as social definitions developed by particular elites on the basis of perceived physical and/or social differences. In this manner, minority groups represent social categories rather than "real" physical groups.

Having completed the above, we turned to psychological explanations of racial attitudes. We concentrated primarily on the "psychopathology of prejudice"—an approach that views prejudiced attitudes as the function of a particular personality type which is supported and reinforced by the social environment in which it operates. With its foundation in Freudian theory, this orientation explains high levels of racism in terms of certain fundamental personality problems which function socially through processes such as frustration-aggression and socially acceptable forms of scapegoating.The neglect of the social context and sociological factors in general was noted with this approach, moving us in the direction of a higher level of analysis.

Chapter 8 brought us to race relations at the group level— the social-psychological approach. Here, we linked the individual to his reference groups through processes such as projection and institutionalization, a sense of group position, his racial identity, socioeconomic characteristics, situational patterning, and level of social conformity. These groups, in turn, were related to their general societal context through the characteristics of the groups involved, elite motivation behind its use of prejudice and discrimination, the relationship between internal and external social environments, and the degree to which the social structure is colonial in form.

Characteristics of the general social structure brought us to major sociological theories of race relations. We showed how these focus on societal characteristics, the importance of initial racial contact, ecological frontiers defining particular patterns of race relations, important demographic variables such as group size, institutional definitions of race, and the effects of status inconsistency on social change. Here, major emphasis was placed on societal factors defining the operation of race as a social definition.

This completes our discussion of the major literature on race which examines the operation of this concept on the individual, group, and societal level. We turn, in Section Three, to synthesize these separate orientations in the form of a general analytical framework, with particular emphasis on a society's colonial characteristics.

Section Three

An Analytical Framework

Chapter 11

Toward a Theoretical Synthesis and Conceptual Framework

In our discussion so far we have analyzed race relations on a number of explanatory levels, using a complexity of factors, attempting to specify various kinds of feedback. In this chapter, we shall attempt to develop a theoretical synthesis of these various elements as well as the conceptual framework they imply. We shall examine levels of analysis, factors involved, their interrelations, and feedback.

LEVELS OF ANALYSIS

We have attempted to analyze the societal operation of race on three major levels: the psychological or individual level, the social-psychological or group level, and the sociological, specifying the relevance of the social structure to societal definitions of race and intergroup relations within it. We see a combination of these three levels comprising social reality, with the major assumption that the societal environment as defined by the dominant elite, normally colonial in character, controls and defines intergroup relations and individual orientations within the groups concerned.

Our approach is essentially *structural:* it is the structure of society which defines and controls group as well as individual processes within it. Therefore, the source of race relations and racial attitudes is to be found in the way a particular society is structured and controlled by an elite which has conquered the indigenous population and imported other race groups for economic purposes.

MAJOR FACTORS

We have specified three major sets of factors behind the social definition of race: societal, group, and individual. The societal concerned the degree to which colonial characteristics were present, the initial kind of intergroup contact, the effects of particular ecological frontiers, and economic change. At the social-psychological level we underlined the relevance of group characteristics, group orientations in reference to the internal-external environment, and the manner in which the individual was integrated with his group environment through the processes of internalization, projection, institutionalization, and racial identity. Finally, we outlined the manner in which the psychoanalytical framework explains individual racial attitudes in terms of the frustration-aggression cycle applying to both dominant and subordinate groups. The major factors we examined were structural, social-psychological, and psychological, with the assumption that societal characteristics define and control the operation of the latter two.

INTERRELATIONSHIPS

A major relationship is implied in the above discussion: race as a social category is defined by the society's ecological, demographic and economic characteristics, which control dominant and minority group orientations. These group orientations, in turn, are patterned by situational, institutional, socioeconomic, and socio-cultural factors, influencing individual personalities through the processes of projection, institutionalization, frustration, and aggression. Finally, all of these factors are affected by economic change in the development of status inconsistency and consequent rejection of the colonial structure as illegitimate. A society's social structure, particularly the degree to which it is colonial, is thus a major determinant in the manner in which race is socially defined, institutionalized, and operates in intergroup relations.

Our approach is based, therefore, on the major proposition that *the more colonial a society's social structure* (i.e., the degree of subordination of indigenous groups and importation of other race groups for economic purposes by a migrant racial elite with certain cultural characteristics), *the more likely and more rigidly race will be used as a social category in matters of political policy, social control, competitive intergroup relations, group identity, as well as individual stereotyping and scapegoating.* Furthermore, the more colonial the structure, the greater the eventual rejection of that structure by subordinate minorities with the development of status inconsistency. Similarly, the more rigid will be the response of the dominant elite to such rejection. Thirdly, in cases where subordinate minorities achieve societal independence and power (e.g., African and Asian countries), the effects of a rigid colonial legacy are reflected in the continuing use of race in matters of political and social policy. Such "reverse racism" reflects the colonial structure, which defined and controlled the social situation before independence was granted to the indigenous population. Colonial contact and domination have far-reaching effects.

The implication of our approach is that the major source of race relations is to be found in the society's social structure, i.e., the degree to which it is *colonial* (a migrant racial elite which develops a system of institutionalized racism for economic and political purposes). Thus, the more colonial the elite, the more racist that system will be on *all* levels—individual, group, and societal. Conversely, the less colonial the elite, the more flexible race relations will be. Furthermore, variations in race relations within the same society (e.g., regional differences) may be attributed to variations in the colonial characteristics of elites at the local level (i.e., community, state control). Specific societies obviously vary in their levels of racism (e.g., South Africa compared with Brazil or Hawaii) as we shall see, while communities and/or states within the same society also differ in the degree to which their policies are racially defined and strictly enforced.

A further implication is that, to a large degree, individual attitudes are determined by participation in a particular social structure. While there is variation according to an individual's socioeconomic characteristics, as we have seen, the general level of racist attitudes in a society is largely determined by the shape of its social structure. This applies to both elite and subordinate groups: racial blindness among the latter, for example, may also be attributed to the racial caste system.

Thirdly, the social structure is also related to its subsequent rejection by subordinate minorities, particularly the indigenous population, with economic change and the development of status inconsistency. Thus, the more racist a social structure, the more it will ultimately be rejected in racial terms.

The implications of our approach are broad and widespread since we view societal characteristics as the ultimate determinants of intergroup relations. However, the diversity of group characteristics within a society has to be taken into account, as we shall see.

FEEDBACK

The feedback process is implied in the above discussion: economic change results in the erosion of the colonial caste system, leading to the development of status inconsistency and rejection of its legitimacy. As specified in the last chapter, different types of inconsistency (i.e., degree and direction of radicalism), affect *both* elite and subordinate groups. However, the general movement is toward an increase in racial conflict and some new form of intergroup accommodation (e.g., independence, separatism, or increased economic and political assimilation). As the colonial system experiences economic development, racial orientations and intergroup relations tend to change.

While race relations need to be analyzed from a structural point of view, then, it should be remembered that this structure is based on dynamic processes.

AN ANALYTICAL FRAMEWORK

It is relevant at this point to draw together the above discussion in the form of a conceptual framework. Retaining the various levels of analysis, relevant factors, their interrelationships, and feedback already specified, it is possible to develop a summary framework as illustrated in Figure 11-1, where the relationships between societal, group, and individual factors are delineated. Such a framework serves to interrelate major factors defining the societal definition of race. A number of qualifications should be raised:

1 Conceptual frameworks are *not* explanatory in and of themselves—they require an explanatory mechanism, which we have attempted to provide in the notion of a colonial society.

2 Change is basic to the framework through the processes of industrialization and economic development.

3 The relationship between societal factors and group orientations is interactive rather than one-way or static. Thus subordinate minorities react to the dominant elite, which in turn takes such reactions into account in its implementation of political policy. If we accept Park's cycle approach, described in the last chapter, such an interactive process is an important element in the society's ongoing movement toward accommodation and eventual assimilation. Here, then, we are taking a systems approach.

4 It is also important to stress that the colonization process may vary in degree in at least two ways. First, it may be either *direct* or *indirect* colonialism. That is, an elite may, after migration, subordinate the indigenous population directly by settling the society on a permanent basis, or it may send representatives to its colonial territory and administer the indigenous population through that colonial machinery, exploiting the country for economic purposes but not effecting large-scale settlement. Secondly, a similar distinction may be made between *internal* and *external* colonialism. The former refers to the

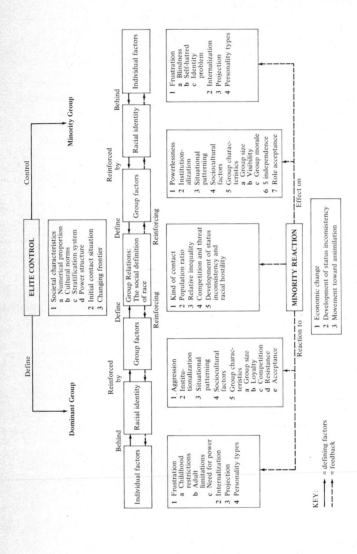

Figure 11-1 A conceptual framework of psychological, social-psychological, and sociological factors defining race relations.

subordination of racial groups within the colonial society, while the latter applies to territories which are annexed by the colonial elite but are not made part of the general society until a much later stage in that society's historical development. (Puerto Rico and Hawaii are useful examples of this.) In reference to our major proposition, it is evident that the more direct and internal the form of colonization, the more rigid race relations will tend to be within that society. Thus, indirect and external forms of colonization tend to be less racist in structure, although they still approximate a caste system. On the other hand, as industrialization occurs in the "mother country," they may become subject to more direct forms of colonization as they are increasingly influenced by the pressures of economic development. (Recent developments in Hawaii may be interpreted this way, as we shall see.) Colonization is thus a relative rather than categorical process.

    5 The framework is useful in highlighting some of the major factors defining race relations on a number of levels, particularly the economic.

    6 It points to relevant research areas, particularly the changing relationship between these sets of variables over time as they relate to an increase or deemphasis on race as a viable source of social differentiation.

    7 Such a framework should be useful in the comparative approach to race relations as the relative influence of these factors is compared within differing societal contexts—a central task in the next section of our discussion, in which we shall apply the framework on national and international levels of analysis.

Most important of the above, perhaps, is the manner in which our framework highlights the importance of a society's structural features for ensuing patterns of race relations within it. Basic to our discussion has been the exploitation of minorities by an elite power group. Relevant to this approach is Benedict's discussion of persecution behind such exploitation, racism being used to legitimize such behavior.[1] Such "racial reasons for persecution" are a function of social inequality and resulting in-group conservatism.

---

[1]R. Benedict, *Science and Politics*, Viking, New York, 1940.

Behind racial exploitation, then, lies social inequality—the general context in which race relations operate. According to Benedict, racism is symptomatic of general social problems causing groups to protect themselves and exploit others, using racism as a basic rationale.

CONCLUSIONS

In this section we have attempted to summarize our previous discussion of approaches to race relations and to develop a conceptual framework within which to analyze major intergroup processes. Our approach was basically structural, underlining the manner in which a society's colonial structure defines and controls the social operation of race within it at both the psychological and group level. We attempted to outline the manner in which a society's structural characteristics (particularly its elite) define the societal operation of race at the group (i.e., relationship) and individual (i.e., attitudinal) level, as well as the way in which these factors are influenced by economic development, leading to a rejection of the racial caste system by subordinate groups.

The above framework completes the first major half of our discussion. The next portion deals with the application of this framework on the international level, as well as an analysis of race relations within the United States. On the international level we shall compare four societies that vary in the degree to which their social structures are colonial—namely, South Africa, the United States, Brazil, and Hawaii. Our analysis of American race relations, on the other hand, will examine the manner in which colonialism operates within a specific society, and in particular, how it affects a hierarchy or plurality of racial groups which relate to the elite under varying historical, social, and economic conditions. In Section Four, we shall attempt to draw together the two halves of our discussion by developing a general theory of race relations and examining its implications for the reduction of racism.

STUDY QUESTIONS

1 Use the conceptual framework outlined in this chapter in an attempt
   to explain the following race relations situations:
   a The position of blacks, both past and present, in American
      society.
   b The position and cultural conservatism of the Chinese in Ameri-
      can society.
   c The exclusion of American Indians from American society in
      general.
   d The racial conservatism of middle-class whites in American
      society.
   e The development of violent and nonviolent social movements
      among American blacks.

Section Four

The Framework Applied

Chapter 12

Race Relations on the Inter-Societal Level: A Comparative Analysis

We now move to the second major part of our analysis—application of the conceptual framework on a number of levels. In this chapter we shall compare several societies according to the predominant pattern of race relations within them, examining the degree to which these settings differ in their colonial characteristics. In the following chapter we shall concentrate on varying intergroup relations within the United States, highlighting the heterogeneity of group characteristics and racial situations within this society. In both analyses we shall draw together our conclusions in a comparative framework of differing societal and group situations.

Throughout our discussion so far, we have emphasized the degree to which a society's structural characteristics are colonial, i.e., domination of indigenous and imported groups by a migrant elite and their exploitation for economic purposes. Societies obviously vary in the degree to which such circumstances define race relations within them. In this chapter we shall illustrate this variety by placing four societies on a continuum of colonialism to demonstrate the varying effects of differing historical and social circumstances on prevailing modes of intergroup relations. In this respect we shall examine race relations within South Africa, the United States, Brazil, and Hawaii in descending order of colonialism and, thereby, racism. We shall concentrate on these societies' historical and structural characteristics in relation to such racism.

SOUTH AFRICA

South Africa is, perhaps, the best example of a colonial society. Controlled by a racial and ethnic minority (i.e., white Afrikaners), this heterogeneous or plural society represents one of the most potentially threatening and insecure settings for any minority within it. Each racial group is differentiated by a number of ethnic and cultural divisions: whites vary by language and ethnicity (there are eight major languages spoken), Asians differ by religion and caste (there are at least five main language groups), blacks are divided historically and ethnically by tribal background (there are nine major groups), while coloureds or mulattoes differ according to whether they speak English or Afrikaans. This pluralism is further complicated by varying levels of urbanization and economic achievement.

    In such a society, the migrant minority elite defines its situation as one of extreme threat, racially as well as ethnically, internally and externally. Institutionalized racism (i.e., "apartheid") represents a societal form of social control, designed to protect this elite and ensure its monopoly of political and economic power in a highly threatening situation. The urgency of such an approach is further aggravated by the elite's Calvinistic background, which rationalizes domination on religious and moral grounds. Social control and racial separatism represent the major reactions of a racial-ethnic minority with Calvinistic and capitalistic motives in a racially plural society which poses a continuous political, physical, economic, and cultural threat to the elite in power. Furthermore, the society's historical development is one of racial, ethnic, and economic conflict. Conflict and intergroup threat are traditional to this social system, magnifying the extent to which racism operates as a mechanism of elitist control. The effects of economic development only increase perceived racial threat on the part of the elite as well as relative deprivation among subordinate minorities.

The South African situation is thus highly complex in terms of social composition but relatively simple in the manner its controlling elite reacts in a typically colonial manner—i.e., the attempt to institutionalize and perpetuate political and economic control on a racial basis. The policy of "separate development," for example, simply coincides with such colonial goals in the attempt to maintain and further develop racial-ethnic differences to ensure elite domination on a stable and lasting basis.

Any examination of South Africa's history highlights the above points: the predominance of racial and ethnic conflict, economic threat, and the development of minority-group nationalism, all of which occur within the context of a colonial minority, which, having broken the major ties binding it to its homeland (i.e., Holland), urgently attempts to ensure its racial, cultural, and economic security. Viewing the history of this society as a series of frontiers, it is possible to delineate a number of colonial, war, economic, and political factors which have contributed to the evolution of a highly racist society.

The earliest historical situation of significance was initial *colonial contact.*[1] In the early part of the seventeenth century, the Dutch East India Company attempted to settle and develop the Cape region of South Africa. The company was Calvinistic in policy and authoritarian in practice, attempting to maximize economic pay off. During the 1650s, slaves arrived, and non-whites were generally defined in a subordinate manner. Complicating the company's development were similar attempts by the British to take over the Cape; during the late 1700s and early nineteenth century, the latter attacked and eventually took over. The first major *war frontier* thus occurred against the British, who possessed similar colonial aspirations. Later, conflict between

---

[1]For relevant discussions of South Africa's historical development see, for example, J. Fisher, *The Afrikaners,* Cassell, London, 1969; N. J. Rhoodie, *Apartheid and Racial Partnership in Southern Africa,* Academica, Pretoria, 1969.

these two groups served to reinforce and aggravate the antagonism between those two ethnic groups—a basic factor relating to
economic and cultural competition in the South African situation.

As the Afrikaner Boers, or farmers, resented the control of
both the British and Dutch, they decided to move inland during
the 1830s. The "Great Trek" took place as the Afrikaners moved
away from the Cape and British domination. This brought them
into conflict with the African tribes in the area. Throughout the
nineteenth century, conflict between these two race groups took
place. The second *war frontier* was a racial conflict, reinforcing
the social definitions of blacks as savage and threatening, requir-
ing rigid control. Initial racial contact was thus negative, as is
typical of most colonial situations. The viability of such negativism in ensuing race relations cannot be underestimated.

Meanwhile, conflict with the British continued, particularly
as the latter attempted to further develop and consolidate their
control of the country. Matters came to a head in 1879 with the
First War of Independence and again with the Boer War of 1901.
Both events, particularly the latter, were instances of fierce
conflict, resulting in a high level of bitterness among the
Afrikaners and a determination to maintain their independence.
The third *war frontier* thus reverted to ethnic conflict. However,
as with racial competition, this conflict reveals a high level of
historical continuity and is reflected in the Afrikaners' contemporary fear of English liberalism, culture, and economic power.

The early twentieth century may be viewed essentially as a
political frontier. The Afrikaners attained self-government of
their own provinces, became active in South African politics, and
formed their own party. They attempted political coalitions with
the English but achieved only limited success.

Economic factors came to the fore in the 1930s with the
Great Depression. Prior to the beginning of this century, Indian
labor had been imported to Natal to work the cane fields, the
English had competed with the Afrikaners for control of the
diamond and gold fields, while Chinese labor was recruited during
the early 1900s. The racial-ethnic basis of the economic structure
was well established. Aggravating the potential interracial threat
implicit in such a system was a general strike in the 1920s and a

depression in the following decade. In both instances the perceived economic threat of nonwhites was high, establishing an economic basis for racism and white domination.

The postdepression years saw an increase in Afrikaner politics, controversy over support for the Germans in World War II, the gradual monopolization of political power by Afrikaners in the Nationalist Party, and formalization of the policy of "separate development." This was clearly a *political frontier* of some significance, particularly as the country moved toward a republic and greater independence from British influence.

The 1960s saw the beginning of great industrial and urban development—a significant *economic frontier.* Such development saw an increase in nonwhite nationalism, an increase in perceived racial threat with urban migration, an increase in external pressure against South Africa, and further elaboration of the apartheid policy. The results of these factors include further implementation of residential and educational segregation, an increase in the control of migration and law enforcement in general, the banning of nonwhite political movements, imprisonment without trial, further implementation of internal self-government for certain race groups, and an attempt to develop "friendly" relations with neighboring and economically dependent black governments.

At the same time, however, the economic demands of increased industrialization have made the maintenance of role assignment or job reservation on a strictly racial basis increasingly difficult. Certain racial barriers have become slightly more flexible but remain under the control of the white elite. That elite, however, appears to lack complete agreement concerning the full implementation of societal racism, as recent political disagreements have demonstrated. Nevertheless, white domination remains the cornerstone of political policy.

Contemporary analyses of the South African situation vary in focus: some concentrate on the potential conflict within it;[2] others look at its structural features, such as the effects of

[2]See, for example, P. B. Baker, "Is Apartheid an Insoluble Problem?" *Race,* **6**, pp. 263–266; L. Kuper, "Racialism and Integration in South African Society," *Race,* **4**, 1963, pp. 26–31.

urbanization and attempts by the white elite to restrict those effects;[3] while some writers describe the effects of the apartheid system on the deprived blacks within it, resulting in high levels of crime, poverty, disease, and deviant behavior.[4] Whatever the orientation, there is general agreement that South Africa represents a case of extreme colonialism: a racial, ethnic, and numerical minority migrates to another society, subordinates the local and highly heterogeneous population, competes with other colonial powers, imports other race groups for economic purposes, and attempts to institutionalize racism on a societal level in order to monopolize the political and economic control of all other minorities in this very plural society. The major result is that race is an overwhelming criterion in all social action—more or less regardless of the social characteristics of those involved—within the racial caste system.

A racial-cultural minority has thus succeeded in the building and reinforcement of a racial caste system. Given their Calvinistic culture, minority situation, and negative contact with all other race groups, all the major elements of colonialism exist for the development of a rigid and racist society. Race represents the major method of social control and racism its pseudoscientific rationale,[5] elaborated by an insecure minority. While industrialization may result in restricted modification of ths caste system, it is unlikely that there will be any immediate change in the power monopoly. The latter will develop on either an evolutionary or revolutionary basis.

Whatever the case, the South African situation is the most complete illustration of the colonial situation, providing a yardstick for the analysis of other societies on a structural basis. Given the framework we developed in the last section, this society possesses most of the negative structural, historical, group, and individual factors resulting in a highly racist society,

---

[3]L. Bloom, "Some Problems of Urbanization in South Africa," *Phylon,* **25**, 1964, pp. 347–361.

[4]See N. Mkele, "The Effects of Apartheid," *New Society,* **2**, 1963, pp. 6–7.

[5]Thus, the South African government has its own Bureau of Racial Affairs (S.A.B.R.A.), set up to clarify the principles of racial separation. The bureau publishes a *Journal of Racial Affairs,* which provides "scientific credence" and empirical support for the apartheid system.

i.e., the rigid use of race as a social category in matters of political policy, social control, competitive intergroup relations, group identity, and individual stereotyping and scapegoating. Van den Berghe shows, for example, in a study of racial attitudes in Durban[6] that among Africans, Indians, and whites, racism and prejudice is strongest among the third group. He also found no clear relationship between racial social distance and parental occupation or education within the same group. According to these data, then, racial attitudes in South Africa are most negative among whites and tend to be undifferentiated by socioeconomic characteristics, highlighting the society's racist norms.

The general effects of the society's colonial structure appear to be operative here: race is the major criterion of political policy, intergroup relations, and individual attitudes, particularly among the white elite. We turn next to race relations within the United States.

THE UNITED STATES

The structural characteristics of American society are surprisingly colonial: a minority group of white Protestants migrates to another society, attempts to drive off or exterminate the indigenous Indian population for economic reasons but rationalized in religious and philosophical terms, sets up a plantation slavery system, and imports other race groups for economic purposes, submitting them to social and economic discrimination. Under these circumstances, race is a very "real" social category, utilized as a mode of social control and economic exploitation in the attempt to maximize the development of white, Protestant capitalism.

Of basic importance to race relations in this society, as in South Africa, are the values of the white elite and the kind of institutional structure which has evolved on the basis of these societal orientations. Traditional "American" values are well conceptualized in the notion of the Protestant Ethic— individualism, moralism, puritanism, materialism, and, from a

---

[6]P. L. van den Berghe, "Race Attitudes in Durban, South Africa," *Journal of Social Psychology,* **57**, 1962, pp. 55–72.

religious point of view, a sense of "manifest destiny"—an ethnocentric definition of one's own culture as more civilized than another and divinely ordained to overcome the latter. Other race groups are viewed from this value standpoint: Indians were "savages"; Negroes, "barbaric"; Orientals, "clannish" and "treacherous"; Mexicans, "inferior"; and various white ethnic groups, "un-American." Given the relative monopoly of political and economic power by white Protestants, changes in the race relations hierarchy are viewed as competitive and threatening. Minorities have to "earn the right" to be accepted on the elite's own terms—i.e., they should become part of the white conservative bourgeoisie.

The structure which evolved from this set of values, as in the typical colonial situation, was designed to favor the dominant elite politically, socially, and economically. Minorities (e.g., the Indians) were either excluded completely from this structure or included in it on grossly unequal terms, with little or no resources. Thus, the notion of community facilities, community development, and local politics allowed the elite to build a colonial society with minorities at its political, social, and economic mercy, neatly "packaged" into separate areas, or ghettos.

Where minorities were not markedly different racially and culturally from the elite, conformed to American values, and were not defined as threatening, they were permitted to assimilate into the society's mainstream on a gradual basis (i.e., white ethnic immigrants). Other groups, however, have been subject to deculturation (i.e., blacks), internment (i.e., Japanese), immigration control and economic exploitation (i.e., Mexicans), as well as to social, economic, and political discrimination (e.g., Jews). Given the society's political and economic power elite and institutionalized inequality, each race group, relatively speaking, occupies a certain general slot in the stratification system.

Since legitimate change is effected through the political structure, and resources are distributed unequally in the stratification system, change in race relations is slow. Structural change is particularly difficult the higher the racial, economic, and cultural dissimilarity between the controlling elite and the minority concerned. While racial policies in the society do not conform strictly to the South African apartheid system and whites constitute the numerical and effective majority, then, given America's structural inequality and the dependence of minorities on it, race relations within this setting in some respects parallel the colonial "type." It is, perhaps, for this very reason that racial exploitation and violence have become so visible in recent years, since the more rigid and colonial the society's social structure, the greater the eventual problem of race. We turn to examine the historical evolution of this structure in more detail.

As with South Africa, the development of American race relations may be divided into a number of distinct frontiers. Bogardus, for example, delineates the periods of enslavement, enfranchisement, disenfranchisement, segregation, desegregation, and integration as crucial to American white-Negro relations.[7] We shall discuss eight frontiers considered vital to the development of race relations within the society as a whole.

The initial stage was essentially a *colonial frontier,* with major emphasis on the establishment of white rule in an alien land controlled by Indians. At this stage, the in-group values of ethnocentrism, puritanism, manifest destiny, and eventually, racism are at the forefront of intergroup contact. Indians are considered a barbaric, savage race which needs to be conquered and controlled as the settlers move inland. Such a period is typically colonial: greatest emphasis is placed on in-group solidarity, economic development, and control of a situation threatened by a savage race. Given the conditions of physical and social threat, the need for self-preservation and economic development, it is not surprising to see a high level of ethnocentrism during this initial period. Negative contact with other groups, particularly the Indians, has had viable historical repercussions, as can be seen through to the present era.

The above orientations are further reflected in the ensuing *plantation frontier,* based on the slavery system. Such a "paternalistic" system, as described by van den Berghe, viewed Negroes in purely economic and materialistic terms.[8] They were

---

[7]E. S. Bogardus, "Stages in White-Negro Relations in the United States." *Sociology and Social Research,* **45**, 1960, pp. 74–79.

[8]P. L. van den Berghe, *Race and Racism,* Wiley, New York, 1967.

to be bought and sold, used and abused, and to function as general scapegoats for the frustrations of the dominant elite. While some family servants might be treated on pseudointimate terms, the predominant relationship was one of oppressive domination for economic purposes. Furthermore, as van den Berghe points out, an important characteristic of American slavery was the manner in which it broke up the Negro family structure and culture, resulting in his deculturation and self-hatred.[9] Thus, this minority was not only physically and economically dependent on the elite, it became culturally dependent as well—an important difference in comparing this race relations situation with that in the other three societies.

With the advent of the Civil War, the plantation era moved into the *war frontier.* This period had a number of significant effects on race relations: the power structure of the South was weakened, and for a restricted period Negroes achieved a limited degree of freedom and social status. However, the latter had little effect on the power structure and did not last. Furthermore, social segregation on a racial basis increased as the paternalistic order began to break down. Thus, the South began to adjust to the effects of the war in such a way as to maintain racial slavery, but in a new guise. Institutionalized racism did not break down; it simply adapted to a new situation—a basic process in colonial race relations.

During the 1850s and for the rest of the century, the above adaptation process continued, but with increased urgency during what was essentially an *economic frontier,* resulting in increased racial competition generally. Capitalism developed at a high rate as big business furthered its power and consolidation, with the concomitant development of industrialization and urbanization. Immigration from Europe increased sharply, as did the general motivation for economic achievement. The restricted changes in race relations of the previous frontier were reversed: racial segregation increased, the Negro vote was restricted through various franchise tests, and economically this minority was little better off than it had been during its plantation days. Emancipa-

---

[9]P. L. van den Berghe, ibid. Note that I am following his ordering of historical periods in American race relations.

tion meant little socially, economically, or politically. In 1896, the Supreme Court's "separate-but-equal" doctrine further legitimized a traditional caste system, but in terms which made it appear more positive, at least philosophically.

The first half of the twentieth century returned the society to a *war frontier,* but on an external basis. Given the increased immigration of Negroes to the north, their participation in the war effort, and the effects of "New Deal" policies following the depression, it is possible to see the racial caste structure becoming unsettled and beginning to break down, if only slightly. Participation in World War II further contributed to this trend, as individuals from both races came together under new circumstances. On the other hand, the development of racial ghettos and the economic threat Negroes posed to immigrant workers reinforced previous patterns of segregation and racism.

The postwar years may be seen as a period of economic rebuilding, or another *economic frontier.* Segregation and other forms of official discrimination were frowned on, and a number of important legal decisions concerning such matters were made. However, the general caste structure of race relations remained virtually intact. On the other hand, Negro awareness of and reaction to this structure was beginning to increase—the forerunner of a new definition of the racial scene.

The 1960s, perhaps, may be seen as an important *political frontier.* While dynamic economic development took place, the importance of political events for race relations was high. Beginning with President Kennedy and continuing with Johnson, the "Great Society" concept was applied to social policy, with at least an attempt made to implement certain racial changes. This was particularly true in the face of Negro revolt, reflecting an increased sense of relative deprivation and aspiration for greater equality. A redefinition of race relations was made, particularly by black social movements, ranging from the nonviolent to the revolutionary. While such orientations were clearly significant, it would be naïve to overestimate the degree to which they resulted in structural change. A rising white blacklash in reaction to racial rioting combined with the assassination of effective leadership appear to have slowed down the pace of the movement toward greater racial parity.

Finally, the 1970s may be viewed as an *economic frontier* with rather conservative effects. Economic developments have made for greater control of social policy, an increased sense of economic competition, and, more importantly, greater political awareness of the silent middle-class majority, with its traditional values of independence, law, and order. All of these factors, coupled with the economic burden of the Vietnam war, have made for a decline in the move toward more positive and more equalitarian race relations. Given economic problems and brushes with the law, black social movements have moved from rhetoric to matters of economic policy, making them, in at least some respects, less radically active.

The political elite, it would appear, perceives racial problems as a matter of tokenism—adjustments in the present structure to give it the appearance of being more equalitarian and open to advancement, without respect to racial background. Recent analyses, for example, highlight the correlation between economic values and social change, a tendency among the white elite to ignore "hard-core" problems, and the stability of the Negro's ghetto environment over time.[10] Such characteristics may be viewed as a function of the society's colonial structure, which has maintained remarkable stability throughout its historical development.

Racially, then, the American social system closely parallels, at least in some respects, the typically colonial situation. A group of white Protestants moves to a foreign environment, subordinates the indigenous population, and then develops the society economically, using a system of racial slavery. While political and economic factors result in the formal breakdown of such a system, the form remains basically the same, since political policy is both elitist and conservative for capitalistic reasons. Certain minority advances are made but result in few, if any, viable structural modifications. The biggest danger lies in mistaking a change in social definition for a change in structure.

[10]See J. A. Moss, "Currents of Change in American Race Relations," *British Journal of Sociology*, **11**, 1960, pp. 232–243; M. Duberman, "Black Power in America," *Partisan Review*, **35**, 1968, pp. 34–48; G. Osofsky, "The Enduring Ghetto," *Journal of American History*, **55**, 1968, pp. 243–255.

Furthermore, while we have restricted our discussion to blacks, other race groups have been affected in a similarly colonial fashion with disastrous historical results. Thus, Indians remain generally tangential to American society on reservations reminiscent of the South African apartheid system, while the Japanese find it difficult to forget their internment as a threat to the society's security. The Chinese remain in a cultural and physical ghetto, as do the Puerto Ricans, while Mexicans continue to be exploited economically and to retain their position of low social status. The American Creed is thus a myth applying to the white majority, particularly its middle-class, Protestant sector.

Considering the extent to which the American Creed has dominated the value system of this society, many are at a loss to explain the recent development of racial nationalism and outbreaks of violence. Resorting to "blaming the victim" is one way of "explaining" such behavior, but this approach is clearly blind, reflecting the prejudices of a colonial elite when the "natives" become insubordinate. Clearly, it is the racial structure of American society—based on the Protestant Ethic, capitalism, and economic exploitation on a racial bias—which accounts for racial disillusionment, alienation, and rejection of the system as "illegitimate" as relative deprivation develops with industrialization. Since the society's political, economic, educational, and social structure is defined and controlled on the basis of racial criteria, it is clearly a rigid and inflexible system which perpetuates social and cultural pluralism despite the "melting-pot" notion of some decades past. To the extent that the society is racially controlled, it is inflexible and ridden with potential conflict.

The central problem, quite clearly, is its decolonization—a particularly difficult problem, since the political elite reflects and is dependent on the economic elite—which, to a large extent, is racially and socially homogeneous. Since such elitism occurs at the neighborhood, community, state, and national level, social change in racial power is a particularly slow and agonizing process. Within such a setting, the group and individual factors specified in our conceptual framework operate to maintain racism among the elite and self-hatred and/or aspiration toward white-defined values among subordinate minorities. However, the latter phenomena are subject to change through industrialization, consequent status inconsistency, and the development of minority-group nationalism. The structure of the society, however, tends to remain racist and relatively inflexible, as race remains a major factor in the society's stratification system, intergroup relations, and individual attitudes in general. In this manner, the society's colonial structure places it, to a surprising degree, nearer the South African end of the continuum.

SOUTH AFRICA AND THE UNITED STATES AS COLONIAL SOCIETIES: A SUMMARY

Before considering Brazil and Hawaii, it is worth bringing together those characteristics that place South Africa and the United States at the upper end of the colonial continuum, i.e., the manner in which they highlight those features most characteristic of the colonial situation.

In both the above cases, we are presented with a white, Protestant minority which migrates to another society in order to develop a new home and maximize economic achievement. Contact with the indigenous population is negative and conflict-ridden, resulting in high levels of racism in the competition for resources. Ensuing frontiers tend to take on a certain similarity: internal and external conflict occurs, heightening internal threat and competition, while economic development, both negative and positive, tends to aggravate intergroup relations. Political frontiers may also increase intraracial competition and conflict over policy, while later economic development begins to disturb the racial caste system, resulting in increased relative deprivation and racial conflict. Furthermore, common to both situations is the importation of external race groups for economic purposes—a process which increases intergroup competition on all levels of the social system. From a normative standpoint, both societies possess dominant elites which are highly ethnocentric, puritanical, and imbued with Protestant Ethic values of individualism and materialism. Social distance between elite and subordinate groups is maximized, despite a relatively high level of sexual exploitation and miscegenation.

The typical colonial situation, then, involves a migrant white Protestant minority which subordinates an indigenous population, imports other race groups for economic purposes, and utilizes race as a mode of social control in order to ensure the monopoly of political, economic, and social power. As industrialization takes place, however, minorities develop a sense of relative deprivation and begin to reject the legitimacy of the society's power structure. Elite reaction to such "rebellion" is conservative but tends, eventually, to lead to some new form of racial accommodation. In this manner, race relations, even within a colonial situation, are dynamic rather than static.

We turn now to the second two societies on the continuum, Brazil and Hawaii.

BRAZIL

Brazil is one of the most fascinating societies with respect to the social operation of race. Known for its flexible and fluid definitions of race, this society provides us with a useful example to place on the lower end of the colonial continuum.

Several characteristics make this society unique: it was colonized by a Catholic elite—the Portuguese—imbued with little of the Protestant Ethic or the kind of puritanism which finds relations with subordinates shameful. Blacks, imported for slavery purposes, were not deculturized as they were in the American case, and the difference between black and white, from a color standpoint, is one of degree rather than caste. Furthermore, the church attempted to restrain abuse of subordinate groups and, in fact, protected the indigenous Indian population, which was found to be unsuited to slave labor. A factor of further importance was the country's geography: its size and inaccessibility made a highly centralized and efficient form of colonial government impossible. The typical centralized colonial bureaucracy could not operate within such conditions.

The colonial situation in Brazil thus differed from South Africa and the United States on a number of important points: its elite was Catholic rather than Protestant; the indigenous population was not heavily involved in the society's economic development; imported groups were not deculturized, particularly blacks; the church restrained colonial exploitation rather than providing its underlying rationale; and geographical conditions made a centralized colonial bureaucracy impossible. The race relations situation, while still colonial, reveals a more flexible and less castelike pattern than was the case in America and South Africa.

The above differences may be clearly seen in the frontiers of Brazil's historical development. The initial situation was, of course, a *colonial frontier.* Portugal took over the country in the sixteenth century, conquering the local Indians. Considerable miscegenation between the two groups took place, heralding the first period of racial admixture, although the Indians were still defined as slaves. Eventually they were viewed as inefficient, and since labor was required to develop the coffee and rubber industries, the Portuguese decided to import blacks from Africa in large numbers. Three to five million Africans were eventually brought in to work the plantations. The white population was thereby outnumbered, while control of the blacks was paternalistic and nondeculturizing in effect.

The second major period was the *plantation frontier.* During this period, major economic plantations were developed on Brazil's coastal region, while inland the Jesuits developed mission stations for the Indian population. In both cases, control was paternalistic rather than exploitive and was mediated by the church. Miscegenation continued, particularly in the coastal regions, while Indian slavery was outlawed early in the seventeenth century. While clearly colonial, the situation was a great deal more flexible than is typical of such a period. The color line was more of a continuum than a caste division, influenced by the high level of miscegenation.

The early nineteenth century saw the beginning of the *immigrant frontier* in which a large number of whites from Europe migrated to Brazil. Such a development affected the society's demographic structure, largely increasing the white sector of the society. However, given the lower class and Catholic background of the migrants, the continuing high rate of miscegenation, and the absence of a highly centralized colonial bureaucracy, the race relations situation remained fluid well into the present century.

Recent and present developments in Brazil highlight what may essentially be viewed as a competitive *economic frontier.* With continuing European immigration and an increase in the development of industrialization and urbanization, van den Berghe finds evidence of a present decline in miscegenation and an increase in the consciousness of physical appearance (i.e., degree of whiteness), antiblack stereotypes, racial stratification, as well as antiblack segregation and discrimination.[11] With economic development, race relations have become increasingly competitive. As economic competition develops, group boundaries in a traditionally fluid situation begin to crystallize. Under these circumstances, scapegoating becomes a useful technique for reinforcing in-group identity and rationalizing the control and exploitation of other groups in the economic scramble. Thus, racism develops in an otherwise relatively nonracist situation. Racial stereotypes increase and are reinforced in the ongoing process of socialization.

Ironically, then, what was originally a fluid situation appears to be moving toward a more racially conscious society as economic change takes place, while the reverse appears to be developing in the societies we have just discussed. Some may be puzzled and at a loss to explain such a reversal. However, as we shall show in our discussion of Hawaii, there are colonial features in the social structures of most societies which, though not highly visible, may become so and result in intergroup conflict and prejudice. In this, Brazil is no different: it is still a colonial society, though less so than many, and the caste elements in its structure become visible as economic development begins to modify that structure and the perceptions of people within it. The future presents a test of the degree of potential flexibility within that social structure as it adapts to the effects of social change.

Brazil, then, represents an intermediary "type" on the colonial scale and reveals a number of distinct characteristics when compared with highly colonial societies such as South Africa and the United States. These may be summarized as follows:

---

[11]P. L. van den Berghe, *Race and Racism*, Wiley, New York, 1967, pp. 59–76. I am following his historical order here.

1   A Catholic, Portuguese colonial elite
2   The restraining influence of the church on the plantation frontier
3   The lack of a highly centralized, bureaucratic colonial government
4   Limited economic development, given the country's inaccessible geography
5   Little, if any, deculturation of imported black slaves
6   The early outlawing of Indian slavery
7   A high level of miscegenation, resulting in a color continuum rather than a strict racial caste system

All the above factors have contributed to a racial situation which, although still colonial in form, is a great deal more flexible in content than in South Africa and the United States. Contemporary analysts of Brazillian race relations illustrate that colonization is a matter of degree rather than definitive categories: on the one hand there are those who contrast Brazil's history with that of the United States, revealing less racist value systems and detrimental effects.[12] Within this society, prejudice is a matter of class rather than race, while racial identity is not closely related to the "rule of descent," pointing to the flexible rather than rigid operation of "race."[13] However, writers such as Fernandes and Hutchinson point to the persistence of racial inequality and the "paternalism of slaveholding times."[14] Secondly, the widespread existence of anti-Negro stereotypes has been documented in a number of studies carried out by Bastide, van den Berghe, Hammond, and Iannis.[15] Van den Berghe has also suggested that prejudice and discrimination may be increasing in Brazil as it

[12]See C. N. Degler, *Neither Black nor White*, Macmillan, New York, 1971; E. R. Service, "Indian-European Relations in Colonial Latin America," *American Anthropologist*, 57, 1955, pp. 411–425.

[13]See D. Pierson, *Negroes in Brazil*, Southern Illinois University Press, Carbondale, 1942, 1967; M. Harris and G. Kottak, "The Structural Significance of Brazilian Racial Categories," *Sociologia*, 25, 1963, pp. 203–208.

[14]F. Fernandes, "La Persistencia del Pasado," *Revista Mexicana de Sociologia*, 28, 1966, pp. 787–812; H. W. Hutchinson, *Village and Plantation LIfe in Northeastern Brazil*, University of Washington Press, Seattle, 1957.

[15]See R. Bastide, "Race Relations in Brazil," *International Social Science Bulletin*, 9, 1957, pp. 495–512; R. Bastide and P. L. van den Berghe, "Stereotypes, Norms and Interracial Behavior in Sao Paulo, Brazil," *American Sociological Review*, 22, 1957, pp. 689–694; H. R. Hammond, "Race, Social Mobility and Politics in Brazil," *Race*, 4, 1963, pp. 3–13; O. Ianni, "A Ideologia Racial Do Negro e do Mulato em Floriannopolis," *Sociologia*, 20, 1958, pp. 352–365.

moves from a paternalistic to a competitive model of race relations.[16]

In structural terms, then, this society is in marked contrast to the two just described. As these writers show, however, this contrast is a matter of degree on a colonial continuum rather than a set of exclusive categories. In general, however, this society's social structure ranks relatively low on colonialism, making for a stratification system which is more flexible and less caste-bound than the previous two societies. While prejudiced *attitudes* exist, they are not *institutionalized* in a rigid colonial structure based strictly on race.

HAWAII

We turn, finally, to the least racist society on our continuum—Hawaii. This society provides a unique setting in which to examine intergroup relations. With its complex history, introduction of "new" race groups at particular points of its development, and high level of interracial mixture, Hawaii represents a social laboratory to the sociologist interested in the diversity of race relations within a single situation.

Long known for its outward norms of racial tolerance, Hawaii, when compared to the other societies, is unique on a number of accounts: its relative lack of outward racism, the positive nature of initial intergroup contact, the relative absence of a racial caste system, a very high level of racial heterogeneity, and extraordinary level of interracial marriage. As with Brazil, there has been little involvement of the indigenous population in the plantation system and little deculturation of any of the race groups brought into the society. On the other hand, as we shall see later, racist attitudes exist, although to a restricted degree only, while an economic and political racial hierarchy does exist, although it does not operate in a castelike fashion.

Hawaii's initial intergroup situation has been described as the *trading frontier.*[17] During this period, Lind sees contact

---

[16]P. L. van den Berghe, *Race and Racism,* Wiley, New York, 1967, pp. 70–75.

[17]For an important discussion of Hawaii's sociological development, see A. W. Lind, *Hawaii: The Last of the Magic Isles,* Oxford University Press, London, 1969. In Chapter II of that work Lind discusses Hawaii's major historical frontiers: trading, plantation, political, and tourist, and it is largely his approach that I am following here.

between foreigner *(Haole)* and Hawaiian as positive and mutually beneficial, with the groups exchanging products with little conflict.[18] The situation was not typically colonial, since, from a geographical standpoint, Hawaii was a way-station rather than a colonial possession. No attempt was made, therefore, to seize the Islands at this stage and make them a colonial settlement. Furthermore, considering the relatively passive orientation of Hawaiian culture, miscegenation and interracial liaisons developed smoothly. The indigenous society, along with its monarchy, was largely preserved.

The above situation did not remain static, however: foreign economic interests saw Hawaii as a potential source of capital gain, moving the society, during the nineteenth century, into the *plantation frontier.* Since the local population was decimated by disease, the need for labor resulted in the importation of a wide range of race groups: Chinese, Japanese, Korean, Filipino, Portuguese, and Puerto Rican laborers were all involved in the development of the economic system in the Islands. As Lind points out, it was at this point that the notion of race was introduced into Hawaii—comparatively late when compared to the other three societies. Nonetheless, through rigid segregation and control, race became a viable social category in matters of policy and interaction. However, unlike other plantation systems, workers were abused only occasionally. They were contract rather than slave labor, and, as Lind has shown, the caste elements of this period rapidly declined with the demise of this frontier in general. When it came to an end, the various race groups, particularly the Orientals, moved into the urban centers and were able to establish themselves, disadvantaged to a surprisingly restricted extent by their plantation background.

With the formal decline of the plantation system, Hawaii, at the end of the nineteenth century, moved into what may be viewed as a *political frontier.* In 1893, the last Hawaiian monarch was overthrown by mainland whites in a bloodless and conflict-free coup. Hawaii became a United States territory, and white control of the situation was formally institutionalized. The grad-

[18]A. W. Lind, ibid.

ual and conflict-free manner in which such control developed makes Hawaii atypical when compared with the bloody and almost immediate takeover situation common to the other societies, particularly South Africa and the United States. However, it should not be overlooked that such control was effected, and in this respect Hawaii does conform to the colonial type.

An event of major significance during the first half of the twentieth century, was, of course, World War II—in particular Pearl Harbor. This *war frontier* had a major impact on race relations: intergroup relations experienced a high level of strain and anti-Japanese sentiment. However, the general norm of racial tolerance remained intact despite such pressure, while the Japanese deemphasized their racial background and attempted to demonstrate their American loyalty by participating in the general war effort. The effects of the war were thus an increase in awareness of potential racism in the society as well as a gradual movement away from traditional culture toward assimilation.

The late 1950s saw a new *political frontier.* With the achievement of statehood, Hawaii's political and economic incorporation into American society was finally complete. The major effects of such an event have been the society's political and economic control in the hands of whites and Orientals, as well as a marked increase in the general development of economic capital. Furthermore, migration from the United States mainland, both tourist and settler, has increased markedly, bringing new ecological and attitudinal pressures.

The 1960s may thus be viewed as an *economic frontier.* With such development, as Lind has pointed out, have come threats to Hawaii's traditional norms of racial tolerance.[19] He sees the ensuing social pressures increasing the artificiality and insincerity of relationships and upsetting the population balance. In recent years a fairly high level of "hippie" visitors has increased the pressure in certain areas, aggravating local antagonism toward mainland whites. Economic and educational development also appears to account for a rising sense of deprivation among race groups who are lower in the socioeconomic hierarchy, with the

[19]Lind, op. cit., pp. 35–40.

concomitant development of subgroup nationalism and the attempt to develop movements such as the "Third World."[20]

Race groups in Hawaii vary on a number of basic characteristics: migration rate, length of residence, rate of assimilation, size, and level of socioeconomic achievement. These demographic differences (reflecting the society's historical development) are in turn related to attitudes (e.g., social distance and prejudice) and behavior (e.g., outmarriage, divorce, and deviant behavior) within it. The author, for example, examined racial attitudes among elementary school and college students. In both cases there was a clear racial and socioeconomic hierarchy: Orientals (i.e., Japanese, Chinese, and Korean students) tended to show highest levels of prejudice. Filipinos and Negroes rated next, while caucasians rated lowest in overall prejudice. In terms of choice between various races, Orientals constituted an in-group with low internal prejudice, but with fairly high rejection of caucasians, Hawaiians, and Filipinos, while the latter groups, in contrast, showed lower levels of prejudice toward this group.[21]

Race, despite Hawaii's general norms (or myths, perhaps), is clearly a factor in intergroup definition, interracial behavior, and socioeconomic achievement.[22] While evidence of a racial caste system is limited, the vestiges of Hawaii's colonial past appear to operate in the present scene and may increase with further industrialization. In terms of our continuum, however, this society is the least colonial; achievement is not based strictly on race, while institutional segregation is largely absent. The high rate of interracial marriage (one of the world's highest) coupled with the society's general emphasis on racial tolerance contribute to the ongoing process of racial assimilation, while the various

[20]See, for example, "Ethnic Studies Interim Conference, 1971, Report," *Hawaii Pono Journal,* 1, Conference Special, April 1971; W. Hayashi, "Countering Our Pearl Harbor Mentality," *Hawaii Pono Journal,* 1, 2, February 1971, pp. 46–58.

[21]G. C. Kinloch and J. Borders, "Racial Stereotypes and Social Distance among Elementary School Children in Hawaii," *Sociology and Social Research,* 56, 3, 1972, pp. 368–377; see G. C. Kinloch, "Race, Socioeconomic Status, and Social Distance in Hawaii," *Sociology and Social Research,* 57, 1973, pp. 156–167.

[22]For further documentation of racial differences in Hawaii, see G. C. Kinloch, ibid., 1973, and J. Rubano, *Culture and Behavior in Hawaii: An Annotated Bibliography,* University of Hawaii, Social Science Research Institute, Honolulu, 1971. A clear racial hierarchy, with accompanying cultural and socioeconomic variation, is evident. On the other hand, the general norm of nonracial norms and behavior in the general society remains.

racial groups are experiencing social mobility (dependent in large measure on their length of residence in Hawaii) at a relatively constant rate. While racial prejudice exists as a function of economic competition, then, this society, as with Brazil, does not possess a social system based on institutionalized racism—an important difference.

We have attempted to show that Hawaii is one of the world's most unique societies with respect to race relations and represents, perhaps, one of the least colonial in form and content. The major reasons for this were delineated as follows:

1　Hawaii's geographical isolation and function as a way-station rather than colony

2　Positive contact between Hawaiians and whites from their first meeting

3　General norms supporting hospitality and nonracist behavior

4　The hospitable and generally passive quality of Hawaiian culture toward outsiders

5　Little involvement and exploitation of the indigenous population in the society's economic development

6　The use of contract rather than slave labor in the plantation system

7　The relatively rapid breakdown of the plantation frontier

8　An indigenous monarchy which was permitted to remain intact for a lengthy period after colonial contact

9　A gradual and bloodless takeover of the power structure

10　The manner in which World War II hastened assimilation and the breakdown of traditional culture

While it is impossible to account fully for Hawaii's uniqueness, the above factors appear to be important. We have also attempted to highlight some of the society's more colonial characteristics, which place it on our continuum, and account for the continuing use of race in intergroup definition. For, so long as colonial factors continue to operate in a social system, race continues to remain a social problem.

BRAZIL AND HAWAII AS COLONIAL SOCIETIES: A SUMMARY

Brazil and Hawaii provide obvious contrasts to South Africa and the United States: in the case of Brazil, the minority elite was Catholic rather than Protestant, while in the case of Hawaii, the elite was Protestant but allowed the indigenous monarchy to remain intact for a lengthy period. Initial interracial contact was positive rather than negative, particularly in the case of Hawaii, with less colonial motivation behind the elite's migration. The attitude of the elite toward subordinate minorities was less moralistic, and the indigenous population was little involved in the society's economic development. Furthermore, race groups were imported for economic reasons but were not deculturized and, with the breakdown of the plantation system, were assimilated into the society in a less castelike manner. High rates of miscegenation occurred in both cases—a process which is continuing today, particularly in Hawaii.

These two societies, then, represent rather different forms of colonialiam from the previous two, resulting in less use of race as a role sign and caste barrier. The process of racial colonialism should be viewed in terms of its historical and sociological antecedents, dependent upon varying kinds of elites operating under different kinds of geographical, economic, and cultural circumstances. Nevertheless, while Brazil and Hawaii fall on the lower end of the continuum, they remain on it, and, as we have tried to show, with recent economic development, race continues to operate in intergroup relations. While some may be puzzled by this, our analysis suggests that it may be attributed to the colonial characteristics which remain in the social structure of the two societies. Colonialism is thus a matter of degree.

THE COLONIAL CONTINUUM: TOWARD A MODEL

We have seen how race relations appear to be a function of particular levels and kinds of colonial contact: the lower or greater the presence of these characteristics, the more or less rigidly race is used by the elite in matters of intergroup control, political policy, as well as individual attitudes. We have also seen how South Africa and the United States rate high on colonial characteristics, while, relatively speaking, Brazil and Hawaii rate much lower. According to our analysis on the macroscopic level, then, race relations reflect a society's particular colonial experience and the structural characteristics behind them.

It may be useful at this point to draw together our analysis in the form of a model. We have delineated four main structural or independent factors, as follows:

1 Characteristics of the *elite,* i.e., the degree to which it is colonial
2 *Geographical* characteristics of the area, i.e., resources, isolation, size, density
3 The nature of initial *contact* between elite and subordinate groups
4 Characteristics of subordinate *minorities,* i.e., whether migrant or indigenous, and their degree of heterogeneity

The factors are sure to result in the following:

1 Race relations *policies* defined by the dominant elite
2 Ensuing patterns of *race relations*
3 *Change* in these relations attributable to economic development within the society in general, contributing to status inconsistency and a consequent rise in relative deprivation

The general characteristics of such a model are summarized in Figure 12-1. It is these structural characteristics which define the operation of social-psychological (i.e., group) and psychological (i.e., individual personality) factors within them. They represent the most causal factors behind the "race problem" today and should be viewed as such.

Further, it is important to demonstrate the applicability of this model to the four societies we have analyzed in this chapter, showing a continuum of colonial characteristics. Such an analysis is presented in Figure 12-2. A clear continuum of factors, ranging from the highest in the case of South Africa and the lowest in Hawaii, is evident. However, it can be seen that some factors are common to all four situations, accounting for what still constitutes a "race problem" in societies which are less colonial. As emphasized before, colonialism is a matter of degree rather

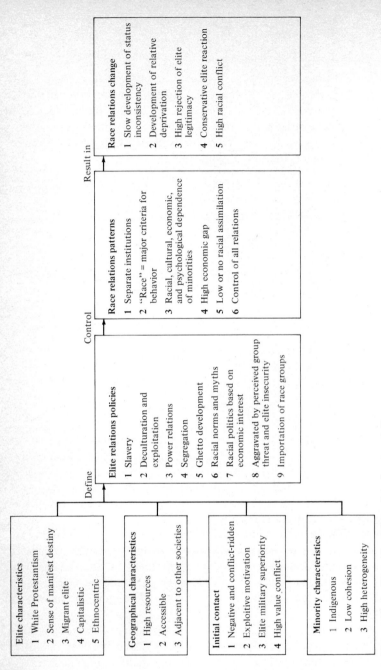

Elite characteristics
1 White Protestantism
2 Sense of manifest destiny
3 Migrant elite
4 Capitalistic
5 Ethnocentric

Geographical characteristics
1 High resources
2 Accessible
3 Adjacent to other societies

Initial contact
1 Negative and conflict-ridden
2 Exploitive motivation
3 Elite military superiority
4 High value conflict

Minority characteristics
1 Indigenous
2 Low cohesion
3 High heterogeneity

Define →

Elite relations policies
1 Slavery
2 Deculturation and exploitation
3 Power relations
4 Segregation
5 Ghetto development
6 Racial norms and myths
7 Racial politics based on economic interest
8 Aggravated by perceived group threat and elite insecurity
9 Importation of race groups

Control →

Race relations patterns
1 Separate institutions
2 "Race" = major criteria for behavior
3 Racial, cultural, economic, and psychological dependence of minorities
4 High economic gap
5 Low or no racial assimilation
6 Control of all relations

Result in →

Race relations change
1 Slow development of status inconsistency
2 Development of relative deprivation
3 High rejection of elite legitimacy
4 Conservative elite reaction
5 High racial conflict

Figure 12-1 The colonial model of race relations.

	Societies			
	South Africa	**United States**	**Brazil**	**Hawaii**
A Societal Factors				
1 Elite characteristics				
a Culture	Protestantism	Protestantism	Catholicism	Prots.–Hwn.
b Manifest destiny	High	High	Medium	Medium
c Elite type	Migrant	Migrant	Migrant	Indigenous
d Capitalistic	High	High	Medium	Medium
e Ethnocentric	High	High	Medium	Medium
2 Geographical characteristics				
a Resources	High	High	Medium	Low
b Accessibility	High	High	Low	Low
c Adjacent	High	High	Medium	Low
3 Initial contact				
a Quality	Negative	Negative	Negative	Positive
b Motivation	Exploitive	Exploitive	Exploitive	Mutual benefit
c Power	Superiority	Superiority	Superiority	Equality
d Value conflict	High	High	Medium	Low
4 Minority characteristics				
a Type	Indigenous	Indig.–Migrant	Indig.–Mig.	Indig.–Mig.
b Cohesion	Low.	Low	Low	Low
c Heterogeneity	High	High	Medium	High
B Resultant Race Relations				
5 Race relation policies				
a Slavery	Yes	Yes	Yes	No
b Deculturation	No	Yes	No	No
c Power relations	High	High	Medium	Medium
d Segregation	High	High	Medium	Medium
e Ghetto development	High	High	Low	Low
f Racial norms	High	High	Medium	Low
g Racial politics	High	High	Medium	Low
h Perceived threat	High	High	Low	Low
i Importation	High	High	High	High
6 Race relations patterns				
a Separate institutions	High	High	Low	Low
b Race = major criteria	High	High	Medium	Low
c Minority dependence	High	High	Low	Low
d Economic gap	High	High	Medium	Low
e Racial assimilation	Low	Low	Medium	High
f Racial control	High	High	Low	Low
7 Race relations change				
a Status inconsistency	Slow	Slow	Slow	Slow
b Relation deprivation	High	High	Low	Low
c Rejection of elite	High	High	Low	Low
d Elite reaction	Conservative	Conservative	Moderate	Moderate
e Racial conflict	High	High	Medium	Low

Figure 12-2 The four societies compared.

than absolute types, and even the most apparently conflict-free societies possess some degree of structural inequality and domination.

Finally, we should point out that this model may be applied to the regional and community level as well as the societal. It is obvious that areas within the same society vary in their degree of historical colonialism (the American South is a useful example), accounting for varying degrees of racism and prejudice within the same setting. Such variations may account for the relatively uneven implementation of elite policies within the same society. It is also evident that the societies which rate highest on our continuum (i.e., South Africa and the United States) have experienced direct and internal colonialism, while Brazil and Hawaii have been influenced more by indirect domination and exploitation.

CONCLUSIONS

In this chapter, we have attempted to apply our conceptual framework on the macroscopic and societal level, showing the relevance of a society's structural characteristics to race relations within it. The relevance of sociological theories of race relations has been obvious: we have shown that the more colonial a society, the more rigidly race is used as a social category in matters of political policy, social control, competitive intergroup relations, group identity, individual stereotyping, and scapegoating. Using four societies as case studies, we demonstrated how South Africa and the United States are relatively more racist than Brazil and Hawaii. Negative race relations and racism are ultimately the function of a society's historical development, particularly the evolution of its *social structure,* for it is the nature of that structure which defines the kind of intergroup relation within it.

Having applied our framework at the sociological level, we turn to social-psychological and individual levels of analysis by examining race relations within the context of a particular society, the United States.

STUDY QUESTIONS

1 Examine initial intergroup contact in South Africa and Hawaii, delineating their distinct differences.

2 Demonstrate the extent to which American society conforms to the colonial "type."

3 Outline the manner in which historical frontier sequences tend to differ in highly colonial, compared with less colonial, societies.

4 Examine how different minorities within the same society (particularly the United States) react to the development of relative deprivation.

5 Compare the historical experiences and reactions of blacks in Brazil and the United States.

READINGS

South Africa

Adam, H., (ed.), *South Africa: Sociological Perspectives,* Oxford University Press, New York, 1971.

Bartlett, Vernon, *The Colour of Their Skin,* Chatto and Windus, London, 1969.

Bloom, Leonard, "Some Problems of Urbanization in South Africa, *Phylon,* 1964, **25**, Winter, pp. 347–361.

Calpin, G. H., (ed.), *The South African Way of Life Values and Ideals of A Multi-Racial Society,* Columbia University Press, New York, 1953.

Carter, G. M., T. Karis, and M. Stultz, *South Africa's Transkei: The Politics of Domestic Colonialism,* Northwestern University Press, Evanston, Ill., 1967.

Duncan, Patrick, B., "Is Apartheid an Insoluble Problem?" *Race,* 1965, **6**, 4, April, pp. 263–266.

Hutt, William H., *The Economics of the Colour Bar: A Study of the Economic Origins and Consequences of Racial Segregation in South Africa,* A. Deutsch, London, 1964.

Kinloch, G. C., *The Sociological Study of South Africa: An Introduction,* Macmillan, Johannesburg, So. Africa, 1972.

Kuper, Leo, Hilstan Watts, and Ronald Davies, *Durban, A Study in Racial Ecology,* Columbia University Press, New York, 1958.

————, "Racialism and Integration in South African Society, *Race,* 1963, **4**, 2, May, pp. 26–31.

————, "The Problem of Violence in South Africa," *Inquiry,* 1964, **7**, 2, Autumn, pp. 295–303.

Lever, Henry, "An Experimental Modification of Social Distance in South Africa," *Human Relations,* 1965, **18**, 2, May, pp. 149–154.

Lewin, J., "Power, Law and Race Relations in South Africa," *Political Quarterly,* 1959, **30**, 4, October–December, pp. 389–399.

MacCrone, Ian D., *Race Attitudes in South Africa,* Witwatersrand University Press, Johannesburg, So. Africa, 1957.

Mittlebeeler, Emmet V., "Race and Jury in South Africa," *Howard Law Journal,* 1968, **14**, 1 Winter, pp. 90–104.

Mkele, Nimrod, "The Effects of Apartheid," *New Society,* 1963, **2**, 46, 15 August, pp. 6–7.

Tiryakian, Edward A., "Sociological Realism: Partition for South Africa?" *Social Forces,* 1967, **46**, 2, December, pp. 208–220.

Van den Berghe, P. L., "Race Attitudes in Durban, South Africa," *Journal of Social Psychology,* 1962, **57**, pp. 55–72.

————, *South Africa: A Study in Conflict,* Wesleyan University Press, Middletown, Conn., 1965.

Watson, S. G. S., and H. Lampkin, "Race and Socioeconomic Status as Factors in the Friendship Choices of Pupils in A Racially Heterogeneous South African School," *Race,* 1968, **10**, 2, October, pp. 181–184.

Williamson, Robert C., "Race Relations in South Africa," *Sociology and Social Research,* 1955, **39**, 3, January–February, pp. 165–170.

————, "Crime in South Africa: Some Aspects of Causes and Treatment," *Journal of Crime and Law Criminology,* 1957, **48**, 2, July–August, pp. 185–192.

United States

Anderson, David D., and Robert L. Wright, (eds.), *The Dark and Tangled Path: Race in America,* Houghton Mifflin, Boston, 1971.

Bailey, Thomas P., *Race Orthodoxy in the South, and Other Aspects of the Negro Question,* Neal Publishing, New York, 1914.

Bartley, Numan V., *The Rise of Massive Resistance: Race and Politics in the South during the 1950s,* Louisiana State University Press, Baton Rouge, 1969.

Blauner, R., *Racial Oppression in America,* Harper & Row, New York, 1972.

Blumrosen, Alfred W., *Black Employment and the Law,* Rutgers University Press, New Brunswick, N.J., 1971.

Bogardus, Emory S., "Racial Distance Changes in the United States during the Past Thirty Years," *Sociology and Social Research,* 1958, **43**, 2, November–December, pp. 127–135.

———, "Stages in White-Negro Relations in the United States," *Sociology and Social Research,* 1960, **45**, 1, October, pp. 74–79.

Boggs, James, *Racism and the Class Struggle,* Monthly Review Publications, New York, 1970.

Bracey, John H., August Meier, and Elliott Rudwick (eds.), *Black Nationalism in America,* Bobbs-Merrill, Indianapolis, 1970.

Brink, William J., and Louis Harris, *Black and White: A Study of U.S. Racial Attitudes Today,* Simon and Schuster, New York, 1967.

Brooks, Alexander D., and Virginia H. Ellison, *Civil Rights and Liberties in the United States,* Civil Liberties Educational Foundation, New York, 1962.

Brown, Ina C., *Race Relations in a Democracy,* 1st ed., Harper, New York, 1949.

Cable, George W., and A. Turner (eds.), *The Negro Question: A Selection of Writings on Civil Rights in the South,* Doubleday, Garden City, N.Y., 1958.

Cousins, Ralph E., et al., *South Carolinians Speak: A Moderate Approach to Race Relations,* Dillon, S.C., 1957.

Cox, Oliver C., *Caste, Class, and Race: A Study in Social Dynamics,* Monthly Review Press, New York, 1959.

Cramer, M. R., "Aspirations of Southern Youth: A Look at Racial Comparisons," *Research Preview,* 1965, **12**, 2, March, pp. 1–11.

Curtis, James C., and Lewis L. Gould (eds.), *The Black Experience in America,* University of Texas Press, Austin, 1970.

Dabbs, James M., *The Southern Heritage,* 1st ed., Knopf, New York, 1958.

Daniel, Bradford, *Black, White, and Gray: Twenty-one Points of View on the Race Question,* Sheed and Ward, New York, 1964.

Doyle, Bertram W., *The Etiquette of Race Relations in the South: A Study in Social Control,* University of Chicago Press, Chicago, 1937.

Du Bois, William E., *The Gift of Black Folk: The Negroes in the Making of America,* Boston, 1924.

Erskine, Hazel, "The Polls: World Opinion of U.S. Racial Problems," *Public Opinion Quarterly,* 1968, **32**, 2, Summer, pp. 299–312.

Feldman, Herman, *Racial Factors in American Industry,* Harper & Brothers, New York, 1931.

Feldstein, Stanley, *The Poisoned Tongue: A Documentary History of American Racism and Prejudice,* Morrow, New York, 1971.

Forman, Robert E., *Black Ghettos, White Ghettos, and Slums,* Prentice-Hall, Englewood Cliffs, N.J., 1971.

Fortune, Timothy T., *Black and White: Land, Labor, and Politics in the South,* Arno, New York, 1968.

Friedman, Lawrence J., *The White Savage: Racial Fantasies in the Postbellum South,* Prentice-Hall, Englewood Cliffs, N.J., 1970.

Gallagher, Buell G., *American Caste and the Negro College,* Columbia University Press, New York, 1938.

Gayle, Addison, *The Black Situation,* Horizon Press, New York, 1970.

Greenberg, Jack, *Race Relations and American Law,* Columbia University Press, New York, 1959.

Grimshaw, Allen D., "Lawlessness and Violence in America and Their Special Manifestations in Changing Negro-White Relationships," *Journal of Negro History,* 1959, **54**, 1, January, pp. 52–72.

————, (ed.), *Racial Violence in the United States,* Aldine, Chicago, 1969.

Halpern, Ben, *Jews and Blacks: The Classic American Minorities,* Herder and Herder, New York, 1971.

Hart, Albert B., *The Southern South,* Association Press, New York, 1910.

Hernton, Calvin C., *Sex and Racism in America: An Analysis of the Influence of Sex on the Race Problem,* Doubleday, Garden City, N.Y., 1965.

————, *Coming Together: Black Power, White Hatred, and Sexual Hang-ups,* Random House, New York, 1971.

Issacs, Harold R., "World Affairs and U.S. Race Relations: A Note on Little Rock," *Public Opinion Quarterly,* 1958, **22**, 3, Fall, pp. 364–370.

Jacobs, Paul, and Saul Landau, (eds.), *To Serve the Devil,* Random House, New York, 1971.

Javits, Jacob K., *Discrimination—U.S.A.,* 1st ed., Harcourt, Brace, New York, 1960.

Kennedy, Stetson, *Jim Crow Guide to the U.S.A.: The Laws, Customs, and Etiquette Governing the Conduct of Nonwhites and Other Minorities as Second-Class Citizens,* Lawrence and Wishart, London, 1959.

Killian, Lewis, and Charles Grigg, *Racial Crisis in America: Leadership in Conflict,* Prentice-Hall, Englewood Cliffs, N.J., 1964.

Le Conte, Joseph, *The Race Problem in the South,* Mnemosyne, Miami, Fla., 1969.

Lee, Frank F., "A Cross-Institutional Comparison of Northern and Southern Race Relations," *Sociology and Social Research,* 1958, **42**, 3, January–February, pp. 185–191.

Lubell, Samuel, *White and Black: Test of a Nation,* 1st ed., Harper & Row, New York, 1964.

McGill, Ralph E., *The South and the Southerner,* 1st ed., Little, Brown, Boston, 1963.

McNeil, Elaine O., "Dynamics of Negro-White Relations in the South," *Kansas Journal of Sociology,* 1964, **1**, 1, Winter, pp. 36–41.

Mannix, Daniel P., *Black Cargoes: A History of the Atlantic Slave Trade, 1865,* Viking New York, 1962.

Masotti, Louis H., et al., *A Time to Burn?* Rand McNally, Chicago, 1969.

Matthews, Donald R., and James W. Prothro, "Southern Racial Attitudes: Conflict, Awareness, and Political Change," *American Academy of Political Social Science,* 1962, **344**, November, pp. 108–121.

Mead, Margaret, and James Baldwin, *A Rap on Race,* Lippincott, Philadelphia, 1971.

Mercer, Charles V., "Interrelations among Family Stability, Family Composition, Residence, and Race," *Journal of Marriage and the Family,* 1967, **29**, 3, August, pp. 456–460.

Moss, James A., "Currents of Change in American Race Relations," *British Journal of Sociology,* 1960, **11**, 3, September, pp. 232–243.

Nam, Charles B., and Mary G. Powers, "Variations in Socioeconomic Structure by Race, Residence, and the Life Cycle," *American Sociological Review,* 1965, **30**, pp. 907–1102.

Nolen, Claude H., *The Negro's Image in the South: The Anatomy of White Supremacy,* University of Kentucky Press, Lexington, 1967.

Osofsky, Gilbert, *The Burden of Race: A Documentary History of Negro-White Relations in America,* 1st ed., Harper & Row, New York, 1967.

Pettigrew, Thomas, F., *Racially Separate or Together?* McGraw-Hill, New York, 1971.

Raab, Earl, *American Race Relations Today,* Doubleday, Garden City, N.Y., 1962.

Schmid, Calvin F., and Charles E. Nobbe, "Socioeconomic Differentials among Nonwhite Races," *American Sociological Review,* 1965, **30**, 6, December, pp. 909–922.

Silberman, Charles E., *Crisis in Black and White,* Random House, New York, 1964.

Waskow, Arthur I., *Running Riot: A Journey through the Official Disasters and Creative Disorder in American Society,* Herder and Herder, New York, 1970.

Weltner, Charles L., *Southerner,* 1st ed., Lippincott, Philadelphia, 1966.

Williams, Robin, M., "Social Change and Social Conflict: Race Relations in the United States, 1944–1964," *Sociological Inquiry,* 1965, **35**, 1, April, pp. 8–25.

Workman, William D., *The Case for the South,* Devin-Adair, New York, 1960.

Brazil

Azevedo, T. de, *Social Change in Brazil,* University of Florida Press, Gainesville, 1963.

Baklanoff, E. N., (ed.), *The Shaping of Modern Brazil,* Louisiana University Press, Baton Rouge, 1969.

Bastide, Roger, "Race Relations in Brazil," *International Social Science Bulletin,* 1957, **9**, 4, pp. 495–512.

————, and P. L. van den Berghe, "Stereotypes, Norms and Interracial Behavior in Sao Paulo, Brazil," *American Sociological Review,* 1957, **22**, 6, December, pp. 689–694.

Comas, Juan, "Recent Research on Racial Relations in Latin America," *International Social Science Journal,* 1961, **13**, 2, pp. 271–299.

Degler, C. N., *Neither Black nor White,* Macmillan, New York, 1971.

Fernandes, Florestan, "La Persistencia del Pasado," *Revista Mexicana de Sociologia,* 1966, **28**, 4, October–December, pp. 787–812.

Freyre, G., *Brazil: An Interpretation,* Knopf, New York, 1945.

————, *The Masters and the Slaves: A Study in the Development of Brazilian Civilizations,* Knopf, New York, 1946.

Furtado, C., *Diagnosis of the Brazilian Crisis,* University of California Press, Berkeley, 1965.

Hammond, Harley R., "Race, Social Mobility and Politics in Brazil," *Race,* 1963, **4**, 2, May, pp. 3–13.

Harris, Marvin, and Conrad Kottak, "The Structural Significance of Brazilian Racial Categories," *Sociologia,* 1963, **25**, 3, September, pp. 203–208.

Horowitz, I. L., *Revolution in Brazil: Politics and Society in a Developing Nation,* Dutton, New York, 1964.

Hutchinson, Harry W., *Village and Plantation Life in Northeastern Brazil,* University of Washington Press, Seattle, 1957.

Ianni, Octavio, "A Ideologia Racial Do Negro E Do Mulato Em Florianopolis," *Sociologia,* 1958, **20**, 3, August, pp. 352–365.

Manchester, A. K., *British Preeminence in Brazil, Its Rise and Decline: A Study in European Expansion,* University of North Carolina Press, Chapel Hill, 1933.

Morner, Magnus, (ed.), *Race and Class in Latin America,* Columbia University Press, New York, 1970.

Pierson, Donald, *Negroes in Brazil,* Southern Illinois University Press, Carbondale, 1967.

Prado, C., *The Colonial Background of Modern Brazil,* University of California Press, Berkeley, 1967.

Rodrigues, J. H., *Brazil and Africa,* University of California Press, Berkeley, 1965.

———, *The Brazilians: Their Character and Aspirations,* University of Texas Press, Austin, 1967.

Russel-Wood, A. J. R., "Race and Class in Brazil 1937–1967, a Re-Assessment: A Review," *Race,* 1963, **10**, 2, October, pp. 185–192.

Saldaha, P. H., "Race Mixture among Northeastern Brazilian Populations," *American Anthropology,* 1962, **64**, 4, August, pp. 751–759.

Service, Elman R., "Indian-European Relations in Colonial Latin America," *American Anthropology,* 1955, **57**, 3, June, pp. 411–425.

Smith, T. L., *Brazil: People and Institutions,* Louisiana University Press, Baton Rouge, 1963.

Wagley, Charles, *An Introduction to Brazil,* Columbia University Press, New York, 1963.

———, *Race and Class in Rural Brazil: A UNESCO Study,* 2d ed., Columbia University, New York, 1963.

Hawaii

Abe, Shirley, "Violations of the Racial Code in Hawaii," *Social Process in Hawaii,* 1934, **9–10**, pp. 143–160.

Adams, Romanzo C., "The Unorthodox Race Doctrine of Hawaii," in E. B. Reuter (ed.), *Race and Culture Contacts,* McGraw-Hill, New York, 1934, pp. 143–160.

Arkoff, Abe, Gerald Meredith, and Janice Dong, "Attitudes of Japanese-American and Caucasian-American Students toward Marriage Roles," *Journal of Social Psychology,* 1963, **59**, pp. 11–15.

Bogardus, Emory S., "The Japanese in Hawaii," *Sociology and Social Research,* 1935, **19**, pp. 562–569.

————, "Native Hawaiians and Their Problems," *Sociology and Social Research,* 1935, **19**, pp. 259–265.

Boggs, Joan, "Hawaiian Adolescents and Their Families," in Ronald Gallimore and Alan Howard (eds.), *Studies in a Hawaiian Community: Na Makamaka o Nanakuli,* Pacific Anthropological Records, Honolulu, 1968, pp. 64–79.

Burrows, E. G., *Hawaiian Americans: An Account of the Mingling of Japanese, Chinese, Polynesians and American Cultures,* Yale University Press, New Haven, Conn., 1947.

Cheng, C. K., and D. G. Yamamura, "Interracial Marriage and Divorce in Hawaii," *Social Forces,* 1957, **36**, 1, October, pp. 77–84.

Gallimore, Ronald, and Alan Howard (eds.), *Studies in a Hawaiian Community: Na Makamaka o Nanakuli,* Pacific Anthropological Records No. 1, Honolulu, 1968.

Gardner, A. L., *The Koreans in Hawaii: An Annotated Bibliography,* University of Hawaii, Social Science Research Institute, Honolulu, 1970.

Gilmer, John N., "A Protestant Church in Honolulu," *Social Process in Hawaii,* 1952, **16**, pp. 40–47.

Glick, Clarence E., "A Haole's Changing Conceptions of Japanese in Hawaii," *Social Process in Hawaii,* 1950, **14**, pp. 1–10.

Hayashi, W., "Countering Our Pearl Harbor Mentality," *Hawaii Pono Journal,* **1**, 1971, pp. 46–58.

Hormann, Bernhard L., *Community Forces in Hawaii,* University of Hawaii, Honolulu, 1956.

Howard, Alan, "Adoption and the Significance of Children to Hawaiian Families," in Ronald Gallimore and Alan Howard (eds.), *Studies in a Hawaiian Community: Na Makamaka o Nanakuli,* Pacific Anthropological Records, Honolulu, 1968, pp. 87–101.

Kinloch, Graham C., and J. Borders "Racial Stereotypes and Social Distance among Elementary School Children in Hawaii," *Sociology and Social Research,* **56**, 1972, pp. 368–377.

————, "Race, Socio-economic Status, and Social Distance in Hawaii," *Sociology and Social Research,* **57**, 1973.

Lai, Kum Pui, "Fifty Aged Puerto Ricans," *Social Process in Hawaii,* 1936, **2**, pp. 24–27.

Lind, Andrew W., *Hawaii's Japanese: An Experiment in Democracy,* Princeton University Press, Princeton N.J., 1946.

————, "Race Relations in the Islands of the Pacific," in *Research on Racial Relations,* UNESCO, Paris, 1966, pp. 229–248.

————, "Towards a Theory of Race Relations," paper presented to the

Social Science Seminar, University of Singapore, September 23, 1969 (mimeographed).

———, *Hawaii: The Last of the Magic Isles,* Oxford University Press, London, 1969.

Monahan, Thomas P., "Interracial Marriage and Divorce in the State of Hawaii," *Eugenics Quarterly,* 1966, **13**, pp. 40–47.

Palmer, A. W., *The Human Side of Hawaii's Race Problem in the Mid-Pacific,* Pilgrim, Boston, 1924.

Parkman, Margaret A., and Jack Sawyer, "Dimensions of Ethnic Intermarriage in Hawaii," *American Sociological Review,* 1967, **32**, pp. 593–607.

Peterson, William, "The Classification of Subnations in Hawaii: An Essay in the Sociology of Knowledge," *American Sociological Review,* 1969, **34**, 6, December, pp. 863–877.

Rubano, J., *Culture and Behavior in Hawaii: An Annotated Bibliography,* University of Hawaii, Social Science Research Institute, 1971.

Schmitt, Robert C., *Demographic Statistics of Hawaii: 1776–1965,* University of Hawaii, Honolulu, 1968.

Simpich, F., *Anatomy of Hawaii,* Coward, McCann and Geoghegan, New York, 1971.

Weaver, S. P., *Hawaii, U.S.A.: A Unique National Heritage,* Pageant Press, New York, 1959.

Werner, Emmy E., Kenneth Simonian, and Ruth S. Smith, "Ethnic and Socioeconomic Status Differences in Abilities and Achievement among Preschool and School-age Children in Hawaii," *Journal of Social Psychology,* 1968, **75**, pp. 43–59.

Chapter 13

Intra-Societal Race Relations: An Analysis of the United States

A central topic in our discussion has been the sociological function of race at the societal, group, and individual level within particular situations. In this chapter we shall focus on the effects of race within American society in reference to the colonial model just discussed.

How does race function within the United States? The research literature on this subject may be divided broadly into three major areas: (1) racial differences in socioeconomic achievement and life conditions; (2) variation in racial attitudes toward specific groups on both the individual and group level; and (3) racial differences in culture emerging from and reinforced by the society's caste system. America's racial socioeconomic hierarchy has been well documented: in a detailed study of the 1960 census data, for instance, Schmid and Nobbe delineate a white and Oriental (i.e., Japanese, Chinese) elite, with Filipinos, Negroes, and Indians comprising the lower ranks.[1] This hierarchy reveals some variation with respect to specific variables: whites rate highest on income, for example, while the Japanese and Chinése rank highest occupationally, as do the Japanese in educational status. However, this variation does not affect the hierarchy significantly; furthermore, shifts in the structure over time (1940–1960) are relatively minor. A white-nonwhite socioeconomic hierarchy is clearly visible in this society, despite the widespread notion of the "American Creed."

Racial attitudes, particularly among white elite, tend to be more negative the darker and more different the particular minority in question. Thus, blacks and Indians tend to be rejected most; Mexicans, to a lesser extent; while Orientals, although the object of intense prejudice and discrimination during particular historical periods, are more accepted.[2]

In our previous discussion, we attempted to demonstrate that such prejudice varies according to the individual's background characteristics (i.e., occupational, educational, and income status; age, sex, religion), socialization (i.e., family norms, reference groups, geographical region), and racial experience (kind and extent of interracial experience). It is clear that racial attitudes among whites do vary according to these variables and are affected by social change.[3] However, it can be argued that these differences have little actual effect on the society's racist

[1] C. F. Schmid and C. E. Nobbe, "Socioeconomic Differentials among Nonwhite Races," *American Sociological Review*, **30**, 1965, pp. 909–921; see also C. B. Nam and M. G. Powers, "Variations in Socioeconomic Structure by Race, Residence, and the Life Cycle," *American Sociological Review*, **30**, 1965, pp. 907–1002.

[2] A. Campbell and H. Schuman, "White Beliefs about Negroes," in M. G. Goldschmid (ed.), *Black Americans and White Racism*, Holt, New York, 1970; H. J. Ehrlich, "Stereotyping and Negro-Jewish Stereotypes," *Social Forces*, **41**, 1963, pp. 171–176; "Ethnic Groups in American Life" Series, Prentice-Hall, Englewood Cliffs, N.J.; "Ethnic Groups in Comparative Perspective" Series, Random House, New York; J. D. Forbes, "Race and Color in Mexican-American Problems," *Journal of Human Relations*, **16**, 1968, pp. 55–68; see, for example, A. Pinkney, "Prejudice toward Mexican and Negro Americans: A Comparison," *Phylon*, first quarter, 1963.

[3] For further references, see F. F. Lee, "A Cross-Institutional Comparison of Northern and Southern Race Relations," *Sociology and Social Research*, **42**, 1958, pp. 185–191; D. R. Mathews and J. W. Prothro, "Southern Racial Attitudes: Conflict, Awareness and Political Change," *American Academy of Political and Social Science*, **344**, p. 108–121; J. Morland, "A Comparison of Race Awareness in Northern and Southern Children," *American Journal of Orthopsychiatry*, **36**, 1966, pp. 22–31.; J. W. Vander Zanden, "Desegregation and Social Strains in the South," *Journal of Social Issues*, **15**, 1959, pp. 53–60.

social structure, defined, as it is, by ascriptive characteristics. While there is attitudinal variation within this hierarchy, then, its structure tends to remain stable.

The third aspect of American race relations is cultural variation by race, particularly the degree to which each group conforms to the white Anglo-Saxon Protestant (WASP) elite in motivation and behavior. A number of writers, for example, have highlighted distinct cultural differences between whites and American Indians,[4] whites and Negroes,[5] as well as whites and Mexicans.[6] On the other hand, cultural similarity between the white elite and Orientals, as well as ethnic groups such as Jews, is seen by others.[7] The deculturizing effects of black slavery have also been noted often.[8] What these writers suggest is a cultural dimension to America's racial hierarchy in the degree to which a minority group's culture coincides with or differs from that of the white elite, relating to its eventual level of socioeconomic status and achievement.

The above literature appears to reveal a particular order of race relations in American society: a socioeconomic, attitudinal, and cultural hierarchy, with a white-Oriental elite and nonwhite subordinate minorities, developed and controlled by a WASP elite. Race relations are defined by the degree to which a minority differs from the dominant elite, particularly the extent to which it is rejected, resulting in a particular racial hierarchy, maintained within what is essentially a colonial social system. While societies differ with respect to the degree that their social structures are colonial, race relations within them are also defined by the extent to which minorities differ from the colonial elite.

In our theoretical analysis of race relations, we paid particular attention to the characteristics of a society's elite, since it is those characteristics which define intergroup policies and subse-

---

[4]R. H. Wax and R. K. Thomas, "American Indians and White People," *Phylon*, **22**, 1961, pp. 305–317.

[5]E. E. Baughman, *Black Americans*, Academic Press, New York, 1971.

[6]J. W. Moore, *Mexican Americans*, Prentice-Hall, Englewood Cliffs, N.J., 1970.

[7]See H. H. L. Kitano, *Japanese Americans: The Evolution of a Subculture,* Prentice-Hall, Englewood Cliffs, N.J., 1969; M. Sklare, *America's Jews*, Random House, New York, 1971.

[8]See A. Pinkney, *Black Americans*, Prentice-Hall, Englewood Cliffs, N.J., 1969.

quent minority group reaction. In the case of American society, this emphasis is of particular importance, since it is the white Anglo-Saxon Protestant elite which has defined the society's value system from its colonial foundation through to the present day, revealing a marked continuity in its definition of minorities.

In our analysis of race relations within this society, then, we shall emphasize the nature of this elite as well as the degree and kind of minority-group *differences* compared to it. For, as we have stated, it is the degree to which a minority differs from the dominant elite that defines its position and fate in intergroup relations, particularly the extent to which it is rejected.

In general, it can be seen that when compared to the elite, minorities differ on a number of distinct dimensions:

1   **Historical Context**   The conditions under which the minority came into contact with the elite
2   **Physical Similarity**   The degree of "whiteness"
3   **Cultural Similarity**   The degree to which it differs from the elite in religion, language, values, and institutional structure
4   **Objective Similarity**   The degree of demographic, economic, and occupational similarity to the elite (the minority's resources)
5   **Assimilation Rate**   The resultant level of cultural and social assimilation, particularly the degree of ghetto formation and in-marriage

We shall apply these dimensions to America's minorities with reference to the white elite and consequent intergroup relation. We turn, then, to examine American whites, Orientals, Mexicans, blacks, and Indians. We shall conclude our discussion with a typology of minority-group characteristics and relations in order to draw together our analysis.

AMERICAN WHITES

American whites may be classified into a number of groups: Anglo-Saxon Protestants, European Protestants, Roman Catholics (i.e., the Irish and Italians), and non-Protestant ethnic (e.g.,

Jews). Furthermore, historical conditions have resulted, according to some,[9] in the further differentiation of Northerners and Southerners. The white majority far from represents a unified, homogeneous bloc. Instead, it is differentiated by class, ethnicity, religion, and culture, relating to the white elite differentially according to these characteristics.

Characteristics of the Protestant Ethic are well known: whiteness and purity, individualism, moralism, materialism, economic development plus conservatism, ruralism, high in-group cohesion, a sense of "manifest destiny," ethnocentrism, and suspicion toward outsiders. These values have resulted in high levels of prejudice, discrimination, and oppression, along with the religious and cultural rationalization of such behavior. They constitute the core of American culture and have enabled the elite to maintain its superordinate position politically, economically, and socially over the centuries. The further a minority deviates from these (whether an ethnic or racial minority), the more negativism that group tends to experience. Considering also that the society's institutional structure is controlled and dominated by elite interests and values, the problem of rigid race relations may be seen as inherent in the society's social structure. Such "entrenched" domination makes for an inflexible social system. The basic orientation, at least in the past, has been the adaptation of minorities to the structure rather than the reverse.

The early settlers were mainly English and Scots with high cultural compatibility and skills, resulting in ongoing agricultural and, eventually, industrial development. Considering the religious, linguistic, and institutional similarity of these two groups, intergroup relations were generally positive and harmonious.[10]

European immigrants with similar religions and cultures experienced similarly high levels of assimilation. Thus, the Swedes with their agricultural skills and Lutheran religion, along with Germans and Dutch Protestants, had few problems with assimilation into the dominant culture. On the other hand, Norwegians with their linguistic conservatism, the Finns with a

---

[9]See L. M. Killian, *White Southerners*, Random House, New York, 1970, chap. 1.
[10]See C. H. Anderson, *White Protestant Americans,* Prentice-Hall, Englewood Cliffs, N.J., 1970.

predominance of unskilled workers, along with Irish Catholics, experienced greater problems in terms of acceptance and the assimilation process. Culture and occupational resources were thus most relevant to ethnic minority relations with the dominant elite.

Italian immigrants experienced similar problems to those outlined above. With their poverty-stricken origins, lack of occupational skills, linguistic problems, high rate of immigration, Roman Catholic religion, predominance of older people, color variation, and traditional, rural, commercial, familistic culture, this group was disadvantaged from the beginning of its migration.[11] Furthermore, aspects of their traditional culture such as the *padrone* system which provided contract labor to employers, and negative stereotypes concerning the "Mafia" have contributed further to this minority's comparitively slow economic and social development. As with other minorities, a high level of endogamy only served to further reinforce such negativism. Once again, the relevance of a different religion, traditional culture, and low occupational-economic resources to negative minority status is evident.

Jewish immigrants provide sharp contrast to the Italian case. While representing one of the few non-Christian ethnic groups in American society, this minority, despite its small size, its history of persecution, its cultural visibility, and the early immigrants' lack of training, has been one of the most successful in the achievement of economic and social status. Such success may perhaps be explained in cultural terms: considering the Jews' similarity to American Protestant values in their emphasis on economic development, educational achievement, as well as faith in the value of their own culture, but without detriment to economic and social assimilation, their marked achievement rate may be explicable.

Thus, the efficient utilization of minority-group status (i.e., the organization and use of group resources) may function to advance group achievement. With generational change and the further decline of traditional culture, assimilation on all fronts

---

[11]See, for example, J. Lopreato, *Italian Americans,* Random House, New York, 1970.

will probably proceed at an exponential rate or as fast as the group itself desires.[12] Such *cultural similarity* is obviously an important factor in minority-group achievement.

A broad ethnic differentiation among whites may be made between Southerners and Northerners. While some may find such a classification so broad as to be artificial, Killian has recently argued that white Southerners do in fact constitute a minority,[13] both in status and culture. While similar to the North in religion and language, the particular social, economic, demographic, and racial history of the South has made for rather different values and life styles, i.e., the manner in which these structural variables operate in the social system. Thus, economically, educationally, and politically, the South tends to operate rather differently when compared to other areas in the country. The heavy emphasis on rural white values, Protestant fundamentalism, and racism has made the Americanization of the South a long, tortuous process. On the other hand, a more cynical view may see Southern culture as the only real "American way of life" left in a highly pluralistic society. Whatever the case, Southerners may be seen as an ethnic group, although one whose boundaries are rather indistinct and whose potential assimilation is high. Structural characteristics of the area, however, as well as a regional self-concept, continue to retard this process.

In our discussion of American whites, then, we have emphasized the degree to which various minorities differ in culture (particularly religion, language, plus level of traditional culture) and resources (i.e., skills and economic strength) from the Protestant elite. Negative initial intergroup contact serves to aggravate these differences. Thus, more similar groups such as the Scots, Swedes, Germans, Dutch, and Jews have experienced high levels of assimilation and socioeconomic success, while Southerners and Italians have been less successful, resulting in lower levels of assimilation as well as higher levels of stereotyping and negative status. Institutionalized inequality tends to

[12]For a discussion of Jews, see M. Sklare, *America's Jews,* Random House, New York, 1971.
[13]L. M. Killian, op. cit.

entrench such differences, while the conservative effects of endogamy and traditional communal culture reinforce them.

Furthermore, economic development increases intergroup competition and subsequent ethnic prejudice. Even ethnic relations are a structural problem, given the characteristics of a society's elite. Attitudes, behavior, achievement, intergroup relations, and political policy are all the function of a specific social environment, particularly its historical, structural, and cultural features. We turn now to view their operation in American race relations as well, looking first at the American Japanese.

JAPANESE AMERICANS

The Japanese as a race are comparative to the Jews as an ethnic group: they exhibit high in-group cohesion, are non-Christian in religion, value education highly, and have made significant and rapid socioeconomic progress. As Kitano also points out, they immigrated as a farming class but were essentially middle class in background and education.[14] They have shown a relatively high rate of cultural assimilation over the generations and a remarkable ability to operate within a capitalist economic system with a tendency characteristic of the white elite. In their economic development they have used their communal culture and extended family system to their advantage rather than as barriers to achievement. In general, this race group has adapted positively to American society, utilizing its cultural and physical resources to its own advantage. Its economic and cultural similarity to the white elite, as well as a general emphasis on middle-class values, perhaps, have been major factors in this development.

Despite the above progress, however, the Japanese have suffered severe setbacks in intergroup relations. Perceived as physically different from whites, along with a foreign, heathen religion, they were imported into the United States for labor purposes and began under negative conditions. With World War

---

[14]H. H. L. Kitano, *Japanese Americans: The Evolution of a Subculture,* Prentice-Hall, Englewood Cliffs, N.J., 1969.

II, they were viewed as a national threat and, as is well known, were interned as prisoners of war. Furthermore, their high level of economic success brought them into competition with whites, who reacted with bitter resentment. Their geographical concentration has also increased their visibility, aggravating racist views of this group as a national and economic threat. Nonetheless, as Kitano emphasizes, negative experiences such as the internment camps hastened the acculturation process and ultimately contributed to the ongoing assimilation of this group into white American society.[15]

The Japanese, then, represent a race group which entered American society under negative conditions, were viewed as physically and culturally alien, and were subject to harsh, racist treatment. However, considering this group's resources and cultural similarity to the white elite, in some respects, its development and ongoing assimilation have proved remarkable. As an upwardly mobile physical minority, however, the case of the Japanese highlights the importance of cultural resources which parallel those of the dominant elite. These, along with physical similarities which place them generally among whites, puts this group at the forefront, perhaps, of racial assimilation.[16] Other groups are clearly not as fortunate.

MEXICAN AMERICANS

The Mexican minority is clearly among the most disadvantaged in American society. Historically, contact between the societies has been negative, while immigration has occurred mainly in response to the demand for cheap labor within the United States. Resources brought by the migrants were very low: they lacked education, occupational skills, and financial resources; were Catholic rather than Protestant; had and continue to have language problems; practiced endogamy like other minorities; and developed ghettos. High levels of illegal immigration have made

[15]H. H. L. Kitano, ibid.
[16]It should be noted that the Chinese are in a similar position, but are not discussed here because of their small population in the United States as a minority, as well as because of the similarity of their case to that of the Japanese.

their contact with the law negative, as well as bringing them into a competitive position with other minorities. Their oscillating migration between Mexico and the United States has also contributed to their being defined as "outsiders," while their work habits are perceived as "lazy." Their geographical concentration in the South, notably Texas, has also increased their visibility and competition with surrounding groups, while their perceived variation in color has further retarded the assimilation process. Furthermore, their large family size has aggravated the problem of economic resources as has their traditional participation in low-paying, insecure, migrant labor.[17]

Mexicans in America, then, represent a minority which has entered the society under negative conditions to occupy unskilled work roles. Religious and linguistic dissimilarity, along with low occupational skills, little economic resources, and a traditional, noncapitalistic culture, has resulted in a highly disadvantaged minority position, aggravated by competition with other minorities and unstable patterns of migration. Their historical, economic, and cultural problems have retarded the process of assimilation and the acquisition of political, social, and economic resources. Once again, it can be seen that the level of a minority's similarity to the elite defines its position and assimilation into the dominant society.

BLACK AMERICANS

Black Americans also may be viewed as among the most disadvantaged and, in many respects, the most oppressed in modern America. They were forcibly imported for economic reasons, subjugated under a system of slavery, deculturized through the destruction of their family system, represented as the principal reason for civil war, segregated at the end of that conflict, and controlled by a society through institutionalized racism. Physically most different from the majority elite as well as other minorities, blacks continue to be hampered by high rates of mortality, disease, large families with a matriarchal structure, lack of

[17]For a useful discussion of this minority, see J. W. Moore, *Mexican Americans,* Prentice-Hall, Englewood Cliffs, N.J., 1970.

education and occupational skills, and the continuance of ghettos through the enforcement of residential segregation.[18]

While change in these characteristics is undeniable, this group remains one of the most oppressed, relative to other minorities in the society. Considering the historical tradition behind this minority's treatment and the long-term effects—cultural, economic, and psychological—ensuing from it, change in black-white relations remains one of the most problematic issues in modern America. Stereotypes defining blacks tend to represent much of what the white elite rejects: blackness, overt sexuality, low economic status, conspicuous consumption, permissiveness, insubordination, and lack of cleanliness. If one accepts the psychoanalytic explanation of racial attitudes, such stereotypes represent the elite's insecurity and projection of its self-rejection.

Whatever the case, it is not surprising that blacks, after rejecting themselves in reaction to such stereotypes,[19] have recently begun to reject such negativism in the movement toward black pride and separatism. Nevertheless, this minority continues to be the object of most white racism, remains the center of the "race problem" in political and social terms, and finds the process of assimilation the most difficult, ambivalent, and frustrating issue in its relationship with the white elite.

As we have attempted to demonstrate, the source of this problem is historical, cultural, and economic. Given the characteristics of such factors in the case of blacks, it is not surprising that with economic change the most virulent forms of racial rejection, rage, nationalism, and violence have originated within this group, one at the center of the colonization process. However, given the dependency effects of this process, such a reaction is complex, ambivalent, and does not characterize the group as a whole. Black-white relations continue to be among the most complex and ambivalent in the general society. This minority has been simultaneously the most oppressed and dependent group of all. In some respects, therefore, it is the most *American* minority, with the least power and independence.

---

[18]See A. Pinkney, *Black Americans,* op. cit.
[19]See, for example, W. H. Grier and P. M. Cobbs, *Black Rage,* Bantam Books, New York, 1968.

AMERICAN INDIANS

Considering the attempted extermination of American Indians, their almost complete exclusion from the society through the reservation system, and their continued dependence on the state, economically and politically, it is difficult to see this group as an "American" minority. However, as the "original" Americans, their present situation in American society reflects their relationship to the white elite and its racial policies.[20]

While American Indians are obviously differentiated by tribe, resources, and historical situation, their position as a minority is remarkably uniform: defined as "barbaric savages" who deserved extermination as the whites moved inland and wanted their land, Indian tribes were slaughtered, their chiefs captured, and the people eventually relegated to arid reservations. Even today, this minority is dependent upon the federal government through the Bureau of Indian Affairs for economic aid and political advice. Such a process is typically colonial: an indigenous people is deprived of its resources and placed aside in the status of wards, while outsiders are brought in to develop the economic system.[21] While this status has undergone some modification, the power structure and dependency relationship remain essentially the same.

Complicating the Indian case is traditional Indian culture, particularly the extent to which it stands in opposition to the Protestant Ethic, with the emphasis of the former upon naturalism, communalism, ruralism, agriculture, and nonmaterialistic values. Such values hinder rather than contribute to a group's socioeconomic achievement in a capitalistic economic system. Indians stand condemned as "different" and "unsuited" to American society, and therefore, according to these values, they should not participate fully within it. Their deep commitment to such a culture further aggravates white rejection of them and

[20]Note that this was not always the case, since initial white-Indian relations were positive rather than negative. However, as white migration and the desire for Indian land and mineral wealth grew, race relations became negative and conflict-ridden, with the whites' eventual response being the attempt to exterminate the Indians.

[21]Brazil and Hawaii are good examples of this. The reservation system is also similar to South Africa's "homelands" plan, where African tribes are assigned to specific geographic areas for residence and economic development. In this way, they remain dependent on the white elite and remain under its control.

reinforces the notion that they should be "looked after" as "naïve children"—a typical, colonial dependency status. The Indian's belief in the value of his own culture and lack of desire for cultural assimilation, coupled with tribal disunity, have resulted in his general isolation from American society and his difficulty in relating to it when he does leave the reservation, given the characteristics of his cultural background.

America's Indian minority constitutes, perhaps, one of its most tragic: proud in his cultural heritage, yet humiliated politically, economically, and socially, he stands alone at the outskirts of a capitalistic system which has rejected him and has removed most of his resources. The status of colonial dependence does little but cause frustration, and it places this group among the society's most deprived and rejected minorities. Once again, the effects of negative historical contact and cultural dissimilarity on intergroup relations and minority-group status can be seen.[22]

INTERGROUP RELATIONS
IN AMERICAN SOCIETY: A TYPOLOGY

In our discussion of America's racial minorities, we have compared them to the white elite on a number of criteria: the nature of historical contact, their physical similarity, objective resources (i.e., occupational and economic), degree of cultural similarity (i.e., language, religion, and economic motivation), and consequent level of assimilation into the general society. We view these factors as defining a minority's social and socioeconomic position in American society as they have affected the elite's view of these groups and their consequent treatment. Considering the degree to which such minorities vary with respect to these factors, it is possible to delineate a *minority-group continuum* with respect to contact, physical similarity, resources, cultural similarity, and assimilation. The continuum ranges from those most similar to the white elite and highly assimilated to those most different and excluded. Such a typology is presented in Figure 13-1.

[22]For a discussion of this minority, see M. L. Wax, *Indian Americans, Unity and Diversity,* Prentice-Hall, Englewood Cliffs, N.J., 1971.

Group	White Protestants	Jews	Southerners	Orientals	Italians	Blacks	Mexicans	Indians
Factor								
Historical contact	+	+	–	–	+	–	–	–
Physical similarity	High	High	High	Medium	High	Low	Medium	Low
Resources								
1 Occupational	High	High	Low	Medium	Low	Low	Low	Low
2 Economic	High	High	Low	Medium	Low	Low	Low	Low
Cultural similarity								
1 Religion	High	Low	High	Low	Low	High	Low	Low
2 Language	High	High	High	Low	Low	High	Low	Low
3 Protestant Ethic	High	High	High	High	Low	Low	Low	Low
Assimilation level	High	High	Medium	Medium	Medium	Low	Low	Low

Figure 13-1 A typology of minorities in American society.

The continuum inherent within this typology represents a definition of race relations defined by the white elite in reference to its own culture and formed within a specific historical context. It can be seen that Protestants, Jews, and Southerners tend to rate highly on similarity; Orientals, Italians, and blacks, less so; while Mexicans and Indians rate lowest in general. From this model it can be seen that the white-nonwhite hierarchy delineated at the beginning of our discussion is confirmed on a number of physical, cultural, demographic, and socioeconomic characteristics. Secondly, we postulate that those of medium-to-low similarity and resources as compared to the elite:

    1 Experience most social, physical, and socioeconomic discrimination

    2 Are most vulnerable to control and exploitation by the elite

    3 Experience the elites' most conservative reaction when social change is attempted

    4 Experience similarly conservative reaction from minorities that are higher in the similarity hierarchy than they

    5 Tend, eventually, to be the most militant in their rejection of the social system's legitimacy, particularly its domination by the white elite, resulting in high levels of nationalism and separatism

    6 Possess a fairly high proportion of apathetic membership because of their dependence on the elite and the traditionally colonial control by it

    7 Tend to cooperate least with minorities in positions similar to themselves because of the competitive nature of their situation

    8 Are least differentiated economically owing to their long history of discrimination

    9 Possess least power and access to the white elite and its resources, since they are the most dependent on that elite

    10 Experience the lowest rate of social, physical, and socioeconomic assimilation, irrespective of their own cultural aspirations

We are emphasizing here, then, that a group's historical, physical, cultural, and socioeconomic position in a society is a determining factor in its relationship with other minorities and the white elite, i.e., the manner in which it generally functions as a minority. The more negative these factors, the more disadvantaged that group will be, and the more it will function as a caste rather than moving toward assimilation. These boundaries also define the function of psychological processes within each minority, such as social blindness, prejudice, frustration, and racial aggression. The more positive their characteristics, on the other hand, and the less threatening they are perceived by the elite, the more assimilated socially and culturally the particular minority, depending on its level of cultural conservatism and traditional norms. Minority-group relations should thus be analyzed in reference to their historical, physical, cultural, and socioeconomic position relative to the society's dominant colonial elite in order to understand the operation of intergroup relations within a particular social system.

CONCLUSIONS

In this chapter we have examined race relations within a particular society in reference to that society's white elite. We delineated the elite's values as an emphasis upon whiteness and purity, individualism, moralism, materialism, economic development and conservatism, ruralism, high in-group cohesion, a sense of "manifest destiny," ethnocentrism, and suspicion toward outsiders. We then attempted to demonstrate that a minority's degree of physical and cultural variation from such values and its resources to cope with the economic system, coupled with the circumstances under which it first came into contact with the elite, define its place in the society, its relationship to other minorities, its general level of assimilation, and its reaction to its social situation on an ongoing and dynamic basis. Such a model is summarized in Figure 13-2.

Thus, while we have attempted to show that on a comparative and international level race relations are a function of the degree to which the elite and social structure is colonial in form, race relations within a particular society are also a function of the degree of dissimilarity between the colonial elite and the subordi-

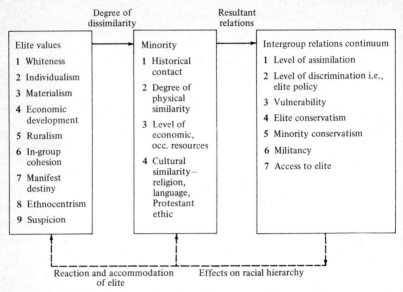

Figure 13-2 Major factors behind minority-group relations on the intrasocietal level.

nate minorities under its control. Intergroup relations are ulti- mately a *structural problem,* reflecting elite and minority-group characteristics, as well as dominant motives behind societal development. These *motives* and *characteristics* define the man- ner and degree to which race (and other group boundaries) operates in the process of intergroup relations in a stratified social setting.

Therefore, in general the more colonial an elite and the more dissimilar the minorities under its control, the more rigidly race will be utilized in matters of political policy and social control. In this matter, America tends to rate highly on both, thereby accounting for a race problem which appears to be surprisingly widespread, conflict-ridden, oppressive, and resistant to positive social change. The seeds of the problem, according to our analysis, should be sought in the nature of the social structure at elite and group levels rather than the personality structure of particular individuals within it.

STUDY QUESTIONS

1 Delineate the extent and characteristics of the racial continuum in American society.
2 Outline the extent to which assimilation into the dominant white elite has taken place in American society.
3 What factors do you believe most retard assimilation in this society?
4 To what extent is each minority in American society further differentiated by nonracial characteristics (e.g., ethnicity, tribalism, religion, geographic origins, sex)?
5 Examine the manner in which American politics (particularly among the elite) reflect the racial hierarchy that has been outlined in this chapter.

READINGS

Whites

Anderson, C. H., *White Protestant Americans,* Prentice-Hall, Englewood Cliffs, N.J., 1970.

Berger, G., *Gracnum Berger Speaks on the Jewish Community Center: A Fourth Force in American Jewish Life,* Jewish Education Committee Press, New York, 1966.

Berkson, Issac B., *Theories of Americanization: A Critical Study,* Arno, New York, 1969.

Birmingham, Stephen, *The Grandees: America's Sephardic Elite,* Harper & Row, New York, 1971.

Bisgyer, Maurice, *Challenge and Encounter: Behind the Scenes in the Struggle for Jewish Survival,* Crown, New York, 1967.

Campbell, Angus, *White Attitudes toward Black People,* Institute for Social Research, Ann Arbor, Mich., 1971.

———, and H. Schuman, "White Beliefs about Negroes," in M. L. Goldschmid (ed.), *Black Americans and White Racism,* Holt, New York, 1970.

Child, Irvin L., *Italian or American? The Second Generation in Conflict,* Yale University Press, New Haven, Conn., 1943.

Chyet, Stanley F., (ed.), *Lives and Voices: A Collection of American Jewish Memoirs,* Jewish Publication Society of America, Philadelphia, 1972.

Cohen, George, *The Jews in the Making of America,* Stratford, Boston, 1924.

Cohen, Naomi W., *Not Free to Desist: The American Jewish Committee, 1906–1966,* Jewish Publication Society of America, Philadelphia, 1972.

Cook, James G., *The Segregationists,* 1st ed., Appleton Century Crofts, New York, 1962.

Covello, Leonard, F. Cordasco (ed.), *The Social Background of the Italo-American School Children,* Brill, Leiden, Netherlands, 1967.

Cox, Earnest S., *White America,* White America Society, Richmond, Va., 1923.

Daly, Charles P., and J. Kohler, (ed.), *The Settlement of Jews in North America,* Cowen, New York, 1893.

Davis, Mac, *Jews Fight Too!* Jordan Publishing, New York, 1945.

Doreshkin, Milton, *Yiddish in America: Social and Cultural Foundations,* Fairleigh Dickinson University Press, Rutherford, N.J. 1969.

Duker, Abraham, G., "On Negro-Jewish Relations: A Contribution to a Discussion," *Jewish Social Studies,* 1965, **27**, 1, January, pp. 18–22.

Epstein, Benjamin R., and Arnold Forster, *Some of My Best Friends,* Farrar, Straus & Cudahy, New York, 1962.

Ets, Marie H., *Rosa: The Life of an Italian Immigrant,* University of Minnesota Press, Minneapolis, 1970.

Evans, M. S., *Black and White in the Southern States: A Study of the Race Problem in the United States from a South African Point of View,* Longmans, London, 1915.

Federal Writers' Project, *The Italians of New York,* Arno, New York, 1969.

Forster, Arnold, *A Measure of Freedom: An Anti-Defamation League Report,* 1st ed., Doubleday, Garden City, N.Y., 1950.

———, and Benjamin R. Epstein, *The Trouble-makers: An Anti-Defamation League Report,* 1st ed., Doubleday, Garden City, N.Y., 1952.

Fredrickson, George M., *The Black Image in the White Mind: The Debate on Afro-American Character and Destiny, 1817–1914,* Harper & Row, New York, 1971.

Gilbert, Arthur, *A Jew in Christian America,* Sheed and Ward, New York, 1966.

Glanz, Rudolf, *Studies in Judaica Americana,* Ktav Publishing House, New York, 1970.

Goldberg, Israel, *The Jews in America: A History,* World Publishing, Cleveland, 1954.

Goldstein, Israel, *Transition Years: New York–Jerusalem, 1960–1962,* Jerusalem, R. Mass, 1962.

Herman, Simon N., and Erling Schild, "Ethnic Role Conflict in a Cross-Cultural Situation," *Human Relations*, 1960, **13**, 3, August, pp. 215–288.

Irish, Donald P., "Reactions of Caucasian Residents to Japanese-American Neighbors," *Journal of Social Issues*, 1952, **8**, pp. 10–17.

Janowsky, Oscar I., (ed.), *The American Jew: A Reappraisal*, Jewish Publication Society of America, Philadelphia, 1964.

Johnson, David C., "White Resistance to Racial Integration," *Dialog*, 1964, **3**, pp. 112–117.

Johnson, Guy B., "Racial Integration in Southern Higher Education," *Social Forces*, 1956, **34**, 4, May, pp. 309–312.

Joseph, Samuel, *Jewish Immigration to the United States from 1881 to 1910*, Arno, New York, 1914.

Kahane, Meir, *Never Again! A Program for Survival*, Nash, Los Angeles, 1971.

Kertzer, Morris N., *Today's American Jew*, 1st ed., McGraw-Hill, New York, 1967.

Kiell, Norman, *The Psychodynamics of American Jewish Life: An Anthology*, Twayne, New York, 1967.

Killian, L. M., *White Southerners*, Random House, New York, 1970.

King, Larry L., *Confessions of a White Racist*, Viking, New York, 1971.

Kogan, Lawrence A., "The Jewish Conception of Negroes in the North: An Historical Approach," *Phylon*, 1967, **28**, 4, Winter, pp. 376–385.

Kramer, Judith R., and Seymour Leventman, *Children of the Gilded Ghetto: Conflict Resolutions of Three Generations of American Jews*, Yale University Press, New Haven, Conn., 1961.

Kren, George M., "Race and Ideology," *Phylon*, 1962, **23**, 2, Summer, pp. 167–176.

Locke, Hubert G., *The Care and Feeding of White Liberals: The American Tragedy and the Liberal Dilemma*, Newman, New York, 1970.

Lopreato, Joseph, *Italian Americans*, Random House, New York, 1970.

Lotz, Philip H., *Distinguished American Jews*, Association Press, New York, 1945.

McDaniel, Paul A., and Nicholas Babchuk, "Negro Conceptions of White People in a Northeastern City," *Phylon*, 1960, **21**, 1, Spring, pp. 7–19.

Manners, Ande, *Poor Cousins*, Coward, McCann & Geohegan, New York, 1972.

Marcus, Jacob R., *Memoirs of American Jews, 1775–1865,* Jewish Publication Society of America, Philadelphia, 1955.

——, *Studies in American Jewish History: Studies and Addresses,* Hebrew Union College Press, Cincinnati, 1969.

——, *The Colonial American Jew 1492–1776,* Wayne University Press, Detroit, 1970.

Musmanno, Michael A., *The Story of the Italians in America,* 1st ed., Doubleday, Garden City, N.Y., 1965.

Myer, Dillon S., *Uprooted Americans: The Japanese Americans and the War Relocation Authority during World War II,* University of Arizona Press, Tucson, 1971.

Piedmont, Eugene B., "Changing Racial Attitudes at a Southern University: 1947–1964," *Journal of Negro Education,* 1967, **36,** 1, Winter, pp. 32–41.

Pisani, Lawrence F., *The Italian in America: Social Study and History,* 1st ed., Exposition Press, New York, 1957.

Ringer, Benjamin B., *The Edge of Friendliness: A Study of Jewish-Gentile Relations,* Basic Books, New York, 1967.

Rolle, Andrew F., *The Immigrant Upraised: Italian Adventures and Colonists in an Expanding America,* 1st ed., University of Oklahoma Press, Norman, 1968.

Rosenthal, Gilbert S. (ed.), *The Jewish Family in a Changing World,* Yosloff, New York, 1970.

St. John, Robert, *Jews, Justice, and Judaism: A Narrative of the Role Played by the Bible People in Shaping American History,* Doubleday, Garden City, N.Y., 1969.

Schappe, Morris Urman (ed.), *A Documentary History of the Jews in the United States 1654–1875,* Schocken Books, New York, 1971.

Schrag, Peter, *The Decline of the WASP,* Simon and Schuster, New York, 1971.

Segal, Bernard E., "Contact, Compliance, and Distance among Jewish and Non-Jewish Undergraduates," *Social Problems,* 1965, **13,** 1, Summer, pp. 66–74.

Sherman, Charles B., *The Jew within American Society: A Study in Ethnic Individuality,* Wayne State University Press, Detroit, 1960.

Simonhoff, Harry, *Jewish Notables in America, 1776–1865: Links of an Endless Chain,* Greenberg, N.Y., 1956.

Sklare, Marshall, and Joseph Greenblum, *Jewish Identity on the Surburban Frontier: A Study of Group Survival in the Open Society,* Basic Books, New York, 1967.

——, *America's Jews,* Random House, New York, 1971.

Stalvey, Lois M., *The Education of a WASP,* Morrow, New York, 1970.

Steiner, Jesse F., *The Japanese Invasion: A Study in the Psychology of Inter-racial Contacts,* A. C. McClurg, Chicago, 1917.

Stemons, James S., *As Victim to Victims: An American Negro Laments with Jews,* Fortuny's, New York, 1941.

Strong, Donald S., *Organized Anti-Semitism in America: The Rise of Group Prejudice during the Decade 1930–1940,* American Council on Public Affairs, Washington, D.C., 1941.

Tait, Joseph W., *Some Aspects of the Effect of the Dominant American Culture upon Children of Italian-Born Parents,* Columbia University, New York, 1942.

Teller, Judd L., *Strangers and Natives: The Evolution of the American Jew from 1921 to the Present,* Delacorte Press, New York, 1968.

Terry, Robert W., *For Whites Only,* Eerdmans, Grand Rapids, Mich., 1970.

Van den Haag, Ernest, *The Jewish Mystique,* Stein and Day, New York, 1969.

Weyl, Nathaniel, *The Creative Elite in America,* Public Affairs Press, Washington, D.C., 1966.

Whyte, William F., *Street Corner Society: The Social Structure of an Italian Slum,* University of Chicago Press, Chicago, 1943.

Winter, Nathan H., *Jewish Education in a Pluralist Society: Samson Benderly and Jewish Education in the United States,* New York University Press, New York, 1966.

Yaffe, James, *The American Jews,* Random House, New York, 1968.

Japanese

Bloom, Leonard, *Removal and Return: The Socio-economic Effects of the War on Japanese Americans,* University of California Press, Berkeley, 1949.

Bunch, Ralph E., "The Political Orientations of Japanese Americans," Ph.D. thesis, University of Oregon, Eugene, 1968.

Daniels, Roger, *The Politics of Prejudice: The Anti-Japanese Movement in California, and the Struggle for Japanese Exclusion,* University of California Press, Berkeley, 1962.

Flowers, Montaville, *The Japanese Conquest of American Opinion,* Doran, New York, 1917.

Girdner, Audrie, and Anne Loftis, *The Great Betrayal: The Evacuation of the Japanese Americans during World War II,* Macmillan, London, 1969.

Grodzins, Morton, *Americans Betrayed: Politics and the Japanese Evacuation,* University of Chicago Press, Chicago, 1949.

Ichihashi, Yamato, *Japanese in the United States: A Critical Study of the Problems of the Japanese Immigrants and Their Children,* Oxford University Press, London, 1932.

Kitagawa, Daisuke, *Issei and Nisei: The Internment Years,* Seabury, New York, 1967.

Kitano, Harry H. L., *Japanese Americans: The Evolution of a Subculture,* Prentice-Hall, Englewood Cliffs, N.J., 1969.

Leighton, A. H., *The Governing of Men: General Principles and Recommendations Based on Experience at a Japanese Relocation Camp,* Princeton University Press, Princeton, N.J., 1945.

McWilliams, Carey, *Prejudice: Japanese-Americans: Symbol of Racial Intolerance,* Little, Brown, Boston, 1944.

Miyamoto, S. Frank, "The Process of Intergroup Tension and Conflict," in E. W. Burgess and D. J. Bogue (eds.), *Contributions to Urban Sociology,* University of Chicago Press, Chicago, 1964, pp. 389–403.

Peterson, William, *Japanese Americans: Oppression and Success,* Random House, New York, 1971.

Smith, Bradford, *Americans from Japan,* 1st ed., Lippincott, Philadelphia, 1948.

Sone, Monica, *Niesei Daughter,* 1st ed., Little, Brown, Boston, 1953.

Mexicans

Alba, Victor, *The Mexicans: The Making of a Nation,* Praeger, New York, 1967.

Beals, Ralph L., and Norman D. Humphrey, *No Frontier to Learning: The Mexican Student in the United States,* University of Minnesota Press, Minneapolis, 1957.

Carter, Thomas P., *Mexican Americans in School: A History of Educational Neglect,* College Entrance Examination Board, New York, 1970.

Fogel, Walter, *Education and Income of Mexican-Americans in the Southwest,* University at Los Angeles, Los Angeles, 1965.

Forbes, J. D., "Race and Color in Mexican-American Problems," *Journal of Human Relations,* **16,** 1968, pp. 55–68.

Gonzales, Nancie L. (ed.), *The Spanish-Americans of New Mexico: A Heritage of Pride,* University of New Mexico Press, Albuquerque, 1969.

Grebler, Leo, "The Naturalization of Mexican Immigrants in the United States," *International Migration Review*, 1966, **1**, 1, Fall, pp. 17–32.

———, et al., *The Mexican-American People: The Nation's Second Largest Minority*, Free Press, New York, 1970.

Kelly, Arthur R., *Physical Anthropology of a Mexican Population in Texas: A Study in Race-Mixture*, Tulane University, New Orleans Middle American Research Institute, New Orleans, 1947.

Madsen, William, *Mexican-Americans of South Texas*, Holt, New York, 1964.

Moore, J. W., *Mexican Americans*, Prentice-Hall, Englewood Cliffs, N.J., 1970.

Menefee, Selden C., *Mexican Migratory Workers of South Texas*, U.S. Government Printing Office, Washington, D.C., 1941.

Paredes, Americo, "Texas' Third Man: The Texas-Mexican," *Race*, 1963, **4**, 2, May, pp. 49–58.

Penalosa, Fernando, "The Changing Mexican-American in Southern California," *Sociology and Social Research*, 1967, **51**, 4, July, pp. 405–517.

Tuck, Ruth D., *Not with the Fist: Mexican-Americans in a Southwest City*, Harcourt, Brace, New York, 1946.

Blacks

Allen, Robert L., *Black Awakening in Capitalist America: An Analytic History*, Doubleday, Garden City, N.Y., 1969.

Baldwin, James, *Notes of a Native Son*, Dial Press, New York, 1955.

———, *Nobody Knows My Name: More Notes of a Native Son*, Dial Press, New York, 1961.

Baughman, Emmett E., *Black Americans: A Psychological Analysis*, Academic Press, New York, 1971.

Bigham, John A. (ed.), *Select Discussions of Race Problems: A Collection of Papers of Especial Use in Study of Negro American Problems*, Atlanta University Press, Atlanta, 1916.

Billingsley, Andrew, *Black Families in White America*, Prentice-Hall, Englewood Cliffs, N.J., 1968.

Boesel, David, and Peter H. Rossi, *Cities under Siege: An Anatomy of the Ghetto Riots, 1964–1968*, Basic Books, New York, 1971.

Brotz, Howard, *The Black Jews of Harlem: Negro Nationalism and the Dilemmas of Negro Leadership*, Free Press of Glencoe, New York, 1964.

Cleage, Albert B., *Black Christian Nationalism: New Directions for the Black Church,* Morrow, New York, 1972.

Conrad, Earl, *The Invention of the Negro,* Eriksson, New York, 1966.

Cronon, Edmond D., *Black Moses: The Story of Marcus Garvey and the Universal Negro Improvement Association,* University of Wisconsin Press, Madison, 1955.

Cross, Theodore L., *Black Capitalism: Strategy for Business in the Ghetto,* 1st ed., Atheneum, New York, 1969.

Dowd, Jerome, *The Negro in American Life,* Century, New York, 1926.

Drake, St. Clair, and Horace R. Cayton, *Black Metropolis: A Study of Negro Life in a Northern City,* Harcourt, Brace, New York, 1945.

Duberman, Martin, "Black Power in America," *Partisan Review,* 1968, **35,** 1, Winter, pp. 34–48.

Du Bois, William E., *Black Reconstruction,* Saifer, Philadelphia, 1935.

——, *Black Folk, Then and Now: An Essay in the History and Sociology of the Negro Race,* Henry Holt and Co., New York, 1939.

——, *Dusk of Dawn: An Essay toward an Autobiography of a Race Concept,* Harcourt, Brace, New York, 1940.

——, *The Philadelphia Negro: A Social Study,* B. Blom, New York, 1967.

Dykeman, Wilma, and James Stokely, *Neither Black nor White,* Rinehart, New York, 1957.

Edlefsen, J. B., "Social Distance Attitudes of Negro College Students," *Phylon,* 1956, **17,** 1, March, pp. 79–83.

Edward, H., *Black Students,* Free Press, New York, 1970, pp. 205–227.

Epstein, Edwin M., and David R. Hampton, *Black Americans and White Business,* Dickenson, Encino, Calif., 1971.

Forbes, J. D., "Race and Color in Mexican-American Problems," *Journal of Human Relations,* 1968, **16,** pp. 55–63.

Frazier, Edward F., *Black Bourgeoisie,* Free Press, Glencoe, Ill., 1957.

Hayden, Thomas, *Rebellion in Newark: Official Violence and Ghetto Response,* Random House, New York, 1967.

Heller, Celia S., and Alphonso Pinkney, "The Attitudes of Negroes toward Jews," *Social Forces,* 1965, **43,** 3, March, pp. 364–369.

Hesslink, George K., *Black Neighbors: Negroes in a Northern Rural Community,* Bobbs-Merrill, Indianapolis, 1968.

Hill, Roy L., *Rhetoric of Racial Revolt,* Golden Bell Press, Denver, 1964.

Himes, Joseph S., "Negro Teen-age Culture," *AAAPSS,* 1961, **338,** November, pp. 91–101.

Jamal, Hakim A., *From the Dead Level: Malcolm X and Me,* A. Deutsch, London, 1971.

Johnson, Charles R., *Black Humor,* Johnson Publishing, Chicago, 1970.

Kronus, Sidney, *The Black Middle Class,* Merrill, Columbus, Ohio, 1971.

Lincoln, Charles E., *The Black Muslims in America,* Beacon Press, Boston, 1961.

Little, Malcolm, and George Breitman (eds.), *Malcolm X Speaks: Selected Speeches and Statements,* Grove Press, New York, 1966.

———, and Archie Epps (eds.), *The Speeches of Malcolm X at Harvard,* Morrow, New York, 1968.

———, and George Breitman (eds.), *By Any Means Necessary: Speeches, Interviews and a Letter,* Pathfinder Press, New York, 1970.

Lomax, Louis E., *The Negro Revolt,* 1st ed., Harper, New York, 1962.

Middleton, Russell, and John Moland, "Humor in Negro and White Subcultures: A Study of Jokes among University Students," *American Sociological Review,* 1959, **24**, 1, February, pp. 61–69.

———, "Negro and White Reactions to Racism," *Sociometry,* 1959, **22**, 2, June, pp. 175–183.

Miller, Kelly, *Out of the House of Bondage,* Arno, New York, 1914.

Mitchell, Glenford E., and William H. Peace (eds.), *The Angry Black South,* Corinth Books, New York, 1962.

Myrdal, Gunnar, *An American Dilemma: The Negro Problem and Modern Democracy,* Harper, New York, 1944.

Nearing, Scott, *Black America,* Vanguard, New York, 1929.

Osofsky, Gilbert, *Harlem: The Making of a Ghetto,* Harper & Row, New York, 1966.

———, "The Enduring Ghetto," *Journal of American History,* 1968, **55**, 2, September, pp. 243–255.

Pettigrew, Thomas F., *A Profile of the Negro American,* Van Nostrand, Princeton, N.J., 1964.

Scanzoni, John H., *The Black Family in Modern Society,* Allyn and Bacon, Boston, 1971.

Searles, Ruth, and J. Allen Williams, "Negro College Students' Participation," *Social Forces,* 1962, **40**, 3, March, pp. 215–220.

Staples, Robert, *The Black Family: Essays and Studies,* Wadsworth, Belmont, Calif., 1971.

Van Der Slik, Jack R. (ed.), *Black Conflict with White America: A Reader in Social and Political Analysis,* Merrill, Columbus, Ohio, 1970.

Wagerly, C. W., and M. Harris, "The Situation of the Negro in the

United States," *International Social Science Bulletin,* 1957, **9**, 4, pp. 427–438.

Weaver, E. K., "Racial Sensitivity among Negro Children," *Phylon,* 1956, **17**, 1, March, pp. 52–60.

Wish, Harvey (ed.), *The Negro since Emancipation,* Prentice-Hall, Englewood Cliffs, N.J., 1964.

Young, Richard P. (ed.), *Roots of Rebellion: The Evolution of Black Politics and Protest since World War II,* Harper & Row, New York, 1970.

Indians

Arny, William Frederick M., *Indian Agent in New Mexico: The Journal of Special Agent W. F. M. Arnv, 1870,* Stagecoach Press, Sante Fe, N.Mex., 1967.

Atkin, Edmond, and Wilbur R. Jacobs (ed.), *Indians of the Southern Colonial Frontier: The Edmond Atkin Report and Plan of 1775,* University of South Carolina Press, Columbia, 1954.

Brophy, William A., et al., *The Indian: America's Unfinished Business: Report,* University of Oklahoma Press, Norman, 1966.

Caughey, John W., *McGillivray of the Creeks,* University of Oklahoma Press, Norman, 1938.

Colton, Calvin, *Tour of the American Lakes and among the Indians of the North-west Territory in 1830,* F. Westley and A. H. Davis, London, 1833.

Dale, Edward E., *The Indians of the Southwest: A Century of Development under the United States,* 1st ed., University of Oklahoma Press, Norman, 1949.

Deloria, Vine, *Of Utmost Good Faith,* Straight Arrow Books, San Francisco, 1971.

De Vorsey, Louis, *The Indian Boundary in the Southern Colonies, 1763–1775,* University of North Carolina Press, Chapel Hill, 1966.

Ellis, Richard N., *General Pope and U.S. Indian Policy,* University of New Mexico, Albuquerque, 1970.

Fey, Harold E., and D'Arcy McNickle, *Indians and Other Americans: Two Ways of Life Meet,* Harper, New York, 1959.

Forbes, Jack D., *The Indian in America's Past,* Prentice-Hall, Englewood Cliffs, N.J., 1964.

Fritz, Henry E., *The Movement for Indian Assimilation, 1860–1890,* University of Pennsylvania Press, Philadelphia, 1963.

Gaines, George S., *Dancing Rabbit Creek Treaty,* Birmingham Printing Company, Birmingham, Ala., 1928.

Gessner, Robert, *Massacre: A Survey of Today's American Indian,* J. Cape and H. Smith, New York, 1931.

Hagan, William T., *American Indians,* University of Chicago Press, Chicago, 1961.

Harmon, George D., *Sixty Years of Indian Affairs, Political, Economic, and Diplomatic, 1789–1850,* The University of North Carolina Press, Chapel Hill, 1941.

Hoopes, A. W., *Indian Affairs and Their Administration: With Special Reference to the Far-West, 1849–1860,* University of Pennsylvania Press, Philadelphia, 1932.

Horsman, Reginald, *Expansion and American Indian Policy, 1783–1812,* Michigan State University Press, Lansing, 1967.

Jacobs, Wilbur R., *Diplomacy and Indian Gifts: Anglo-French Rivalry along the Ohio and Northwest Frontiers, 1748–1763,* Stanford University Press, Stanford, Calif., 1950.

————, *Wilderness Politics and Indian Gifts: The Northern Colonial Frontier, 1748–1763,* University of Nebraska Press, Lincoln, 1966.

Kinney, Jay P., *A Continent Lost—A Civilization Won: Indian Land Tenure in America,* Johns Hopkins, Baltimore, 1937.

Kneale, Albert H., *Indian Agent,* Caxton, Caldwell, Idaho, 1950.

LaFarge, Oliver, *As Long as the Grass Shall Grow,* Alliance Book Corporation, New York, 1940.

Lindquist, Gustavus E., *The Indian in American Life,* Friendship Press, New York, 1944.

Lummis, Charles F., Robert Easton, and Mackenzie Brown (eds.), *Bullying the Moqui,* Prescott College Press, Prescott, Ariz., 1968.

Manypenny, George W., *Our Indian Wards,* R. Clarke and Co., Cincinnati, 1880.

Mohr, Walter H., *Federal Indian Relations, 1774–1788,* University of Pennsylvania Press, Philadelphia, 1933.

Morse, Jedidiah, *A Report to the Secretary of War of the United States on Indian Affairs,* S. Converse, New Haven, Conn., 1822.

Nammack, Georgiana C., *Fraud, Politics, and the Dispossession of the Indians: The Iroquois Land Frontier in the Colonial Period,* University of Oklahoma Press, Norman, 1969.

Parker, Thomas V., *The Cherokee Indians, with Special Reference to Their Relations with the United States Government,* Grafton Press, New York, 1907.

Peake, Ora B., *A History of the United States Indian Factory System, 1795–1822,* Sage Books, Denver, 1954.

Peithmann, Irvin M., *Broken Peace Pipes: A Four-Hundred-Year History of the American Indian,* Charles C Thomas, Springfield, Ill., 1964.

Pound, Merritt B., *Benjamin Hawkins, Indian Agent,* University of Georgia Press, Athens, 1951.

Priest, Loring B., *Uncle Sam's Stepchildren: The Reformation of United States Indian Policy, 1865–1887,* Rutgers University Press, New Brunswick, N.J., 1942.

Prucha, Francis P., *American Indian Policy in the Formative Years: The Indian Trade and Intercourse Acts, 1780–1834,* Harvard University Press, Cambridge, Mass., 1962.

Richardson, R. N., *The Commanche Barrier to South Plains Settlement: A Century and a Half of Savage Resistance to the Advancing White Frontier,* Clark, Glendale, Calif., 1933.

Schmeckebier, Laurence F., *The Office of Indian Affairs: Its History, Activities and Organization,* Johns Hopkins, Baltimore, 1927.

Slotkin, James S., *The Peyote Religion: A Study in Indian-White Relations,* Free Press, Glencoe, Ill., 1956.

Sorkin, Alan L., *American Indians and Federal Aid,* Brookings Institution, Washington, D.C., 1971.

Steiner, Stanley, *The New Indians,* 1st ed., Harper & Row, New York, 1967.

Tatum, Lawrie, *Our Red Brothers and the Peace Policy of President Ulysses S. Grant,* University of Nebraska Press, Lincoln, 1970.

Turner, Katherine C., *Red Men Calling on the Great White Father,* 1st ed., University of Oklahoma Press, Norman, 1951.

Tyler, Samuel L., *Indian Affairs: A Study of the Changes in Policy of the United States toward Indians,* Brigham Young University, Provo, Utah, 1964.

U.S. Congress, Senate, Committee on Indian Affairs, *Plains and Rockies,* Wagner-Camp, Washington, D.C., 1824.

U.S. Congress, House, Committee on Indian Affairs, *Remove Indians Westward,* Gales and Seaton Printers, Washington, D.C., 1829.

Van Elvery, Dale, *Disinherited: The Lost Birthright of the American Indian,* Morrow, New York, 1966.

Wax, M. L., *Indian Americans: Unity and Diversity,* Prentice-Hall, Englewood Cliffs, N.J., 1971.

Wax, Rosalie H., and Robert K. Thomas, "American Indians and White People," *Phylon,* 1961, **22,** 4, Winter, pp. 305–317.

Chapter 14

Summary
of Section Four

In this section of our discussion we attempted to apply the conceptual framework developed in Section Three to race relations on the international and national level as we move toward a general theory of varying patterns of race relations, based on the colonial model.

In Chapter 12 we delineated a colonial model of race relations which related a particular combination of elite, geographical, and minority characteristics, along with the consequences of highly negative intergroup contact, to ensuing race relations policies, patterns, and social change. We based our discussion on the major assumption that *the more colonial a society* (i.e., the more it conformed to this combination of factors), *the more rigidly race will tend to be used as a social category in matters of political policy, social control, competitive intergroup relations, group identity, individual stereotyping, and scapegoating.*

Thus, the more a society's elite conformed to a migrant WASP elite, which subordinates a society's indigenous population, settled this society on a permanent basis, and imported other minorities for purposes of economic exploitation, the more racist it tends to be in its social structure. We then applied this model to a number of societies, delineating a continuum of race relations from the most racist in South Africa and the United States, through Brazil, to the least racist in Hawaii. These comparative data highlighted the degree to which negative race relations and racism are ultimately the function of a society's historical development, particularly the evolution of its social structure.

Our analysis of race relations within American society emphasized that they are structured by a socioeconomic, attitudinal, and cultural hierarchy in which a minority's relationship to the white elite is defined *by the degree to which it differs from that elite in terms of color, culture, occupational and economic resources, as well as the nature of its initial entrance into intergroup relations* (i.e., historical contact). Thus, groups rating low in similarity and resources comprised the society's lower ranks (i.e., blacks, Indians, Mexicans), while groups with greater resources and similarity are closer to the elite in terms of status and assimilation (i.e., white ethnic groups, Orientals). Race relations within a society are defined, then, by a physical, historical, socioeconomic, and cultural continuum controlled by a particular elite.

From our analysis, it is evident that *race relations are defined by the degree to which a society's elite conforms to the colonial model and the social-physical characteristics of the minorities under its control.* The more colonial the elite and the more heterogeneous the minorities under its control, the more racist the social structure will tend to be at the societal, group, and individual level. It is with this proposition in mind that we turn to the conclusions of our analysis in which we shall attempt to develop a general theory of race relations and examine its implications for social change and the decline of racism.

Section Five

Conclusions

Chapter 15

Toward a General Theory of Race Relations

At this point, before attempting to examine the policy implications of our analysis, we shall try to draw together our discussion in the form of a general theory which attempts to explain and account for various patterns of race relations.

So far, we have examined definitions of race and theories which attempt to explain racism on the individual (psychological), group (social-psychological), and societal (sociological) level. Out of these approaches we developed a multilevel conceptual framework which we applied on the international and national level.

We emphasized that race is a *social definition*—an artificial and imposed category that has evolved out of a society's historical development, particularly the extent to which that development was *colonial* in nature. We also attempted to show that such definitions change over time, particularly with industrialization, resulting in the redefinition of particular race groups as well as their view of the dominant elite. Race and race relations are dynamic rather than static and should be viewed from a developmental perspective, dependent, as they are, on an ongoing and changing social structure.

First, viewing race in this dynamic way, we proceeded to examine its operation on three levels: the societal, group, and individual. We explored this major social problem as an attitude, the focus of intergroup relations, and the basis of the social structure in the form of institutionalized racism. A basic assumption, then, is that race is a *structural problem* that needs to be examined on all levels of the social system, as does the manner in which it is affected by social change, particularly industrialization.

Secondly, we saw how race operated differently in varying societies, depending on the degree to which their structure was colonial, while race relations within a particular society are dependent on the characteristics of minorities within it, particularly their degree of dissimilarity to the dominant elite. Our basic approach, then, is *structural* in our emphasis upon a particular kind of social structure (i.e., colonial elite) which defines policies toward indigenous and imported minorities. Such policies, in turn, define the operation of racial attitudes on both group and individual levels.

Thirdly, economic development affects the acceptance of elite policies by minority groups, leading eventually to conflict and some new form of accommodation in intergroup relations. Race relations according to our analysis, then, are the function of a society's historical-structural development, resulting in a particular kind of institutional structure, relations and attitudes within it, and the manner in which it is affected by economic change. *The more colonial that structure is, the more racist and rigid intergroup relations are within it.* This basic assumption brings us to our general model representing the foundation of our theory.

A MODEL OF RACE RELATIONS

We have formulated the basic premise that the more colonial a society's social structure (i.e., the degree of subordination of indigenous groups and importation of other race groups by a migrant racial elite for economic purposes), the more likely and more rigidly race will be used as a social category in matters of political policy, social control, competitive intergroup relations, group identity, as well as individual stereotyping and scapegoating. Basic to our model is the degree to which a society's superordinate elite is *colonial,* the prototype being a small, migrant, white, Anglo-Saxon, Protestant group which subordinates the indigenous population and imports others under slaverylike conditions for the principal purpose of economic exploitation. Such an elite normally experiences *negative contact* with the local population, which it continues to *define negatively* from that point onward, imports a *variety of minority groups,* and sets up a social structure based on *institutionalized racism.* Within such a setting, *race* is the most pervasive criteria in the *social and organizational definition of behavior.* It is also basic to *group identity* and through the processes of *socialization* and *individual conformity* controls the *individual's definition of intergroup norms and social situations* on both the elite and minority level.

As economic development takes place and status inconsistency results, minorities begin to *reject the legitimacy of the colonial structure* and their place within it. The governing *elite* tends to *react conservatively* to such a reaction, attempting to suppress it. But such conservatism increases *minority pressure* and subsequent *power* as minorities eventually come to some new form of *accommodation* with the elite. They thereby increase their power, independence, and rejection of the elite, increasingly controlling their situation on their own terms, often in a nationalistic and separatist fashion. We thus see colonialism as the major explanatory factor in the evolution of societal (i.e., institutional), group, and individual racism as well as the eventual development of racial nationalism, conflict, and rejection of the colonial system. Furthermore, this process may occur on the local, community level as well as the societal, accounting for varying levels of racism and conflict within the same society.

The model we are suggesting, then, is based on a particular *colonial sequence* following a number of stages as summarized in Figure 15-1. It is a structural approach that attempts to account

Stage 1: → Contact	Stage 2: → Institutionalized racism	Stage 3: → Social definition of race	Stage 4: → Group definition of race	Stage 5: → Individual definition of race	Stage 6: → Economic and social change	Stage 7: → Decline of colonialism
1 Migrant WASP colonial elite	1 Elite development of racist structure	1 High use of "race" in societal definition of behavior and role assignment	1 High use of "race" in organizational definitions of behavior	1 High absorption of racism through socialization	1 Dramatic effects of economic development	1 Eventual racial accommodation
2 Indigenous population with perceived negative characteristics	2 High social and economic inequality = caste barrier	2 High use of "race" in societal definition of intergroup political policy and social behavior	2 High use of "race" in subgroup identity	2 High conformity to racist norms	2 High minority eventual rejection of elite	2 High minority control
3 Negative contact and conflict over resources				3 High racial definition of intergroup relation	3 Elite conservative rejection of elite	3 Eventual decline of colonial status
4 Negative definition of subordinate groups				4 High racial definition of social situations	4 High minority pressure	4 Eventual assimilation
5 Import variety of minority groups					5 High general rejection of elite	5 Use of achieved criteria in role assignment
					6 High general pressure against elite	

Figure 15-1 The colonial sequence.

for varying levels of racism on both intersocietal and national levels as the *degree* of a society's (or community's) *colonialism* accounts for the *degree* to which *race* as a *social definition* is *institutionalized,* defines *intergroup relations,* and is part of an individual's *social attitudes* and *personality structure.* Race relations are basically a structural and sociological problem on *any* level of analysis and need to be viewed as such. We turn now to translate this model into theoretical form.

TOWARD A GENERAL THEORY OF RACE RELATIONS

Taking the colonial sequence outlined in our model, it is possible to develop a theory by expressing it in a set of sequential propositions, utilizing the initial degree and nature of colonial contact to account for the society's racist structure and its eventual rejection by subordinate minorities.[1] We are attempting to synthesize structural, group, and individual levels of analysis by utilizing colonialism as the major independent factor—an approach we have attempted to illustrate and justify on both the comparative and societal level in our previous discussion.

The general propositions of our theory may be stated as follows:

Stage 1   Contact

1 The more colonial a society's migrant elite (i.e., the more it conforms to the WASP type), the more negative the initial contact between the elite and other race groups (e.g., wars and attempted extermination).

2 The more negative the initial interracial contact, the more negatively subordinate minorities will be defined by the elite, such negativism being aggravated by marked physical and social differences between the elite and its minorities, both indigenous and imported.

[1]The full axiomatic, deductive theory is presented in the Appendix. For discussion of this *type* of theory, see H. L. Zetterberg, *On Theory and Verification in Sociology,* Bedminster Press, Toronto, 1965; K. D. Bailey, "Evaluating Axiomatic Theories," in E. F. Borgatta and G. W. Bohrnstedt (eds.), *Sociological Methodology, 1970,* Jossey-Bass, San Francisco, 1970, pp. 48–74; K. C. Land, "Formal Theory," in H. L. Costner (ed.), *Sociological Methodology 1971,* Jossey-Bass, San Francisco, 1971, pp. 175–220.

Stage 2   Institutionalized Racism

3   The more negatively subordinate minorities are defined, the more racist will be the social structure developed by the elite (i.e., degree of institutionalized racism).

4   The more racist the society's social structure, the more social and economic inequality it will contain (i.e., racial caste elements.)

Stage 3   The Social Definition of Race

5   The more social and economic inequality in the social structure, the more race will be utilized in role assignment and the societal definition of behavior (i.e., race as a role sign).

6   The more race is utilized in the societal definition of behavior and role assignment, the more it will be utilized in the societal definition of intergroup relations as the main criterion of political policy and social behavior.

Stage 4   The Group Level

7   The more race is utilized in the societal definition of intergroup relations, the more it will be a major factor in organizational definitions of behavior (i.e., institutional theories of race relations).

8   The more race is a major factor in organizational definitions of behavior, the more it will function as the major criterion of subgroup identity in the social system.

Stage 5   Individual Attitudes

9   The more race is utilized in subgroup identity, the more the individual, whether a member of the elite or a minority, will absorb racist norms through the process of socialization.

10   The more the individual absorbs racist norms through socialization, the more he will tend to conform to them.

11   The more the individual conforms to racist norms, the more he will tend to define intergroup relations in racial terms.

12   The more the individual defines intergroup relations in racial terms, the more he will also tend to define social situations in general in racial terms.

Stage 6   Economic and Social Change

13   The more the individual defines social situations in general in racial terms, the more dramatic (i.e., effective) will be the effects of high rates of economic development as status inconsistency and relative deprivation increase.

14   The higher the level of status inconsistency and relative deprivation, the greater a minority's eventual rejection of the colonial structure as being illegitimate.

15   The greater a minority's rejection of the colonial structure as being illegitimate, the more conservative will be the elite's reaction to such a development.

16   The more conservative the elite's reaction to a minority's rejection of the colonial structure, the higher the eventual level of minority-group pressure against that elite.

17   The greater the level of minority-group pressure against the dominant elite, the greater the general rejection of that elite's power monopoly.

18   The greater the general rejection of the elite's power monopoly, the greater the general pressure brought to bear on that elite.

Stage 7   Accommodation and the Decline of Colonialism

19   The greater the general pressure brought to bear on the colonial elite, the more likely it will eventually develop some new relationship to the minorities under its control (i.e., racial accommodation).

20   The greater the accommodation between the colonial elite and its minorities, the more control they will eventually have over their own situation (i.e., an increase in power).

21   The more control minorities exert over their own situation, the greater the eventual decline of their colonial status.

22   The greater the eventual decline of a minority's colonial status, the greater its assimilation into the general social system.

23   The greater a minority's assimilation into the general social system, the greater the use of bureaucratic-achieved rather than colonial-ascriptive criteria in the process of societal role assignment.

Such an approach may be viewed as a *structural, sequential* theory, emphasizing the relevance of a society's colonial elite to the subsequent evolution of a system of institutionalized racism, which operates at the societal, group, and individual level. The economic demands of such a system, in turn, upset its racial caste boundaries, resulting in competition, conflict, and an eventual new form of accommodation. Some of this approach's major implications may be seen as follows:

1 The source of any society's mode of intergroup relations is located in its initial colonial elite and the ensuing developments.

2 The more heterogeneous a society's minorities (i.e., physically, culturally, socially), the more complex and competitive ethnic and race relations will tend to be.

3 The more insecure a society's colonial elite (i.e., physically, culturally, socially), the more rigidly and extensively it will utilize racism in matters of social control and political policy.

4 The higher a society's rate of economic development, the more rapidly the racial caste system will break down. Thus, ironically, the more successful a colonial system, the quicker it will disappear, whereas more traditional societies will experience slower rates of change.

5 The more a society experiences economic development, the more groups within it will be economically and socially differentiated, making for a variety of views on race. Such variety tends to contribute to the process of social change.

6 Finally, colonial characteristics and experience may vary, even within the same society. This approach can be applied to race relations on the community and regional level as well as the societal, although the society's general structure defines the boundaries within which such differences operate.

A major implication of this theory is that race relations represent a particular kind of *institutional arrangement* which has evolved out of certain historical, social, and economic circumstances. This "arrangement" represents a structure developed by a colonial elite to further economic development and to protect its power monopoly. Additionally, this structure defines behavior on both the group and individual level. As we turn to consider social change in race relations, it is obvious that it is only as this institutional structure is modified that intergroup relations within it will change and the societal use of race decline. As we stated at the beginning of this book, race relations reflect a society's social structure, and as we have seen, it is those characteristics, which are colonial in nature and operation, that require investigation.

Thus, it is only as the social sciences begin to understand and investigate the colonial structure in detail that the process of decolonization will become clearer. Such a focus, we contend, should be central to the sociology of race relations if that field is to make a major contribution to the understanding of race relations and positive social change. In this venture, the importance of theory should be obvious. The one developed here is clearly temporary and requires further development. However, the emphasis on structure is both relevant and important to the understanding of *relations* rather than *attitudes*. We turn now to examine the implications of our theory for social change and the decline of racism.

STUDY QUESTIONS

1 Take the theory developed in this chapter and apply it in detail to the following:
   a Race relations in South Africa compared with those in the United States
   b A comparison of the white elites in Brazil and Hawaii
   c The importance of racial heterogeneity in South Africa and the United States
   d The effects of economic change on race relations in Brazil and Hawaii
   e Intergroup minority relations within the United States

Chapter 16

Race Relations and Social Change: The Reduction of Racism

From our analysis, it has been clear that race relations are basically a question of *social structure:* a migrant elite dominates an indigenous population and imports a variety of racial minorities for economic purposes. It then erects an institutional structure which exploits and controls these minorities on the group and individual level through the implementation of segregation and discrimination. This *colonial structure* serves the elite and is self-reinforcing through social inequality and controlled socialization. As it becomes more industrialized, subordinate minorities perceive the elite in a new light and may begin to reject its legitimacy. However, through techniques such as cooptation, tokenism, and the image of social concern, the elite may adjust to such pressure in a manner which results in little change in power. In fact, changes initiated by the elite may further reinforce their power monopoly despite their apparently ameliorative intentions.[1] Change in race relations is thus a slow process, and an interactive one, between the dominant elite and subordinate minorities.

The reduction of racism as an analytical problem is hardly a new topic; there is a large body of material relating to positive social change in race relations. This discussion may be divided into four major approaches: researchers advocating *structural change* (e.g., urban renewal, economic aid, improved police-community relations); the development of *community organizations*, both social and political, in order to maximize minority group resources; the importance of positive *socialization* in educational programs; and the contribution of educational and social *desegregation.*

The structural approach is illustrated by Taueber, who emphasizes that income redistribution will alleviate the problems of residential segregation, while Northwood perceives that urban renewal must be developed and controlled if it is to contribute positively to race relations. Cross deals with the need of the police to handle all situations impartially and objectively if race relations are to be improved. Coleman is also known for his attempt to develop a social resource approach to black achievement in American society: delineating a minority's resources, he then attempts to handle the problem of resource conversion.[2] According to this approach, the solution to race relations is viewed in terms of a change in the utilization of the society's resources and assets.

Community organizations, on the other hand, are also seen as major tools of social change by certain researchers: Rogler, for example, discusses the characteristics of a successful Puerto Rican action group, while Halstead examines black power and sees its need for white aid if it is to be successful. Thirdly,

[1]For a useful discussion of this problem within the context of the colonial model, see J. Prager, "White Racial Privilege and Social Change: An Examination of Theories of Racism," *Berkeley Journal of Sociology,* **17**, 1972–73, pp. 117–150.

[2]K. E. Taueber, "The Effect of Income Redistribution on Racial Residential Segregation," *Urban Affairs Quarterly,* **4**, 1970, pp. 5–14; L. K. Northwood, "The Threat and Potential of Urban Renewal: A Workable Program for Better Race Relations," *Journal of Intergroup Relations,* **2**, 1961, pp. 101–114; G. J. Cross, "The Negro, Prejudice, and the Police," *Journal of Criminal Law, Criminology and Police Science,* **55**, 1964, pp. 405–411; J. S. Coleman, *Resources for Social Change: Race in the United States,* Wiley, New York, 1971.

Tomlinson studies the evolution of a "riot ideology" among blacks and relates it to the local social setting.[3] Social change in this approach is viewed as a function of minority-group orientations and ensuing social movements which interact with the power elite to gain concessions and resources.

A more microscopic approach is taken by those who view stereotypes as the basis of the race problem. Tajfel, for instance, suggests specific techniques for reducing the individualistic qualities of emotional stereotypes, while Richmond perceives small-group discussion as most effective in the process of reeducation. Clark discusses some suggestions for effective leadership action prior to desegregation, while Rubin has highlighted the strong association between prejudice and an individual's level of self-acceptance.[4] Positive change, according to this material, occurs predominantly through individual socialization and the reduction of stereotypes. Relevant research, therefore, concentrates on the characteristics of stereotypes and factors behind them.

Finally, the desegregation of institutions, particularly in education, is seen by many to represent the most viable solution to race. In addition to studying the factors associated with this process (i.e., resistance or support), many studies relate it to an increase in educational achievement, positive self-esteem, and the evaluation of an individual's own race group.[5] Institutional

[3]L. H. Rogler, "The Growth of an Action Group: The Case of a Puerto Rican Migrant Voluntary Association," *International Journal of Comparative Sociology,* **9**, 1968, pp. 223–234; M. Halstead, "Race, Class and Power: A Paradigm of the Means of Power for the Negro American," *Human Mosaic,* **2**, 1968, pp. 133–146; T. M. Tomlinson, "The Development of a Riot Ideology among Urban Negroes," *American Behavior Scientist,* **11**, 1968, pp. 17–31.

[4]H. Tajfel, "Stereotypes," *Race,* **5**, 1963, pp. 3–14; A. H. Richmond, "Teaching Race Questions," *Phylon,* **17**, 1956, pp. 239–249; D. Clark, "Leadership Education in an All-White Neighborhood," *Journal of Inter-Group Relations,* **3**, 1961–1962, pp. 38–44; I. M. Rubin, "Increased Self-Acceptance: A Means of Reducing Prejudice," *Journal of Personality and Social Psychology,* **5**, 1967, pp. 233–238.

[5]See, for example, D. Gottlieb and W. O. TenHouten, "Racial Composition and the Social Systems of Three High Schools," *Journal of Marriage and the Family,* **17**, 1965, pp. 204–222; G. B. Johnson, "Racial Integration in Southern Higher Education," *Social Forces,* **34**, 1956, pp. 309–312; D. E. Muir and C. D. McGlamery "The Evolution of Desegregation Attitudes of Southern University Students," *Phylon,* **29**, 1968, pp. 105–118; E. B. Piedmont, "Changing Racial Attitudes at a Southern University: 1947–1964," *Journal of Negro Education,* **36**, 1967, pp. 32–41; D. G. Singer, "Reading, Writing, and Race Relations," *Transaction,* **4**, 1967, pp. 27–31; M. R. Yarrow, J. D. Campbell, and L. J. Yarrow, "Acquisition of New Norms: A Study of Racial Desegregation," *Journal of Social Issues,* **14**, 1958, pp. 8–28.

integration, according to this approach, represents a major solution to the caste elements of race.

Major approaches to changing race relations, then, focus on structural innovation, social movements, individual socialization, and educational desegregation. This focus on structure and process is useful but is severely limited: its emphasis is basically assimilationist, with little radical implications for the racial caste system. Thus, whether the individual is referring to desegregation, urban renewal, or reeducation, the implication is that these processes will lead to the greater assimilation of minorities into the social system on the elite's own terms. While their relationship to that elite will change, the power structure will remain substantially the same. There is a need, therefore, to examine the kind of structural change on a societal level which will make racism sociologically irrelevant.

Our view here, then, is that structural change has to take place before any viable change in actual race relations occurs, for it is the colonial social structure which maintains the operation of racism on all levels of the social system, particularly the elite's vested interests—political, economic, social, and psychological—in the continuing operation of such a system. Race relations are ultimately a question of power and the social structure, particularly the kinds of economic motivation behind the foundation and development of the social system.

A basic problem within the colonial situation, therefore, is the social definition of people and groups as "things" which have a certain status in the socioeconomic hierarchy. Role assignment and reward are then based on this status, and any suggestions that it be changed are viewed as threatening, competitive, and disloyal. Racial progress within such an environment is slow, uneven, and beset with backlashes at various stages of its development. However, if the race problem is not viewed as structural, the alternative is psychological reductionism, in which people's attitudes only have to be modified in order to deal with the problem. No real change in the social order ensues and race continues to function as the basis of role assignment, group identity, and individual prejudice. For race to lose its significance, it must possess no significance in the social structure. The reduction of racism is thus a structural problem. What, then, is the structure of institutionalized racism? We turn to examine this before viewing the various alternatives for social change.

INSTITUTIONALIZED RACISM

Institutionalized racism represents a social system in which race is the major criterion of role assignment, role rewards, and socialization on a positive or negative basis, depending upon the structure of the racial caste hierarchy. After colonial contact takes place, elite monopoly of political, economic, social, cultural, and psychological resources develops, resulting in a social system which is oppressive of all minorities.

Any society's institutional system performs a number of tasks: decision making and social control, training for role behavior, socialization and the absorption of social norms, and the provision of physical facilities and care. The institutional system may be delineated as follows:

Control

1. The political system
2. The legal system
3. The military system

Socialization

1. The educational system
2. The media
3. Religion
4. The family system

Physical Facilities

1. The economic system
2. Medicine
3. Welfare and housing
4. Transportation

In the colonial situation, these institutions operate in a racist way as follows:

Control

1   Elite control of the political system, exclusion of minority participation, and the suppression of subordinate-group political movements.
2   A legal system designed to protect the privileged elite and oppress subordinate minorities.
3   A military system in the elite's total control, used for internal oppression.

Socialization

1   Educational facilities and policies based on race and community resources. Socialization emphasizes the superiority of the elite and the importance of patriotism.
2   A media system which ignores subordinate minorities and/or portrays them in negative and segregated ways.
3   Religion rationalizes racial domination, reinforces a paternalistic relationship toward minorities, and helps the latter accept their subordinate status.
4   The family propogates racist norms and the importance of power relations and racial identity. The effects of deculturation are also felt in the evolution of matriarchal structures.

Physical Facilities

1   An economic system based on racial discrimination in role assignment and reward—the basis of the caste system.
2   Medical facilities based on race and community resources. Typically, there are segregated and inferior treatment and facilities for minorities.
3   Inadequate welfare and housing facilities for minorities, with particular emphasis on residential segregation and the maintenance of ghettos controlled by the elite.
4   Segregated and inferior transport facilities for minorities.

This structure defines the use of race on societal, group, and individual levels in accordance with the society's imposed racial hierarchy and is designed to maintain and further develop the elite's privileged position. Racism is the tool and rationalization of economic exploitation as well as being at the base of the eventual rejection of such oppression by subordinate minorities (i.e., "reverse racism"). Racism among minorities may also be the function of intergroup competition as they vie for economic and social resources within the colonial system, particularly as economic change takes place. The social definition and use of race thus reflects a particular kind of institutional structure formed and elaborated under certain historical conditions. Its "reality"—psychological, social-psychological, and sociological—is dependent on the foundation and shape of the social system, as well as the manner in which it is affected by economic change.

SOCIAL CHANGE: THE ALTERNATIVES

A number of possible types of race relations policies exist as follows:

   1   Maintenance of segregation: i.e., the colonial caste system of racial exploitation.
   2   The "separate-but-equal" doctrine: a modification of the first alternative, but only to the point of providing certain segregated social amenities which do not threaten elite dominance or provide avenues to its power monopoly.
   3   An "equal-but-separate" approach: i.e., social and cultural pluralism with little visible discrimination, but a system which remains under the control of a particular group and in which race continues to operate as a role sign.
   4   Racial assimilation: not necessarily physical or cultural, but a social situation in which race has no political, economic, or social significance, since the social system is not based on it in a castelike fashion.

While the fourth item above appears more theoretical than real at this point in history, it would appear to be most desirable, since the first three alternatives assume the continuing significance of race on the group and individual level.

A further complication here is the variety of policy views among both elite and subordinate groups, dependent in the main on their position in the social structure. Elite members range from the reactionary and conservative, through the laissez faire and reformist, to the revolutionary, while subordinates vary from the acquiescent and colonially dependent, through nonviolent reformist, to the militant, separatist, and revolutionary. Despite such heterogeneous perspectives and social movements, however, the central problem remains the same: *the elimination of race as a significant factor in the social system on the societal, group, and individual level.* To achieve such an end implies certain structural changes, and it is to these that we now turn.

DECOLONIZATION: SOME SUGGESTIONS

The basis of decolonization is obvious within the context of our discussion: a change in the society's institutional structure away from a racial foundation to one based on achievement and nonascriptive criteria. Such a development, however, involves a broader issue: the elite's self-concept and definition of major societal goals. For, as we have seen, the emphasis on WASP values is predominant in the society's political policies and economic development. Within such an environment, groups and individuals are defined as "things," i.e., where they fit into the economic structure. Major policy issues and social change focus mainly on such criteria in the usual capitalistic, materialistic, and ethnocentric fashion. Programs designed to deal with major social problems concentrate on fitting various groups or categories of people into the economic system under the domination of the white elite. Furthermore, solutions are perceived mainly in monetary terms—i.e., once the funds are provided, it is assured that the problem is largely solved. Consequently, the racist structure remains much the same with a few token changes within it, leaving the self-reinforcing system of exploitation and inequality mainly intact.

An important element in social change, then, is the elite's

major values. Having considered the kinds of values mainly
behind colonial contact and ensuing racism, we would suggest
that a movement away from materialism as the basis of the social
structure toward more emphasis on the quality of life for
everyone in the social system is a most important element.
Instead of perceiving people in terms of resources for an elitist
system, this orientation would emphasize system resources for
the use of those within it.

What we are attempting to suggest, then, is the importance
of an American identity which is less exploitive and more
humanitarian in the movement away from the use of ascriptive
(i.e., racial) criteria in the process of role assignment and reward.
For it is only so long as a society wishes to remain elitist and
exploitive that racism is "required" as a rationalization of that
exploitation, operating on all levels of the social structure.
Without such aims, racism loses its sociological function. We
thus see a decline in the Protestant Ethic as basic to change in
race relations as whole, since it is only the full implementation of
the "American Dream" which will result in the destruction of
racism. An alternative approach here might be to resocialize
the elite into perceiving nonracism as contributing most to the
society's economic and social development, while advancing the
nation that racism is economically inefficient by making economic
discrimination expensive. However, whatever view is taken, the
society's institutional structure is central to the problem of social
change, and we turn to this now.

Changes in the society's institutional structure are also
necessary for the decline of racism, since it is this structure which
is behind the continued utilization of such a policy. Requisite to
institutional change is a decline in elitism, and increase in the
participation of minorities in the decision-making process, and
the societal utilization of economic resources to diminish and
eliminate the caste effects of race. These processes would apply
to the institutional structure as follows:

Control

1   Full participation of minorities in the political system,
the encouragement of minority political movements, and a politi-

cal structure which is not economically based, i.e., open mainly to the control of the wealthy.

2   An open legal system designed to protect minority rights and to encourage their participation, rather than being based on a group or individual's economic resources.

3   A military system governed and controlled by an open political system.

Socialization

1   Integrated educational facilities based on societal rather than community resources. Nonracial socialization which emphasizes the positive contribution of all minorities to American society as well as the importance of political participation and critique. Interracial interaction under noncompetitive, positive social conditions. Access to educational institutions based on nonracial, noneconomic criteria.

2   A media system which highlights the "normality" of interracial and nonracial interaction, portraying minorities in positive rather than negative ways.

3   The identification of religion with nonracism, providing a positive contribution to the politicalization of minorities and increased political participation.

4   An emphasis in family counseling on noncompetitive, equalitarian relations; nonracist socialization; the encouragement of interracial adoption policies; and the importance of personal rather than materialistic values.

Physical Facilities

1   An economic system based on nonracial role assignment, emphasizing individual potential rather than objective qualifications alone.

2   The provision of medical facilities based on societal rather than racial, community, and individual resources. Propogation of medical information through the mass media.

3   The provision of adequate nonracial welfare services and housing facilities, with enforcement of residential integration and the breakdown of ghettos based on outside economic interests.

4   The provision of adequate and integrated transport facilities.

Such proposals may appear hopelessly utopian and theoretical. However, they highlight, as has our analysis throughout this text, the *structural* features behind racism—features that are dependent on the dominant elite. Change in race relations is ultimately an *elite problem,* since it is the dominant elite which is and has been primarily responsible for the evolution of institutionalized racism. Therefore, just as race relations begin with a particular elite, they continue to be an elite problem. We would emphasize, therefore, that any viable structural change has to come from that elite if it is to affect race relations within the society as a whole. Furthermore, it is primarily the elite which can exert control of the backlash problem as it redefines the major criteria for a "sense-of-group position," despite the variety of individual attitudes within the general society. Minorities also have an important role in convincing the elite that new criteria are both desirable and functional—the interactive process in social change referred to earlier. However, the elite remains the controlling factor in the race relations situation, since it is primarily its own views which define the operation of the society's institutional structure and the change within it. A decline in racism is ultimately dependent on the elite's definition of the situation in racial terms.

We suggest, therefore, that a major sociological effort, both practical and theoretical, be made to further understand how such definitions may be made less racial and more humanitarian, less materialistic and more individual-oriented. For it is only as society moves away from its obsession with ascriptive characteristics that it will become humanitarian and less exploitive, more concerned with human development than with power and social control.

While the effects of industrialization may lead us generally in this direction in the long run, it is important that the social sciences make a viable contribution to such a development. In our discussion we have attempted to make at least a limited move in this direction, utilizing the colonial model on a number of levels of the social system. It is hoped its fuller elaboration will contribute further to the decline and ultimate destruction of racism.

STUDY QUESTIONS

1 Analyze the major dimensions of "institutionalized racism" in your home town.
2 Demonstrate the relationship between institutionalized racism and individual prejudice among both elite and minority-group members.
3 Analyze the relationship between control, socialization, and physical-facility institutions as they maintain the racial status of blacks, Indians, and Mexicans in American society.
4 Discuss what you consider to be the most effect methodology(ies) in "deinstitutionalizing" racism.
5 Discuss the effects, both positive and negative, of backlash on the above process.

READINGS

Auerback, Aline S., and Sandra Roche, *Creating a Preschool Center: Parent Development in an Integrated Neighborhood Project,* Wiley, New York, 1971.

Bettelheim, Bruno, and Morris Janowitz, *Social Change and Prejudice,* Free Press of Glencoe, New York, 1964.

Caliver, Ambrose, *Education of Teachers for Improving Minority Relationships,* U.S. Government Printing Office, Washington, D.C., 1944.

Canty, Donald, *A Single Society: Alternatives to Urban Apartheid,* Praeger, New York, 1969.

Clark, Dennis, "Leadership Education in an All-White Neighborhood," *Journal of Intergroup Relations,* 1961–1962, **3,** 1, Winter, pp. 38–44.

Coleman, J. C., *Resources for Social Change: Race in the United States,* Wiley, New York, 1971.

Cramer, Richard M., "School Desegregation and New Industry: The Southern Community Leaders' Viewpoint," *Social Forces,* 1963, **41,** 4, May, pp. 384–389.

Cross, Granville, J., "The Negro, Prejudice, and the Police," *Journal of Law, Criminology and Police Science,* 1964, **55,** 3, September, pp. 405–411.

Curry, Jesse E., and Glen D. King, *Race Tensions and the Police,* Charles C Thomas, Springfield, Ill., 1962.

Dean, John P., and Alex Rosen, *A Manual of Intergroup Relations,* University of Chicago Press, Chicago, 1955.

Dentler, Robert A., "Barriers to Northern School Desegregation," *Daedalus,* 1966, **95,** 1, Winter, pp. 45–62.

———, Bernard Mackler, and Mary E. Warshauer (eds.), *The Urban R's: Race Relations as the Problem in Urban Education,* Praeger, New York, 1967.

Dixon, Vernon J., and Badi G. Foster (eds.), *Beyond Black or White: An Alternate America,* Little, Brown, Boston, 1971.

Du Bois, Rachel D. (ed.), *Build Together Americans: Adventures in Intercultural Education for the Secondary School,* Hinds, Hayden and Eldredge, New York, 1945.

———, *Neighbors in Action: A Manual for Local Leaders in Intergroup Relations,* 1st ed., Harper, New York, 1950.

Eysenck, Hans J., *Race, Intelligence and Education,* Temple Smith, London, 1971.

Fischer, John H., "Race and Reconciliation: The Role of the Shcool," *Daedalus,* 1966, **14,** pp. 24–43.

Gottlieb, David, and Warren O. TenHouten, "Racial Composition and the Social Systems of Three High Schools," *Journal of Marriage and the Family,* 1965, **27,** 2, May, pp. 204–212.

Grimshaw, Allen D., "Police Agencies and the Prevention of Racial Violence," *Journal of Crime, Law, Criminology and Police Science,* 1963, **54,** 1, March, pp. 110–113.

Halstead, Michael, "Race, Class and Power: A Paradigm of the Means of Power for the Negro American," *Human Mosaic,* 1968, **2,** 2, Spring, pp. 133–146.

Hamnett, Ian, "The Maseru Stockfell Club: A Multi-Racial Experiment in Southern Africa," *Race,* 1966, **8,** 2, October, pp. 175–184.

Height, Dorothy I., *Step by Step with Interracial Groups,* Woman's Press, New York, 1948.

Helper, Hinton R., *Miscegenation: The Theory of the Blending of the Races, Applied to the American White Man and Negro,* H. Dexter, Hamilton, New York, 1864.

Ingle, Dwight J., "Racial Differences and the Future," *Science,* 1964, **146,** 3642, October 16, pp. 375–379.

Janis, Irving L., and Daniel Katz, "The Reduction of Intergroup Hostility: Research Problems and Hypotheses," *Journal of Conflict Resolution,* 1959, **3,** 1, March, pp. 85–100.

Janowitz, Morris, *Social Control and Escalated Riots,* University of Chicago, Chicago, 1968.

Katz, Daniel, "Consistent Reactive Participation of Group Members and Reduction of Intergroup Conflict," *Journal of Conflict Resolution,* 1959, **3,** 1, March, pp. 28–40.

Laue, James H., and Leon M. McCorkle, "The Association of Southern Women for the Prevention of Lynching: A Commentary on the Role of the 'Moderate,'" *Sociological Inquiry,* 1965, **35**, 1, Winter, pp. 80–93.

LeMelle, Tilden J., and Wilbert J. Le Melle, *The Black College: A Strategy for Achieving Relevancy,* Praeger, New York, 1969.

Lippitt, Ronald, *Training in Community Relations: A Research Exploration toward New Group Skills,* Harper, New York, 1949.

MacIver, Robert M., *The More Perfect Union: A Program for the Control of Inter-group Discriminations in the United States,* Macmillan, New York, 1948.

McKee, James B., "Community Power and Strategies in Race Relations: Some Critical Observations," *Social Problems,* 1958–59, **6**, 3, Winter, pp. 195–203.

Marrow, Alfred J., *Living Without Hate: Scientific Approaches to Human Relations,* 1st ed., Harper, New York, 1951.

Morsell, John A., "Schools, Courts, and the Negro's Future," *Harvard Educational Review,* 1960, **30**, 3, Summer, pp. 170–194.

Muir, Donal E., and Donald McGlamery, "The Evolution of Desegregation Attitudes of Southern University Students," *Phylon,* 1968, **29**, 2, Summer, pp. 105–118.

Northwood, L. K., "The Threat and Potential of Urban Renewal: A 'Workable Program' for Better Race Relations," *Journal of Intergroup Relations,* 1961, **2**, 2, Spring, pp. 101–114.

Orleans, Peter, and William R. Ellis, (eds.), *Race, Change, and Urban Society,* Sage Publications, Beverly Hills, Calif., 1971.

Pastalan, Leon A., "An Experiment in Structured Assimilation," *Phylon,* 1964, **25**, 4, Winter, pp. 331–336.

Pettigrew, Thomas F., "Social Psychology and Desegregation Research," *American Psychology,* 1961, **16**, 3, March, pp. 105–112.

Powdermaker, Hortense, *Probing Our Prejudices: A Unit for High School Students,* Harper, New York, 1944.

Richmond, Anthony H., "Teaching Race Questions," *Phylon,* 1956, **17**, 3, October, pp. 239–249.

Rogler, Lloyd H., "The Growth of an Action Group: The Case of a Puerto Rican Migrant Voluntary Association," *International Journal of Comparative Sociology,* 1968, **9**, 3–4, September–December, pp. 223–234.

Rubin, Irwin M., "Increased Self-Acceptance: A Means of Reducing Prejudice," *Journal of Personality and Social Psychology,* 1967, **5**, 2, February, pp. 233–238.

Stinchcombe, Arthur L., Mary McDill, and W. Dollie, "Is There a Racial

Tipping Point in Changing Schools?" *Journal of Social Issues,* 1969, **25**, 1, January, pp. 127–134.

Stroup, Atlee L., and Joseph Landis, "Change in Race-Prejudice Attitudes as Related to Changes in Authoritarianism and Conservatism in a College Population," *Southwestern Social Science Quarterly,* 1965, **46**, 3, December, pp. 255–263.

Taueber, Karl E., "The Effect of Income Redistribution on Racial Residential Segregation," *Urban Affairs Quarterly,* 1963, **4**, 1, September, pp. 5–14.

Theobald, Robert, *An Alternative Future for America: Essays and Speeches,* Swallow Press, Chicago, 1968.

Tillman, James A., "The Quest for Identity and Status: Facets of the Desegregation Process in the Upper Midwest," *Phylon,* 1961, **22**, 4, Winter, pp. 329–339.

Tomlinson, T. M., "The Development of a Riot Ideology among Urban Negroes," *American Behavior Scientist,* 1968, **11**, 4, March–April, pp. 27–31.

Towler, Juby E., *The Police Role in Racial Conflicts,* Charles C Thomas, Springfield, Ill., 1964.

Vander Zanden, James W., "Desegregation and Social Strains in the South," *Journal of Social Issues,* 1959, **15**, 4, pp. 53–60.

———, "The Non-Violent Resistance Movement against Segregation," *American Journal of Sociology,* 1963, **68**, 5, March, pp. 544–559.

Watson, Goodwin B., *Action for Unity,* Harper, New York, 1947.

Watts, Lewis G., "Social Integration and the Use of Minority Leadership in Seattle, Washington," *Phylon,* 1960, **21**, 2, pp. 136–143.

Williams, J. Allen, "Reduction of Tension through Intergroup Contact: A Social Psychological Interpretation," *Pacific Sociological Review,* 1964, **7**, 2, Fall, pp. 81–84.

Williams, Robin M., *The Reduction of Intergroup Tensions: A Survey of Research on Problems of Ethnic, Racial, and Religious Group Relations,* Science Research Council, New York, 1947.

Woofter, T. J. (ed.), *Cooperation in Southern Communities,* Commission on Interracial Cooperation, Atlanta, 1921.

Wright, Nathan, *Let's Work Together,* 1st ed., Hawthorn, New York, 1968.

Yarrow, Marian R., John D. Campbell, and Leon J. Yarrow, "Acquisition of New Norms: A Study of Racial Desegregation," *Journal of Social Issues,* 1958, **14**, 1, pp. 8–28.

An Axiomatic Deductive Theory of Race Relations

The following theory is in temporary form, since testing and further elaboration will obviously result in its modification.

ABREVIATIONS

P = proposition
T = theorem

DEFINITIONS OF KEY CONCEPTS

Colonial Elite A migrant (usually WASP) elite, which subordinates an indigenous population, imports other race groups for purposes of economic exploitation, and rationalizes its power monopoly on the basis of its assumed racial superiority.

Colonial Status Applied to a subordinate group under the political, economic, and social control of a colonial elite.

Racist Policy utilizing assumed physical criteria on the societal, group, or individual level of social structure, behavior, or attitude.

Societal Definitions of Behavior Generally accepted forms of behavior and ways of viewing such behavior.

Organizational Definitions of Behavior Forms and views of behavior accepted by particular subgroups in society.

Subgroup Identity The major criteria utilized by a particular subgroup in defining its social boundaries.

Status Inconsistency The degree of inconsistency in the relationship between racial and socioeconomic status.

Relative Deprivation The social-psychological gap between a group's aspirations and its actual socioeconomic achievement level.

Conservative Reaction The dominant elite's attempt to maintain its political, economic, and social control of the colonial situation.

Racial Accommodation The dominant elite's recognition of subordinate minority groups' rights to political, economic, and social participation in the greater society.

Assimilation Greater participation in the society's political, economic, and social institutions.

Colonial-Ascriptive Criteria The utilization of ascribed racial criteria in role assignment and reward.

Bureaucratic-Achieved Criteria The utilization of achieved and nonracial criteria in role assignment and reward.

STAGE 1 CONTACT

P1 *The more colonial a society's migrant elite, the more negative will be the initial contact between that elite and other race groups.*

P2 *The more negative the initial interracial contact, the more negatively subordinate minorities will be defined by the elite, such negativism being aggravated by marked physical and social contrasts between the elite and its minorities, both indigenous and imported.*

T1   The more colonial a society's migrant elite, the more negatively subordinate minorities will be defined by that elite.

STAGE 2   INSTITUTIONAL RACISM

P3   *The more negatively subordinate minorities are defined, the more racist will be the social structure developed by the colonial elite (i.e., degree of institutionalized racism).*

T2   The more colonial a society's migrant elite, the more racist will be the social structure developed by the elite.

T3   The more negative the initial interracial contact, the more racist the social structure developed by the elite will be.

P4   *The more racist the society's social structure, the more social and economic inequality it will contain.*

T4   The more colonial a society's migrant elite, the more social and economic inequality the subsequent social structure will contain.

T5   The more negative the initial interracial contact, the more social and economic inequality the subsequent social structure will contain.

T6   The more negatively subordinate minorities are defined, the more social and economic inequality the subsequent social structure will contain.

STAGE 3   THE SOCIAL DEFINITION OF "RACE"

P5   *The more social and economic inequality in the social structure, the more "race" will be utilized in the societal definition of behavior and role assignment (i.e., race as a role sign).*

T7   The more colonial a society's migrant elite, the more race will be utilized in the societal definition of behavior and role assignment.

T8   The more negative the initial interracial contact, the more race will be utilized in the societal definition of behavior and role assignment.

T9   The more negatively subordinate minorities are defined, the more race will be utilized in the societal definition of behavior and role assignment.

T10   The more racist the society's social structure, the more race will be utilized in the societal definition of behavior and role assignment.

P6   *The more race is utilized in the societal definition of behavior and role assignment, the more it will be utilized in the societal definition of intergroup relations as the main criterion of political policy and social behavior.*

T11   The more colonial a society's migrant elite, the more race will be utilized in the societal definition of intergroup relations.

T12   The more negative the initial interracial contact, the more race will be utilized in the societal definition of intergroup relations.

T13   The more negatively subordinate minorities are defined, the more race will be utilized in the societal definition of intergroup relations.

T14   The more racist the society's social structure, the more race will be utilized in the societal definition of intergroup relations.

T15   The more social and economic inequality in the social structure, the more race will be utilized in the societal definition of intergroup relations.

STAGE 4   GROUP DEFINITIONS OF "RACE"

P7   *The more "race" is utilized in the societal definition of intergroup relations, the more it will be a major factor in organizational definitions of behavior (i.e., institutional theories of race relations).*

T16   The more colonial a society's migrant elite, the more race will be a major factor in organizational definitions of behavior.

T17   The more negative the initial interracial contact, the more race will be a major factor in organizational definitions of behavior.

T18   The more negatively subordinate minorities are defined, the more race will be a major factor in organizational definitions of behavior.

T19   The more racist the society's social structure, the more race will be a major factor in organizational definitions of behavior.

T20   The more social and economic inequality in the social structure, the more race will be a major factor in organizational definitions of behavior.

T21   The more race is utilized in the societal definition of behavior and role assignment, the more it will be a major factor in organizational definitions of behavior.

P8 *The more race is a major factor in organizational definitions of behavior, the more it will function as the major criterion of subgroup identity in the social system.*

T22 The more colonial a society's migrant elite, the more race will function as the major criterion of subgroup identity.

T23 The more negative the initial interracial contact, the more race will function as the major criterion of subgroup identity.

T24 The more negatively subordinate minorities are defined, the more race will function as the major criterion of subgroup identity.

T25 The more racist the society's social structure, the more race will function as the major criterion of subgroup identity.

T26 The more social and economic inequality in the social structure, the more race will function as the major criterion of subgroup identity.

T27 The more race is utilized in the societal definition of behavior and role assignment, the more it will function as the major criterion of subgroup identity.

T28 The more race is utilized in the societal definition of intergroup relations, the more it will function as the major criterion of subgroup identity.

STAGE 5 INDIVIDUAL ATTITUDES

P9 *The more race is utilized in subgroup identity, the more the individual, whether a member of the elite or a minority, will absorb racist norms through the process of socialization.*

T29 The more colonial a society's migrant elite, the more the individual will absorb racist norms.

T30 The more negative the initial interracial contact, the more the individual will eventually absorb racist norms.

T31 The more negatively subordinate minorities are defined, the more the individual will absorb racist norms.

T32 The more racist the society's social structure, the more the individual will absorb racist norms.

T33 The more social and economic inequality in the social structure, the more the individual will absorb racist norms.

T34 The more race is utilized in the societal definition of behavior and role assignment, the more the individual will absorb racist norms.

T35 The more race is utilized in the societal definition of intergroup relations, the more the individual will absorb racist norms.

T36 The more race is a major factor in organizational definitions of behavior, the more the individual will absorb racist norms.

P10 *The more the individual absorbs racist norms through socialization, the more he will tend to conform to them.*

T37 The more colonial a society's migrant elite, the more individuals within society will tend to conform to racist norms.

T38 The more negative the initial interracial contact, the more individuals within society will tend to conform to racist norms.

T39 The more negatively subordinate minorities are defined, the more individuals within society will tend to conform to racist norms.

T40 The more racist the society's social structure, the more individuals within society will tend to conform to racist norms.

T41 The more social and economic inequality in the social structure, the more individuals within society will tend to conform to racist norms.

T42 The more race is utilized in the societal definition of behavior and role assignment, the more individuals within society will tend to conform to racist norms.

T43 The more race is utilized in the societal definition of intergroup relations, the more individuals within society will tend to conform to racist norms.

T44 The more race is a major factor in organizational definitions of behavior, the more individuals within society will tend to conform to racist norms.

T45 The more race is utilized in subgroup identity, the more individuals within society will tend to conform to racist norms.

P11 *The more the individual conforms to racist norms, the more he will tend to define intergroup relations in racial terms.*

T46 The more colonial a society's migrant elite, the more individuals will tend to define intergroup relations in racial terms.

T47 The more negative the initial interracial contact, the more individuals will tend to define intergroup relations in racial terms.

T48 The more negatively subordinate minorities are defined, the more individuals will tend to define intergroup relations in racial terms.

T49 The more racist the society's social structure, the more individuals will tend to define intergroup relations in racial terms.

T50 The more social and economic inequality in the social structure, the more individuals will tend to define intergroup relations in racial terms.

T51 The more race is utilized in the societal definition of behavior and role assignment, the more individuals will tend to define intergroup relations in racial terms.

T52 The more "race" is utilized in the societal definition of intergroup relations, the more individuals will tend to define intergroup relations in racial terms.

T53 The more race is a major factor in organizational definitions of behavior, the more individuals will tend to define intergroup relations in racial terms.

T54 The more race is utilized in subgroup identity, the more individuals will tend to define intergroup relations in racial terms.

T55 The more the individual absorbs racist norms through socialization, the more he will tend to define intergroup relations in racial terms.

P12 *The more the individual defines intergroup relations in racial terms, the more he will also tend to define social situations in general in racial terms.*

T56 The more colonial a society's migrant elite, the more individuals will tend to define social situations in general in racial terms.

T57 The more negative the initial interracial contact, the more individuals will tend to define social situations in general in racial terms.

T58 The more negatively subordinate minorities are defined, the more individuals will tend to define social situations in general in racial terms.

T59 The more racist the society's social structure, the more individuals will tend to define social situations in general in racial terms.

T60 The more social and economic inequality in the social structure, the more individuals will tend to define social situations in general in racial terms.

T61 The more race is utilized in the societal definition of behavior and role assignment, the more individuals will tend to define social situations in general in racial terms.

T62 The more race is utilized in the societal definition of intergroup relations, the more individuals will tend to define social situations in general in racial terms.

T63 The more race is a major factor in organizational definitions of behavior, the more individuals will tend to define social situations in general in racial terms.

T64 The more race is utilized in subgroup identity, the more individuals will tend to define social situations in general in racial terms.

T65 The more the individual absorbs racist norms through socialization, the more he will tend to define social situations in general in racial terms.

T66 The more the individual conforms to racist norms, the more individuals will tend to define social situations in general in racial terms.

STAGE 6   ECONOMIC AND SOCIAL CHANGE

P13 *The more the individual defines social situations in general in racial terms, the more dramatic (i.e., effective) will be the individual effects of high rates of economic development as status inconsistency and relative deprivation increase.*

T67 The more colonial a society's migrant elite, the more dramatic will be the individual effects of high rates of economic development as status inconsistency and relative deprivation increase.

T68 The more negative the initial interracial contact, the more dramatic will be the individual effects of high rates of economic development as status inconsistency and relative deprivation increase.

T69 The more negatively subordinate minorities are defined, the more dramatic will be the individual effects of high rates of economic development as status inconsistency and relative deprivation increase.

T70 The more racist the society's social structure, the more dramatic will be the individual effects of high rates of economic development as status inconsistency and relative deprivation increase.

T71 The more social and economic inequality in the social structure, the more dramatic will be the individual effects of high rates of economic development as status inconsistency and relative deprivation increase.

T72 The more race is utilized in the societal definition of behavior and role assignment, the more dramatic will be the individual effects of high rates of economic development as status inconsistency and relative deprivation increase.

T73 The more race is utilized in the societal definition of intergroup relations, the more dramatic will be the individual effects of high rates of economic development as status inconsistency and relative deprivation increase.

T74 The more race is a major factor in organizational definitions of behavior, the more dramatic will be the individual effects of high rates of economic development as status inconsistency and relative deprivation increase.

T75 The more race is utilized in subgroup identity, the more dramatic will be the individual effects of high rates of economic development as status inconsistency and relative deprivation increase.

T76 The more the individual absorbs racist norms through socialization, the more dramatic will be the effects of high rates of economic development on him as status inconsistency and relative deprivation increase.

T77 The more the individual conforms to racist norms, the more dramatic will be the effects of high rates of economic development on him as status inconsistency and relative deprivation increase.

T78 The more the individual defines intergroup relations in racial terms, the more dramatic will be the effects of high rates of economic development on him as status inconsistency and relative deprivation increase.

P14 *The higher the level of status inconsistency and relative deprivation, the greater a minority's eventual rejection of the colonial structure as illegitimate.*

T79 The more colonial a society's migrant elite, the greater a minority's eventual rejection of the colonial structure as illegitimate.

T80 The more negative the initial interracial contact, the greater a minority's eventual rejection of the colonial structure as illegitimate.

T81 The more negatively subordinate minorities are defined, the greater a minority's eventual rejection of the colonial structure as illegitimate.

T82 The more racist the society's social structure, the greater a minority's eventual rejection of the colonial structure as illegitimate.

T83 The more social and economic inequality in the social structure, the greater a minority's eventual rejection of the colonial structure as illegitimate.

T84 The more race is utilized in the societal definition of behavior and role assignment, the greater a minority's eventual rejection of the colonial structure as illegitimate.

T85 The more race is utilized in the societal definition of intergroup relations, the greater a minority's eventual rejection of the colonial structure as illegitimate.

T86 The more race is a major factor in organizational definitions of behavior, the greater a minority's eventual rejection of the colonial structure as illegitimate.

T87 The more race is utilized in subgroup identity, the greater a minority's eventual rejection of the colonial structure as illegitimate.

T88 The more the individual absorbs racist norms through socialization, the greater a minority's eventual rejection of the colonial structure as illegitimate.

T89 The more the individual conforms to racist norms, the greater a minority's eventual rejection of the colonial structure as illegitimate.

T90 The more the individual defines intergroup relations in racial terms, the greater a minority's eventual rejection of the colonial structure as illegitimate.

T91 The more the individual defines social situations in general in racial terms, the greater a minority's eventual rejection of the colonial structure as illegitimate.

P15 *The greater a minority's rejection of the colonial structure as illegitimate, the more conservative will be the elite's reaction to such a development.*

T92 The more colonial a society's migrant elite, the more conservative will be the elite's reaction to minority rejection of its power as illegitimate.

T93 The more negative the initial interracial contact, the more conservative will be the elite's reaction to minority rejection of its power as illegitimate.

T94 The more negatively subordinate minorities are defined, the more conservative will be the elite's reaction to minority rejection of its power as illegitimate.

T95 The more racist the society's social structure, the more conservative will be the elite's reaction to minority rejection of its power as illegitimate.

T96 The more social and economic inequality in the social structure, the more conservative will be the elite's reaction to minority rejection of its power as illegitimate.

T97 The more race is utilized in the societal definition of behavior and role assignment, the more conservative will be the elite's reaction to minority rejection of its power as illegitimate.

T98 The more race is utilized in the societal definition of intergroup relations, the more conservative will be the elite's reaction to minority rejection of its power as illegitimate.

T99 The more race is a major factor in organizational definitions of behavior, the more conservative will be the elite's reaction to minority rejection of its power as illegitimate.

T100 The more race is utilized in subgroup identity, the more conservative will be the elite's reaction to minority rejection of its power as illegitimate.

T101 The more the individual absorbs racist norms through socialization, the more conservative will be the elite's reaction to minority rejection of its power as illegitimate.

T102 The more the individual conforms to racist norms, the more conservative will be the elite's reaction to minority rejection of its power as illegitimate.

T103 The more the individual defines intergroup relations in racial terms, the more conservative will be the elite's reaction to minority rejection of its power as illegitimate.

T104 The more the individual defines social situations in general in racial terms, the more conservative will be the elite's reaction to minority rejection of its power as illegitimate.

T105 The higher the level of status inconsistency and relative deprivation, the more conservative will be the elite's reaction to minority rejection of its power as illegitimate.

P16 The more conservative the elite's reaction to a minority's rejection of the colonial structure, the higher the eventual level of minority group pressure against that elite.

T106 The more colonial a society's migrant elite, the higher the eventual level of minority-group pressure against that elite.

T107 The more negative the initial interracial contact, the higher the eventual level of minority-group pressure against the colonial elite.

T108 The more negatively subordinate minorities are defined, the higher the eventual level of minority-group pressure against the colonial elite.

T109 The more racist the society's social structure, the higher the eventual level of minority-group pressure against the colonial elite.

T110 The more social and economic inequality in the social structure, the higher the eventual level of minority-group pressure against the colonial elite.

T111 The more race is utilized in the societal definition of behavior and role assignment, the higher the eventual level of minority-group pressure against the colonial elite.

T112 The more race is utilized in the societal definition of intergroup relations, the higher the eventual level of minority-group pressure against the colonial elite.

T113 The more race is a major factor in organizational definitions of behavior, the higher the eventual level of minority-group pressure against the colonial elite.

T114 The more race is utilized in subgroup identity, the higher the eventual level of minority-group pressure against the colonial elite.

T115 The more the individual absorbs racist norms through socialization, the higher the eventual level of minority-group pressure against the colonial elite.

T116 The more the individual conforms to racist norms, the higher the eventual level of minority-group pressure against the colonial elite.

T117 The more the individual defines intergroup relations in racial terms, the higher the eventual level of minority-group pressure against the colonial elite.

T118 The more the individual defines social situations in general in racial terms, the higher the eventual level of minority-group pressure against the colonial elite.

T119 The higher the level of status inconsistency and relative deprivation, the higher the eventual level of minority-group pressure against the colonial elite.

T120 The greater a minority's rejection of the colonial structure as illegitimate, the higher the eventual level of minority-group pressure against the colonial elite.

P17 *The greater the level of minority-group pressure against the dominant elite, the greater the general rejection of that elite's power monopoly.*

T121 The more colonial a society's migrant elite, the greater the eventual general rejection of the elite's power monopoly.

T122 The more negative the initial interracial contact, the greater the eventual general rejection of the elite's power monopoly.

T123 The more negatively subordinate minorities are defined, the greater the eventual general rejection of the elite's power monopoly.

T124 The more racist the society's social structure, the greater the eventual general rejection of the elite's power monopoly.

T125 The more social and economic inequality in the social structure, the greater the eventual general rejection of the elite's power monopoly.

T126 The more race is utilized in the societal definition of behavior and role assignment, the greater the eventual general rejection of the elite's power monopoly.

T127 The more race is utilized in the societal definition of intergroup relations, the greater the eventual general rejection of the elite's power monopoly.

T128 The more race is a major factor in organizational definitions of behavior, the greater the eventual general rejection of the elite's power monopoly.

T129 The more race is utilized in subgroup identity, the greater the eventual general rejection of the elite's power monopoly.

T130 The more the individual absorbs racist norms through socialization, the greater the eventual general rejection of the elite's power monopoly.

T131 The more the individual conforms to racist norms, the greater the eventual general rejection of the elite's power monopoly.

T132 The more the individual defines intergroup relations in racial terms, the greater the eventual general rejection of the elite's power monopoly.

T133 The more the individual defines social situations in general in racial terms, the greater the eventual general rejection of the elite's power monopoly.

T134 The higher the level of status inconsistency and relative deprivation, the greater the eventual general rejection of the elite's power monopoly.

T135 The greater a minority's rejection of the colonial structure as illegitimate, the greater the eventual general rejection of the elite's power monopoly.

T136 The more conservative the elite's reaction to a minority's rejection of the colonial structure, the greater the eventual general rejection of the elite's power monopoly.

P18 *The greater the general rejection of the elite's power monopoly, the greater the general pressure brought to bear on that elite.*

T137 The more colonial a society's migrant elite, the greater the general pressure eventually brought to bear on the colonial elite.

T138 The more negative the initial interracial contact, the greater the general pressure eventually brought to bear on the colonial elite.

T139 The more negatively subordinate minorities are defined, the greater the general pressure eventually brought to bear on the colonial elite.

T140 The more racist the society's social structure, the greater the general pressure eventually brought to bear on the colonial elite.

T141 The more social and economic inequality in the social structure, the greater the general pressure eventually brought to bear on the colonial elite.

T142 The more race is utilized in the societal definition of behavior and role assignment, the greater the general pressure eventually brought to bear on the colonial elite.

T143 The more race is utilized in the societal definition of intergroup relations, the greater the general pressure eventually brought to bear on the colonial elite.

T144 The more race is a major factor in organizational definitions of behavior, the greater the general pressure eventually brought to bear on the colonial elite.

T145 The more race is utilized in subgroup identity, the greater the general pressure eventually brought to bear on the colonial elite.

T146 The more the individual absorbs racist norms through socialization, the greater the general pressure eventually brought to bear on the colonial elite.

T147 The more the individual conforms to racist norms, the greater the general pressure eventually brought to bear on the colonial elite.

T148 The more the individual defines intergroup relations in racial terms, the greater the general pressure eventually brought to bear on the colonial elite.

T149 The more the individual defines social situation in general in racial terms, the greater the general pressure eventually brought to bear on the colonial elite.

T150 The higher the level of status inconsistency and relative deprivation, the greater the general pressure eventually brought to bear on the colonial elite.

T151 The greater a minority's rejection of the colonial structure as illegitimate, the greater the general pressure eventually brought to bear on the colonial elite.

T152 The more conservative the elite's reaction to a minority's rejection of the colonial structure, the greater the general pressure eventually brought to bear on the colonial elite.

T153 The greater the level of minority group pressure against the dominant elite, the greater the general pressure eventually brought to bear on the colonial elite.

STAGE 7 ACCOMMODATION AND THE DECLINE OF COLONIALISM

P19   *The greater the general pressure brought to bear on the colonial elite, the more likely it will eventually develop some new relationship to the minorities under its control (i.e., racial accommodation).*

T154   The more colonial a society's migrant elite, the more likely the elite will eventually develop some new relationship to the minorities under its control.

T155   The more negative the initial interracial contact, the more likely the elite will eventually develop some new relationship to the minorities under its control.

T156   The more negatively subordinate minorities are defined, the more likely the elite will eventually develop some new relationship to the minorities under its control.

T157   The more racist the society's social structure, the more likely the elite will eventually develop some new relationship to the minorities under its control.

T158   The more social and economic inequality in the social structure, the more likely the elite will eventually develop some new relationship to the minorities under its control.

T159   The more race is utilized in the societal definition of behavior and role assignment, the more likely the elite will eventually develop some new relationship to the minorities under its control.

T160   The more race is utilized in the societal definition of intergroup relations, the more likely the elite will eventually develop some new relationship to the minorities under its control.

T161   The more race is a major factor in organizational definitions of behavior, the more likely the elite will eventually develop some new relationship to the minorities under its control.

T162   The more race is utilized in subgroup identity, the more likely the elite will eventually develop some new relationship to the minorities under its control.

T163   The more the individual absorbs racist norms through socialization, the more likely the elite will eventually develop some new relationship to the minorities under its control.

T164   The more the individual conforms to racist norms, the more likely the elite will eventually develop some new relationship to the minorities under its control.

T165   The more the individual defines intergroup relations in racial terms, the more likely the elite will eventually develop some new relationship to the minorities under its control.

T166   The more the individual defines social situations in general in racial terms, the more likely the elite will eventually develop some new relationship to the minorities under its control.

T167   The higher the level of status inconsistency and relative deprivation, the more likely the elite will eventually develop some new relationship to the minorities under its control.

T168   The greater a minority's rejection of the colonial structure as illegitimate, the more likely the elite will eventually develop some new relationship to the minorities under its control.

T169   The more conservative the elite's reaction to a minority's rejection of the colonial structure, the more likely that elite will eventually develop some new relationship to the minorities under its control.

T170   The greater the level of minority-group pressure against the dominant elite, the more likely that elite will eventually develop some new relationship to the minorities under its control.

T171   The greater the general rejection of the elite's power monopoly, the more likely that elite will eventually develop some new relationship to the minorities under its control.

P20   *The greater the accommodation between the colonial elite and its minorities, the more control they will eventually have over their own situation (i.e., an increase in power).*

T172   The more colonial a society's migrant elite, the more control minorities will eventually have over their own situation.

T173   The more negative the initial interracial contact, the more control minorities will eventually have over their own situation.

T174   The more negatively subordinate minorities are defined, the more control minorities will eventually have over their own situation.

T175   The more racist the society's social structure, the more control minorities will eventually have over their own situation.

T176   The more social and economic inequality in the social structure, the more control minorities will eventually have over their own situation.

T177   The more race is utilized in the societal definition of behavior and role assignment, the more control minorities will eventually have over their own situation.

T178   The more race is utilized in the societal definition of intergroup relations, the more control minorities will eventually have over their own situation.

T179   The more race is a major factor in organizational definitions of behavior, the more control minorities will eventually have over their own situation.

T180   The more race is utilized in subgroup identity, the more control minorities will eventually have over their own situation.

T181   The more the individual absorbs racist norms through socialization, the more control minorities will eventually have over their own situation.

T182   The more the individual conforms to racist norms, the more control minorities will eventually have over their own situation.

T183   The more the individual defines intergroup relations in racial terms, the more control minorities will eventually have over their own situation.

T184   The more the individual defines social situations in general in racial terms, the more control minorities will eventually have over their own situation.

T185   The higher the level of status inconsistency and relative deprivation, the more control minorities will eventually have over their own situation.

T186   The greater a minority's rejection of the colonial structure as illegitimate, the more control minorities will eventually have over their own situation.

T187   The more conservative the elite's reaction to a minority's rejection of the colonial structure, the more control minorities will eventually have over their own situation.

T188   The greater the level of minority group pressure against the dominant elite, the more control minorities will eventually have over their own situation.

T189   The greater the general rejection of the elite's power monopoly, the more control minorities will eventually have over their own situation.

T190   The greater the general pressure brought to bear on the colonial elite, the more control minorities will eventually have over their own situation.

P21   *The more control minorities exert over their own situation, the greater the eventual decline of their colonial status.*

T191   The more colonial a society's migrant elite, the greater the eventual decline of the colonial status of minorities in the society.

T192   The more negative the initial interracial contact, the greater the eventual decline of the colonial status of minorities in the society.

T193   The more negatively subordinate minorities are defined, the greater the eventual decline of the colonial status of minorities in the society.

T194   The more racist the society's social structure, the greater the eventual decline of the colonial status of minorities in the society.

T195   The more social and economic inequality in the social structure, the greater the eventual decline of the colonial status of minorities in society.

T196   The more race is utilized in the societal definition of behavior and role assignment, the greater the eventual decline of the colonial status of minorities in the society.

T197   The more race is utilized in the societal definition of intergroup relations, the greater the eventual decline of the colonial status of minorities in the society.

T198   The more race is a major factor in organizational definitions of behavior, the greater the eventual decline of the colonial status of minorities in the society.

T199   The more race is utilized in subgroup identity, the greater the eventual decline of the colonial status of minorities in the society.

T200   The more the individual absorbs racist norms through socialization, the greater the eventual decline of the colonial status of minorities in the society.

T201   The more the individual conforms to racist norms, the greater the eventual decline of the colonial status of minorities in the society.

T202   The more the individual defines intergroup relations in racial terms, the greater the eventual decline of the colonial status of minorities in the society.

T203   The more the individual defines social situations in general in racial terms, the greater the eventual decline of the colonial status of minorities in the society.

T204   The higher the level of status inconsistency and relative deprivation, the greater the eventual decline of the colonial status of minorities in the society.

T205   The greater a minority's rejection of the colonial structure as illegitimate, the greater the eventual decline of the colonial status of minorities in the society.

T206   The more conservative the elite's reaction to a minority's rejection of the colonial structure, the greater the eventual decline of the colonial status of minorities in the society.

T207   The greater the level of minority group pressure against the dominant elite, the greater the eventual decline of the colonial status of minorities in the society.

T208   The greater the general rejection of the elite's power monopoly, the greater the eventual decline of the colonial status of minorities in the society.

T209   The greater the general pressure brought to bear on the colonial elite, the greater the eventual decline of the colonial status of minorities in the society.

T210   The greater the accommodation between the colonial elite and its minorities, the greater the eventual decline of the colonial status of minorities in the society.

P22   *The greater the eventual decline of a minority's colonial status, the greater its assimilation into the general social system.*

T211   The more colonial a society's migrant elite, the greater the eventual assimilation of minorities into the general social system.

T212   The more negative the initial interracial contact, the greater the eventual assimilation of minorities into the general social system.

T213   The more negatively subordinate minorities are defined, the greater their eventual assimilation into the general social system.

T214   The more racist the society's social structure, the greater the eventual assimilation of minorities into the general social system.

T215   The more social and economic inequality in the social structure, the greater the eventual assimilation of minorities into the general social system.

T216   The more race is utilized in the societal definition of behavior and role assignment, the greater the eventual assimilation of minorities into the general social system.

T217   The more race is utilized in the societal definition of intergroup relations, the greater the eventual assimilation of minorities into the general social system.

T218   The more race is a major factor in organizational definitions of behavior, the greater the eventual assimilation of minorities into the general social system.

T219   The more race is utilized in subgroup identity, the greater the eventual assimilation of minorities into the general social system.

T220   The more the individual absorbs racist norms through socialization, the greater the eventual assimilation of minorities into the general social system.

T221   The more the individual conforms to racist norms, the greater the eventual assimilation of minorities into the general social system.

T222   The more the individual defines intergroup relations in racial terms, the greater the eventual assimilation of minorities into the general social system.

T223 The more the individual defines social situations in general in racial terms, the greater the eventual assimilation of minorities into the general social system.

T224 The higher the level of status inconsistency and relative deprivation, the greater the eventual assimilation of minorities into the general social system.

T225 The greater a minority's rejection of the colonial structure as illegitimate, the greater the eventual assimilation of minorities into the general social system.

T226 The more conservative the elite's reaction to a minority's rejection of the colonial structure, the greater the eventual assimilation of minorities into the general social system.

T227 The greater the level of minority-group pressure against the dominant elite, the greater the eventual assimilation of minorities into the general social system.

T228 The greater the general rejection of the elite's power monopoly, the greater the eventual assimilation of minorities into the general social system.

T229 The greater the general pressure brought to bear on the colonial elite, the greater the eventual assimilation of minorities into the general social system.

T230 The greater the accommodation between the colonial elite and its minorities, the greater the eventual assimilation of minorities into the general social system.

T231 The more control minorities exert over their own situation, the greater the eventual assimilation of minorities into the general social system.

P23 *The greater a minority's assimilation into the general social system, the greater the use of bureaucratic-achieved rather than colonial-ascriptive criteria in the process of societal role assignment.*

T232 The more colonial a society's migrant elite, the greater the eventual use of bureaucratic-achieved rather than colonial-ascriptive criteria in the process of societal role assignment.

T233 The more negative the initial interracial contact, the greater the eventual use of bureaucratic-achieved rather than colonial-ascriptive criteria in the process of societal role assignment.

T234 The more negatively subordinate minorities are defined, the greater the eventual use of bureaucratic-achieved rather than colonial-ascriptive criteria in the process of societal role assignment.

T235 The more racist the society's social structure, the greater the eventual use of bureaucratic-achieved rather than colonial-ascriptive criteria in the process of societal role assignment.

T236 The more social and economic inequality in the social structure, the greater the eventual use of bureaucratic-achieved rather than colonial-ascriptive criteria in the process of societal role assignment.

T237 The more race is utilized in the societal definition of behavior and role assignment, the greater the eventual use of bureaucratic-achieved rather than colonial-ascriptive criteria in the process of societal role assignment.

T238 The more race is utilized in the societal definition of intergroup relations, the greater the eventual use of bureaucratic-achieved rather than colonial-ascriptive criteria in the process of societal role assignment.

T239 The more race is a major factor in organizational definitions of behavior the greater the eventual use of bureaucratic-achieved rather than colonial-ascriptive criteria in the process of societal role assignment.

T240 The more race is utilized in subgroup identity, the greater the eventual use of bureaucratic-achieved rather than colonial-ascriptive criteria in the process of societal role assignment.

T241 The more the individual absorbs racist norms through socialization, the greater the eventual use of bureaucratic-achieved rather than colonial-ascriptive criteria in the process of societal role assignment.

T242 The more the individual conforms to racist norms, the greater the eventual use of bureaucratic-achieved rather than colonial-ascriptive criteria in the process of societal role assignment.

T243 The more the individual defines intergroup relations in racial terms, the greater the eventual use of bureaucratic-achieved rather than colonial-ascriptive criteria in the process of societal role assignment.

T244 The more the individual defines social situations in general in racial terms, the greater the eventual use of bureaucratic-achieved rather than colonial-ascriptive criteria in the process of societal role assignment.

T245 The higher the level of status inconsistency and relative deprivation, the greater the eventual use of bureaucratic-achieved rather than colonial-ascriptive criteria in the process of societal role assignment.

T246 The greater a minority's rejection of the colonial structure as illegitimate, the greater the eventual use of bureaucratic-achieved rather than colonial-ascriptive criteria in the process of societal role assignment.

T247 The more conservative the elite's reaction to a minority's rejection of the colonial structure, the greater the eventual use of bureaucratic-achieved rather than colonial-ascriptive criteria in the process of societal role assignment.

T248 The greater the level of minority-group pressure against the dominant elite, the greater the eventual use of bureaucratic-achieved rather than colonial-ascriptive criteria in the process of societal role assignment.

T249 The greater the general rejection of the elite's power monopoly, the greater the eventual use of bureaucratic-achieved rather than colonial-ascriptive criteria in the process of societal role assignment.

T250 The greater the general pressure brought to bear on the colonial elite, the greater the eventual use of bureaucratic-achieved rather than colonial-ascriptive criteria in the process of societal role assignment.

T251 The greater the accommodation between the colonial elite and its minorities, the greater the eventual use of bureaucratic-achieved rather than colonial-ascriptive criteria in the process of societal role assignment.

T252 The more control minorities exert over their own situation, the greater the eventual use of bureaucratic-achieved rather than colonial-ascriptive criteria in the process of societal role assignment.

T253 The greater the eventual decline of a minority's colonial status, the greater the eventual use of bureaucratic-achieved rather than colonial-ascriptive criteria in the process of societal role assignment.

Bibliography

Abe, Shirley, "Violations of the Racial Code in Hawaii," *Social Process in Hawaii,* 1945, pp. 9–10, 33–38.

Adam, H. (ed.), *South Africa: Sociological Perspectives,* Oxford University Press, New York, 1971.

Adams, Romanzo C., "The Unorthodox Race Doctrine of Hawaii," in *Race and Culture Contacts* by E. B. Reuter (ed.), McGraw-Hill, New York, 1934, pp. 143–160.

Adorno, T. W., et al., *The Authoritarian Personality,* Harper, New York, 1950.

Alba, Victor, *The Mexicans: The Making of a Nation,* Praeger, New York, 1967.

Alkalimat, A. H. I., "The Ideology of Black Social Science," *Black Scholar,* 1969, sec. 1, 2, pp. 28–36.

Allen, George Cyril, *The Industrial Development of Birmingham and the Black Country, 1860–1927,* A. M. Kelley, New York, 1966.

Allen, Robert L., *Black Awakening in Capitalist America: An Analytic History,* Doubleday, New York, 1969.

Allport, Gordon W. (ed.), *ABC's of Scapegoating,* Anti-Defamation League of B'nai B'rith, New York, 1948.

————, *The Resolution of Intergroup Tensions: A Critical Appraisal of Methods,* National Conference of Christians and Jews, New York, 1952.

————, *The Nature of Prejudice,* Addison-Wesley, Cambridge, Mass., 1958.

Anderson, C. H., *White Protestant Americans,* Prentice-Hall, Englewood Cliffs, N.J., 1970.

Anderson, David D., and Robert L. Wright (eds.), *The Dark and Tangled Path: Race in America,* Houghton Mifflin, Boston, 1971.

Arkoff, Abe, Gerald Meredith, and Janice Dong, "Attitudes of Japanese-American and Caucasian-American Students toward Marriage Roles," *Journal of Social Psychology,* **59,** pp. 11–15.

Arny, William F. M., *Indian Agent in New Mexico: The Journal of Special Agent W. F. M. Arny, 1870,* Stagecoach Press, Sante Fe, N. Mex., 1967.

Ashmore, Harry S., *The Other Side of Jordan,* 1st ed., Norton, New York, 1960.

Atkin, Edmond, and Wilbur R. Jacobs (eds.), *Indians of the Southern Colonial Frontier: The Edmond Atkin Report and Plan of 1755,* University of South Carolina Press, Columbia, S.C., 1954.

Auerbach, Aline Sophie (Buchman), and Sandra Roche, *Creating a Preschool Center: Parent Development in an Integrated Neighborhood Project,* Wiley, New York, 1971.

Austin, Lettie J., Lewis H. Fenderson, and Sophia P. Nelson, *The Black Man and the Promise of America,* Scott, Foresman, Glenview, Ill., 1970.

Azevedo, T. de, *Social Change in Brazil,* University of Florida Press, Gainesville, 1963.

Bagley, C., "Race Relations and Theories of Status Consistency," *Race,* 1970, **11,** 3, pp. 267–289.

Bailey, K. D., "Evaluating Axiomatic Theories," in E. F. Borgatta and G. W. Bohrnstedt (eds.), *Sociological Methodology, 1970,* Jossey-Bass, San Francisco, 1970, pp. 48–74.

Bailey, Thomas P., *Race Orthodoxy in the South, and Other Aspects of the Negro Question,* Neal Publishing, New York, 1914.

Baker, Ray S., *Following the Color Line: An Account of Negro Citizenship in the American Democracy,* Doubleday, Page and Co., New York, 1908.

Baklanoff, E. N. (ed.), *The Shaping of Modern Brazil,* Louisiana University Press, Baton Rouge, 1969.

Baldwin, James, *Notes of a Native Son,* Beacon Press, Boston, 1955.

———, *Nobody Knows My Name: More Notes of a Native Son,* Dial Press, New York, 1961.

Banton, Michael, "Race As a Social Category," *Race,* 1966, **8,** 1, July, pp. 1–16.

———, *Race Relations,* Basic Books, New York, 1967.

Bartlett, Vernon, *The Colour of Their Skin,* Chatto and Windus, London, 1969.

Bartley, Numan V., *The Rise of Massive Resistance: Race and Politics in the South During the 1950s,* Louisiana State University Press, Baton Rouge, 1969.

Baruch, Dorothy (Walter), *Glass House of Prejudice,* Morrow, New York, 1946.

Bastide, Roger, "Race Relations in Brazil," *International Social Science Bulletin,* 1957, **9,** 4, pp. 495–512.

———, and Pierre van den Berghe, "Stereotypes, Norms and Interracial Behavior in Sao Paulo, Brazil," *American Sociological Review,* 1957, **22,** December 6, pp. 689–694.

———, "Color, Racism, and Christianity," *Daedalus,* 1967, **96,** 2, pp. 312–327.

Baughman, Emmett E., *Black Americans: A Psychological Analysis,* Academic Press, New York, 1971.

Beale, Calvin L., "American Triracial Isolates," *Eugenics Quarterly,* **4,** December, 1957, 4, pp. 187–196.

Beals, Ralph L., and Norman D. Humphrey, *No Frontier to Learning: The Mexican Student in the United States,* University of Minnesota Press, Minneapolis, 1957.

Bellush, Jewel Lubin, and Stephen M. David, *Race and Politics in New York City: Five Studies in Policy-Making,* Praeger, New York, 1971.

Benedict, Ruth F., and Gene Weltfish, *Race: Science and Politics,* Viking Press, New York, 1959.

Bennett, Lerone, *Confrontation: Black and White,* Johnson, Chicago, 1965.

Berger, Graenum, *Graenum Berger Speaks on the Jewish Community Center: A Fourth Force in American Jewish Life,* Jewish Education Committee Press, New York, 1966.

Berkson, Isaac B., *Theories of Americanization: A Critical Study,* Arno, New York, 1969.

Bernard, J., "The Conceptualization of Intergroup Relations with Special Reference to Conflict," *Social Forces,* 1951, **29,** pp. 243–246.

Bernstein, Saul, *Alternatives to Violence: Alienated Youth and Riots, Race, and Poverty,* Association Press, New York, 1967.

Berreman, Gerald D., "Caste as Social Process," *Southwestern Journal of Anthropology,* 1967, **23,** 4, Winter, pp. 351–370.

Berry, Brewton, *Race Relations: The Interaction of Ethnic and Racial Groups,* Houghton Mifflin, Boston, 1951.

Berry, Wendell, *The Hidden Wound,* Houghton Mifflin, Boston, 1970.

Bettelheim, Bruno, and Morris Janowitz, *Dynamics of Prejudice: A Psychological and Sociological Study of Veterans,* 1st ed., Harper, New York, 1950.

————, and ————, *Social Change and Prejudice,* Free Press of Glencoe, New York, 1964.

Bibby, Harold Cyril, *Race, Prejudice, and Education,* Praeger, New York, 1960.

Bigham, John Alvin (ed.), *Select Discussions of Race Problems;* A Collection of Papers of Especial Use in Study of Negro-American Problems: With the Proceedings of the Twentieth Annual Conference for Study of Negro Problems, Held at Atlanta University, May 24, 1915, Atlanta University Press, Atlanta, 1916.

Billingsley, Andrew, *Black Families in White America,* Prentice-Hall, Englewood Cliffs, N.J., 1968.

Birmingham, Stephen, *The Grandees: America's Sephardic Elite,* Harper & Row, New York, 1971.

Bisgyer, Maurice, *Challenge and Encounter: Behind the Scenes in the Struggle for Jewish Survival,* Crown, New York, 1967.

Blalock, Hubert M., "Power Analysis of Racial Discrimination," *Social Forces,* 1960, **39,** 1, October, pp. 53–59.

————, *Toward a Theory of Minority-Group Relations,* Wiley, New York, 1967.

Blanford, Benjamin W., *Off the Capes of Delaware: Stories of American Jewish Heroes,* Riverdale Press, Cincinnati, 1940.

Blauner, Robert, "Internal Colonialism and Ghetto Revolt," *Social Problems,* 1969, **16,** 4, Spring, pp. 393–408.

————, *Racial Oppression in America,* Harper & Row, New York, 1972.

Bloom, Leonard, and Ruth Riemer, *Removal and Return: The Socioeconomic Effects of the War on Japanese-Americans,* University of California Press, Berkeley, 1949.

————, "Some Problems of Urbanization in South Africa," *Phylon,* 1964, **25,** 4, Winter, pp. 347–361.

————, *The Social Psychology of Race Relations,* Allen and Unwin, London, 1971.

Blue, John T., Jr., "Patterns of Racial Stratification: A Categoric Typology," *Phylon,* 1959, **20,** 4, Winter, pp. 364–371.

Blumberg, Leonard, "Segregated Housing, Marginal Location, and the Crisis of Confidence," *Phylon,* 1964, **25,** 4, Winter, pp. 321–330.

Blumer, Herbert, "Reflection on Theory of Race Relations," in A. W. Lind (ed.), *Race Relations in World Perspective,* University of Hawaii Press, Honolulu, 1955, pp. 3–21.

———, "Race Prejudice as a Sense of Group Position," *Pacific Sociological Review,* 1958, **1,** 1, Spring, pp. 3–7.

———, "Recent Research on Racial Relations: United States of America," *International Social Science Bulletin,* 1958, **10,** 3, p. 403.

Blumrosen, Alfred W., *Black Employment and the Law,* Rutgers University Press, New Brunswick, N.J., 1971.

Bock, Kenneth E., "Cultural Differences and Race," *Commentary,* 1957, **23,** 2, February, pp. 179–186.

Boesel, David, and Peter H. Rossi (eds.), *Cities under Seige: An Anatomy of the Ghetto Riots, 1964–1968,* Basic Books, New York, 1971.

Bogardus, Emory S., *Immigration and Race Attitudes,* Heath, Boston, 1928.

———, "The Japanese in Hawaii," *Sociology and Social Research,* **19,** 1935, pp. 562–569.

———, "Native Hawaiians and their Problems," *Sociology and Social Research,* **19,** 1935, pp. 259–265.

———, "Racial Distance Changes in the United States during the Past Thirty Years," *Sociology Social Research,* 1958, **43,** 2, November–December, pp. 127–135.

———, "Integration as a Current Concept," *Sociological Social Research,* 1958, **42,** 3, January–February, pp. 207–212.

———, "Race Reactions by Sexes," *Sociology and Social Research,* 1959, **43,** 6, July–August, pp. 439–441.

———, "Stages in White-Negro Relations in the United States," *Sociology and Social Research,* 1960, **45,** 1, October, pp. 74–79.

Boggs, James, *Racism and the Class Struggle: Further Pages from a Black Worker's Notebook,* Monthly Review Press, New York, 1970.

Boggs, Joan, "Hawaiian Adolescents and Their Families," in *Studies in a Hawaiian Community: Na Makamaka o Nanakuli,* Ronald Gallimore and Alan Howard (eds.), Honolulu, 1968, pp. 64–79.

Bonilla, Seda E., "Social Structure and Race Relations," *Social Forces,* 1961, **40,** 2, December, pp. 141–148.

Bosworth, Karl A., *Black Belt Country: Rural Government in the Cotton*

Country of Alabama, Bureau of Public Administration, University of Alabama, University, 1941.

Boxer, Charles R., *Race Relations in the Portuguese Colonial Empire, 1415–1825,* Clarendon Press, Oxford, 1963.

Bracey, John H., Jr., August Meier, and Elliott Rudwick, *Black Nationalism in America,* Bobbs-Merrill, Indianapolis, 1970.

Bradburn, Norman M., Seymour Sudman, and Galen L. Gockel, *Side by Side: Integrated Neighborhoods in America,* Quadrangle, Chicago, 1971.

Brady, Tom P., *Black Monday,* Association of Citizens' Councils, Winona, Miss., 1955.

Brink, William J., and Louis Harris, *Black and White: A Study of U.S. Racial Attitudes Today,* Simon and Schuster, New York, 1967.

Brooks, Alexander D., *Civil Rights and Liberties in the United States: An Annotated Bibliography,* Civil Liberties Educational Foundation, New York, 1962.

Brophy, William A., et al., *The Indian: America's Unfinished Business: Report,* 1st ed., University of Oklahoma Press, Norman, 1966.

Brotz, Howard, *The Black Jews of Harlem: Negro Nationalism and the Dilemmas of Negro Leadership,* Free Press of Glencoe, New York, 1964.

Brown, Barry S., and George W. Albee, "The Effect of Integrated Hospital Experiences on Racial Attitudes: A Discordant Note," *Social Problems,* 1966, **13,** 3, Winter, pp. 324–333.

Brown, Francis J., and Joseph S. Roucek, *Our Racial and National Minorities: Their History, Contributions, and Problems,* Prentice-Hall, New York, 1937.

———, and ———, *One America: The History, Contribution and Present Problems of Our Racial and National Minorities,* Prentice-Hall, New York, 1945.

Brown, Ina C., *Race Relations in a Democracy,* 1st ed., Harper, New York, 1949.

Buckley, W., *Sociology and Modern Systems Theory,* Prentice-Hall, Englewood Cliffs, N.J., 1967.

Bunch, Ralph E., *The Political Orientations of Japanese Americans,* Ph. D. thesis, University of Oregon, Eugene, 1968.

Bunche, Ralph J., *A World View of Race,* Kennikat Press, Port Washington, N.Y., 1936.

Burnstein, Eugene, and Adie V. McRae, "Some Effects of Shared Threat and Prejudice in Racially Mixed Groups," *Journal of Abnormal Social Psychology,* 1962, **64,** 4, April, pp. 257–263.

Burrows, E. G., *Hawaiian Americans: An Account of the Mingling of*

Japanese, Chinese, Polynesian and American Cultures, Yale University Press, New Haven, Conn., 1947.

Cable, George W., and Arlin Turner (eds.), *The Negro Question: A Selection of Writings on Civil Rights in the South,* Doubleday, Garden City, N.Y., 1958.

Caliver, Ambrose, *Education of Teachers for Improving Majority-Minority Relationships,* courses offered for teachers to learn about racial and national minority groups, U.S. Office of Education, U.S. Government Printing Office, Washington, D.C., 1944.

Calpin, G. H., (ed.), *The South African Way of Life: Values and Ideals of A Multi-Racial Society,* Columbia University Press, New York, 1953.

Campbell, Angus, *White Attitudes toward Black People,* Institute for Social Research, Ann Arbor, Mich., 1971.

———, and H. Schuman, "White Beliefs about Negroes," in M. L. Goldschmid (ed.), *Black Americans and White Racism,* Holt, New York, 1970.

Campbell, Byram, *American Race Theorists: A Critique of Their Thoughts and Methods,* Chapman and Grimes, Boston, 1952.

———, *Race and Social Revolution: Twenty-one Essays on Racial and Social Problems,* Truth Seeker, New York, 1958.

Campbell, John, *Negro-Mania,* Campbell and Power, Philadelphia, 1851; reprinted, Mnemosyne, Miami, 1969.

Cantor, Milton, *Black Labor in America,* Negro Universities Press, Westport, Conn., 1969.

Canty, Donald, *A Single Society: Alternatives to Urban Apartheid,* Praeger, New York, 1969.

Carmichael, Stokely S., and C. V. Hamilton, *Black Power: The Politics of Liberation in America,* Vintage Books, New York, 1967, chap. 1.

Carter, G. M., T. Karis, and N. M. Stultz, *South Africa's Transkei: The Politics of Domestic Colonialism,* Northwestern University Press, Evanston, Ill., 1967.

Carter, Robert L., et al., *Equality,* Pantheon, New York, 1965.

Carter, Thomas P., *Mexican Americans in School: A History of Educational Neglect,* College Entrance Examination Board, New York, 1970.

Caughey, John W., *McGillivray of the Creeks,* University of Oklahoma Press, Norman, 1938.

Chadwick-Jones, J. K., "Inter-Group Attitudes: A Stage in Attitude Formation," *British Journal of Sociology,* 1962, **13,** 1, March, pp. 57–63.

Chasteen, Edgar, "Who Favors Public Accommodations: A Demographic Analysis," *Sociological Quarterly,* 1968, **9**, 3, Summer, pp. 309–317.

Cheng, C. K., and Douglas S. Yamamura, "Interracial Marriage and Divorce in Hawaii," *Social Forces,* 1957, **36**, 1, October, pp. 77–84.

Child, Irvin L., *Italian or American? The Second Generation in Conflict,* Yale University Press, New Haven, Conn., 1943.

Cheyet, Stanley F. (ed.), *Lives and Voices: A Collection of American Jewish Memoirs,* 1st ed., Jewish Publication Society of America, Philadelphia, 1972.

Clark, Dennis, "Leadership Education in an All-White Neighborhood," *Journal of Intergroup Relations,* 1961–1962, **3**, 1, Winter, pp. 38–44.

———, *The Ghetto Game: Racial Conflicts in the City,* Sheed and Ward, New York, 1962.

Cleage, Albert B., Jr., *Black Christian Nationalism: New Directions for the Black Church,* Morrow, New York, 1972.

Cohen, George, *The Jews in the Making of America,* Stratford, Boston, 1924.

Cohen, Naomi W., *Not Free to Desist: The American Jewish Committee, 1906–1966,* Jewish Publication Society of America, Philadelphia, 1972.

Coleman, J. D., *Resources for Social Change: Race in the United States,* Wiley, New York, 1971.

Collins, Sydney, *Colored Minorities in Britain: Studies in British Race Relations Based on African, West Indian and Asiatic Immigrants,* Lutterworth Press, London, 1957.

Colton, Calvin, and A. H. Davis, *Tour of the American Lakes and Among the Indians of the North-west Territory in 1830,* University Microfilms, Ann Arbor, Mich., 1956.

Comas, Juan, "Recent Research on Racial Relations in Latin-America," *International Social Science Journal,* 1961, **13**, 2, pp. 271–299.

Comte, A., *The Positive Philosophy of Auguste Comte,* trans. H. Martineau, Blanchard, New York, 1855.

Conant, Melvin, *Race Issues on the World Scene: A Report on the Conference on Race Relations in World Perspective,* University of Hawaii Press, Honolulu, 1954.

Conrad, Earl, *The Invention of the Negro,* P. S. Eriksson, New York, 1966.

Cook, James G., *The Segregationists,* 1st ed., Appleton-Century-Crofts, New York, 1962.

Coser, L., *The Functions of Social Conflict,* Free Press of Glencoe, New York, 1956.

Cousins, E., et al., *South Carolinians Speak: A Moderate Approach to Race Relations,* Dillon, S.C., 1957.

Covello, Leonard, and Francesco Cordasco (eds.), *The Social Background of the Italo-American School Child,* Brill, Leiden, Netherlands, 1967.

Cox, Earnest S., *White America,* White America Society, Richmond, Va., 1923.

Cox, Oliver C., *Caste, Class, and Race: A Study in Social Dynamics,* Monthly Review Press, New York, 1959.

Craige, John H., *Black Bagdad,* Minton, New York, 1933.

Cramer, Richard M., "School Desegregation and New Industry: The Southern Community Leaders' Viewpoint," *Social Forces,* 1963, **41,** 4, May, pp. 384–389.

————, "Aspirations of Southern Youth: A Look at Racial Comparisons," *Research Preview,* 1965, **12,** 2, March, pp. 1–11.

Creger, Ralph, and Erwin L. McDonald, *A Look Down the Lonesome Road,* 1st ed., Doubleday, Garden City, N.Y., 1964.

Cronon, Edmund David, *Black Moses: The Story of Marcus Garvey and the Universal Negro Improvement Association,* University of Wisconsin Press, Madison, 1955.

Cross, Granville, J., "The Negro, Prejudice, and the Police," *Journal of Criminal Law, Criminology and Police Science,* 1964, **55,** 3, September, pp. 405–411.

Cross, Theodore L., *Black Capitalism: Strategy for Business in the Ghetto,* Atheneum, New York, 1969.

Crummel, Alexander, *Africa and America: Addresses and Discourses,* Mnemosyne, Miami, 1969.

Curry, Jesse E., and Glen D. King, *Race Tensions and the Police,* Charles C Thomas, Springfield, Ill., 1962.

Curtis, James C., and Lewis L. Gould (eds.), *The Black Experience in America: Selected Essays,* University of Texas Press, Austin, 1970.

Dabbs, James M., *The Southern Heritage,* 1st ed., Knopf, New York, 1958.

Dahlke, O, H., "Race and Minority Riots: A Study in the Typology of Violence," *Social Forces,* 1952, **30,** pp. 419–425.

Dahrendorf, R., *Class and Class Conflict in Industrial Society,* Stanford University Press, Stanford, Calif., 1959.

Dale, Edward E., *The Indians of the Southwest: A Century of Development under the United States,* 1st ed., University of Oklahoma Press, Norman, 1959.

Daly, Charles P., *The Settlement of Jews in North America,* Cowen, New York, 1893.

Daly, Charles U., (ed.), *Urban Violence,* University of Chicago Center for Policy Study, Chicago, 1969.

Daniel, Branford (ed.), *Black, White, and Gray: Twenty-one Points of View on the Race Question,* Sheed and Ward, New York, 1964.

Daniels, Roger, *The Politics of Prejudice, the Anti-Japanese Movement in California, and the Struggle for Japanese Exclusion,* University of California Press, Berkeley, 1962.

Davidson, Douglas, "Black Culture and Liberal Sociology," *Berkeley Journal of Sociology,* 1969, **14,** pp. 165–175.

Davis, Mac, *Jews Fight Too!* Jordan, New York, 1945.

Davis, Simon, *Race-Relations in Ancient Egypt: Greek, Egyptian, Hebrew, Roman,* Methuen, London, 1953.

Dean, John Peebles, and Alex Rosen, *A Manual of Intergroup Relations,* University of Chicago Press, Chicago, 1955.

DeFleur, Melvin L., and Frank R. Westie, "The Interpretation of Interracial Situations," *Social Forces,* 1959, **38,** 1, October, pp. 17–23.

DeFriese, Gordon H., and W. Scott Ford, "Verbal Attitudes, Overt Acts, and the Influence of Social Constraint in Interracial Behavior," *Social Problems,* 1969, **16,** 4, Spring, pp. 493–504.

Degler, C. N., *Neither Black nor White,* Macmillan, New York, 1971.

Deighton, H. S., "History and the Study of Race Relations," *Race,* 1959, **1,** 1, November, pp. 15–25.

Deloria, Vine, *Of Utmost Good Faith,* Straight Arrow Books, San Francisco, 1971.

Delos, Joseph T., et al., *Race, Nation, Person: Social Aspects of the Race Problem,* a symposium, Barnes & Noble, New York, 1944.

Dentler, Robert A., "Barriers to Northern School Desegregation," *Daedalus,* 1966, **95,** 1, Winter, pp. 45–62.

———, Bernard Mackler, and Mary Ellen Warshauer (eds.), *The Urban R's: Race Relations as the Problem in Urban Education,* Praeger, New York, 1967.

De Reuck, A., and Julie Knight, *Symposium on Caste and Race: Comparative Approaches,* Little, Brown, Boston, 1967.

De Vorsey, Louis, *The Indian Boundary in the Southern Colonies, 1763–1775,* University of North Carolina Press, Chapel Hill, 1966.

Dexter, Harriet Harmon, *What's Right with Race Relations,* 1st ed., Harper, New York, 1958.

Dixon, William H., *White Conquest,* Chatto and Windus, London, 1876.

Dixon, Vernon J., and Badi G. Foster (eds.), *Beyond Black or White: An Alternate America,* Little, Brown, Boston, 1971.

Dollard, J., *Caste and Class in a Southern Town,* Doubleday, Garden City, N.Y., 1957.

Doroshkin, Milton, *Yiddish in America: Social and Cultural Foundations,* Fairleigh Dickinson University Press, Rutherford, N.J., 1969.

Dowd, Jerome, *The Negro in American Life,* Century, New York, 1926.

Doyle, Bertram W., *The Etiquette of Race Relations in the South: A Study in Social Control,* University of Chicago Press, Chicago, 1937.

Drake, St. Clair, and Horace R. Cayton, *Black Metropolis: A Study of Negro Life in a Northern City,* Harcourt, Brace, New York, 1967.

Drimmer, Melvin, *Black History: A Reappraisal,* 1st ed., Doubleday, Garden City, N.Y., 1968.

Duberman, Martin, "Black Power in America," *Partisan Review,* 1968, **35,** 1, Winter, pp. 35–58.

Du Bois, Rachel (Davis) (ed.), *Build together Americans: Adventures in Intercultural Education for the Secondary School,* Hinds, Hayden and Eldridge, New York, 1945.

———, *Neighbors in Action: A Manual for Local Leaders in Intergroup Relations,* 1st ed., Harper, New York, 1950.

Du Bois, William E. B., *The Gift of Black Folk: The Negroes in the Making of America,* Stratford, Boston, 1924.

———, *Black Reconstruction,* Saifer, Philadelphia, 1935.

———, *Black Folk, Then and Now: An Essay in the History and Sociology of the Negro Race,* Henry Holt and Company, New York, 1939.

———, *Dusk of Dawn: An Essay toward an Autobiography of a Race Concept,* Harcourt, Brace, New York, 1940.

———, *The Philadelphia Negro: A Social Study,* B. Blom, New York, 1967.

Duker, Abraham G., "On Negro-Jewish Relations: A Contribution to a Discussion," *Jewish Social Studies,* 1965, **27,** 1, January pp. 18–22.

Dunbar, Ernest (ed.), *The Black Expatriates: A Study of American Negroes in Exile,* 1st ed., Dutton, New York, 1968.

Duncan, Patrick B., "Is Apartheid an Insoluble Problem?" *Race,* 1965, **6,** 4, April, pp. 263–266.

Durham, Laird, *Black Capitalism,* Communication Service Corporation, Washington, D.C., 1970.

Durkheim, E., *The Elementary Forms of Religious Life,* trans. J. Swain, Macmillan, New York, 1926.

Dykeman, Wilma, and James Stokely, *Neither Black nor White,* Rinehart, New York, 1957.

————, and ————, *Seeds of Southern Change: The Life of Will Alexander,* University of Chicago Press, Chicago, 1962.

————, *Prophet of Plenty: The First Ninety Years of W. D. Weatherford,* 1st ed., University of Tennessee Press, Knoxville, 1966.

Edlefsen, J. B., "Social Distance Attitudes of Negro College Students," *Phylon,* 1956, **17,** 1, March, pp. 79–83.

Edwards, Harry, *The Revolt of the Black Athlete,* Free Press, New York, 1969.

————, *Black Students,* Free Press, New York, 1970, pp. 205–227.

Egerton, John, *A Mind to Stay Here: Profiles from the South,* Macmillan, New York, 1970.

Ehrlich, Howard J., "Stereotyping and Negro-Jewish Stereotypes," *Social Forces,* 1962, **41,** 2, pp. 171–176.

Eitzen, D. S., "Status Inconsistency and Wallace Support," *Social Forces,* 1970, **48,** pp. 493–498.

Ellis, Richard N., *General Pope and U. S. Indian Policy,* University of New Mexico Press, Albuquerque, 1970.

Embree, Edwin R., *Brown Americans: The Story of a Tenth of the Nation,* Viking, New York, 1944.

Endler, Norman S., and Elizabet Hoy, "Conformity as Related to Reinforcement and Social Pressure," *Journal of Personality and Social Psychology,* 1967, **7,** 2, October, pp. 197–202.

Epstein, Benjamin R., and Arnold Forster, *Some of My Best Friends . . . ,* Farrar, Straus & Cudahy, New York, 1962.

Epstein, Edwin M., and David R. Hampton, Black Americans and White Business, Dickenson, Encino, Calif., 1971.

Erikson, E., "The Concept of Identity in Race Relations," *Daedalus,* Winter, 1966.

Erskine, Hazel, "The Polls: World Opinion of U.S. Racial Problems," *Public Opinion Quarterly,* 1968, **32,** 2, Summer, pp. 299–312.

Essien-Udom, Essien U., *Black Nationalism: A Search for an Identity in America,* University of Chicago Press, Chicago, 1962.

Ets, Marie Hall, *Rosa: The Life of an Italian Immigrant,* University of Minnesota Press, Minneapolis, 1970.

Etzioni, Amitai, "The Ghetto: A Re-evaluation," *Social Forces,* 1959, **37,** 3, March, pp. 255–262.

Evans, M. S., *Black and White in the Southern States: A Study of the*

Race Problem in the United States from a South African Point of View, Longmans, London, 1915.

Eysenck, Hans Jugen, *Race, Intelligence and Education,* Temple Smith, London, 1971.

Fager, Charles E., *White Reflections on Black Power,* Eerdmans, Grand Rapids, Mich., 1967.

————, *Uncertain Resurrection: The Poor People's Washington Campaign,* Eerdmans, Grand Rapids, Mich., 1969.

Fauset, Arthur H., *Black Gods of the Metropolis: Negro Religious Cults of the Urban North,* University of Pennsylvania Press, Philadelphia, 1944.

Federal Writers' Project: *The Italians of New York,* Arno, New York, 1969.

Feldman, Herman, *Racial Factors in American Industry,* Harper, New York, 1931.

Feldstein, Stanley, *The Poisoned Tongue: A Documentary History of American Racism and Prejudice,* Morrow, New York, 1971.

Fernandes, Florestan, "La Persistencia del Pasado," *Revista Mexicana de Sociologia,* 1966, **28,** 4, October–December, pp. 787–812.

Fendrich, James M., "Perceived Reference Group Support: Racial Attitudes and Overt Behavior," *American Sociological Review,* 1967, **32,** 6, December, pp. 960–969.

Fey, Harold E., and D'Arcy McNickle, *Indians and Other Americans: Two Ways of Life Meet,* 1st ed., Harper, New York, 1959.

Fisher, John H., "Race and Reconciliation: The Role of the School," *Daedalus,* 1966, **14,** pp. 24–43.

Fisher, Sethard, "Review Essay: Negro Life and Social Process," *Social Problems,* 1966, **13,** 3, Winter, pp. 343–353.

————, *Power and the Black Community: A Reader on Racial Subordination in the United States,* Random House, New York, 1970.

Flavin, Martin, *Black and White: From the Cape to the Congo,* Harper, New York, 1950.

Flowers, Montaville, *The Japanese Conquest of American Opinion,* Doran, New York, 1917.

Fogel, Walter, *Education and Income of Mexican-Americans in the Southwest,* University at Los Angeles, Mexican-American Study Project, Report No. 1, Los Angeles, 1965.

Forbes, Jack D., *The Indian in America's Past,* Prentice-Hall, Englewood Cliffs, N.J., 1964.

————, "Race and Color in Mexican-American Problems," *Journal of Human Relations,* 1968, **16,** pp. 55–68.

Forman, Robert E., *Black Ghettos, White Ghettos, and Slums,* Prentice-Hall, Englewood Cliffs, N.J., 1971.

Forster, Arnold, *A Measure of Freedom: An Anti-Defamation League Report,* Doubleday, Garden City, N.Y., 1950.

————, and Benjamin E. Epstein, *The Trouble-makers: An Anti-Defamation League Report,* Doubleday, Garden City, N.Y., 1952.

Fortune, Timothy T., *Black and White: Land, Labor, and Politics in the South,* Arno, New York, 1968.

Franklin, John H., *Color and Race,* Houghton Mifflin, Boston, 1968.

Frazier, E. Franklin, "Sociological Theory and Race Relations," *American Sociological Review,* 1947, **12,** pp. 265–271.

————, "Areas of Research in Race Relations," *Sociology and Social Research,* 1948, **42,** 6, July–August, pp. 424–429.

————, "Race Relations in World Perspective," *Sociology and Social Research,* 1957, **41,** pp. 331–335.

————, *Black Bourgeoisie,* Free Press, Glencoe, Ill., 1957.

————, *Race and Culture Contacts in the Modern World,* 1st ed., Knopf, New York, 1957.

————, and G. Franklin Edwards (eds.), *On Race Relations: Selected Writings,* University of Chicago Press, Chicago, 1968.

Frederickson, George M., *The Black Image in the White Mind: The Debate on Afro-American Character and Destiny, 1817–1914.* Harper & Row, New York, 1971.

Freed, Leonard, *Black in White America,* Grossman, New York, 1969.

Freyre, G., *Brazil: An Interpretation,* Knopf, New York, 1945.

————, *The Masters and the Slaves: A Study in the Development of Brazilian Civilization,* Knopf, New York, 1946.

————, *The Mansions and the Shanties: The Making of Modern Brazil,* Knopf, New York, 1963.

Friedman, Lawrence J., *The White Savage: Racial Fantasies in the Postbellum South,* Prentice-Hall, Englewood Cliffs, N.J., 1970.

Friends, Society of (American Friends Service Committee), *Race and Conscience in America,* a review prepared for the American Friends Service Committee by an authorized working party, University of Oklahoma Press, Norman, 1959.

Fritz, Henry E., *The Movement for Indian Assimilation, 1860–1890,* University of Pennsylvania Press, Philadelphia, 1963.

Furnas, Joseph C., *Goodbye to Uncle Tom,* Sloane, New York, 1956.

Furtado, C., *Diagnosis of the Brazilian Crisis,* University of California Press, Berkeley, 1965.

Gaines, George S., *Dancing Rabbit Creek Treaty,* Birmingham Printing Company, Birmingham, Ala., 1928.

Gallagher, Buell G., *American Caste and the Negro College,* Columbia University Press, New York, 1938.

———, *Color and Conscience: The Irrepressible Conflict,* Harper, New York, 1946.

Gallimore, Ronald, and Alan Howard (eds.), *Studies in a Hawaiian Community: Na makamaka o Nanakuli,* Pacific Anthropological Records No. 1, Honolulu, 1968.

Gardner, Arthur L., *The Koreans in Hawaii: An Annotated Bibliography,* University of Hawaii, Social Science Research Institute, Hawaii Series No. 2, Honolulu, 1970.

Garn, Stanley M. (ed.), *Readings on Race,* Charles C Thomas, Springfield, Ill., 1960.

———, *Human Races,* Charles C Thomas, Springfield, Ill., 1961.

Garrison, Karl C., Jr., "The Behavior of Clergy on Racial Integration as Related to a Childhood Socialization Factor," *Sociology and Social Research,* 1967, **51,** 2, January, pp. 208–219.

Gayle, Addison, *The Black Situation,* Horizon Press, New York, 1970.

Geschwender, J. A., "Explorations in the Theory of Social Movements and Revolutions," *Social Forces,* 1968, **47,** 2, pp. 127–136.

Gessner, Robert, *Massacre: A Survey of Today's American Indian,* J. Cape and H. Smith, New York, 1931.

Giddens, Anthony, "The Psychology of Race Riots," *New Society,* 1964, **69,** January 23, pp. 10–11.

Gilbert, Arthur, *A Jew in Christian America,* Sheed and Ward, New York, 1966.

Gilmer, John N., "A Protestant Church in Honolulu," *Social Process in Hawaii,* **16,** pp. 40–47.

Ginzberg, Eli (ed.), "The Negro Challenge to the Business Community," McGraw-Hill, New York, 1964.

Girdner, Audrie, and Anne Loftis, *The Great Betrayal: The Evacuation of the Japanese-Americans during World War II,* Macmillan, London, 1969.

Gist, Noel P., "Conditions of Inter-group Relations: The Anglo-Indians," *International Journal of Comparative Sociology,* 1967, **8,** 2, September, pp. 199–208.

Glanz, Rudolf, *Jew and Italian: Historic Group Relations and the New Immigration,* Ktav Publishing House, New York, 1970.

———, *Studies in Judaica Americana,* Ktav Publishing House, New York, 1970.

Glaser, Daniel, "Dynamics of Ethnic Identification," *American Sociological Review*, 1958, **23**, 1, February, pp. 31–40.

Glazer, Nathan, "Blacks and Ethnic Groups: The Difference and the Political Difference It Makes," *Social Problems*, 1971, **18**, 4, Spring, pp. 444–461.

Glick, Clarence E., "A Haole's Changing Conceptions of Japanese in Hawaii," *Social Process in Hawaii*, **14**, 1950, pp. 1–10.

Gluckman, M., *Custom and Conflict in Africa*, Blackwell, Oxford, 1955.

Goldberg, Israel, *The Jews in America: A History*, World Publishing, Cleveland, 1954.

Goldsby, Richard A., *Race and Races*, Macmillan, New York, 1971.

Goldstein, Israel, *Transition Years: New York—Jerusalem, 1960–1962*, Jerusalem, Rubin, Mass., 1962.

Gonzalez, Nancie L., *The Spanish-Americans of New Mexico: A Heritage of Pride*, University of New Mexico Press, Albuquerque, 1969.

Goodman, Mary Ellen, *Race Awareness in Young Children*, Collier Books, New York, 1964.

Gossett, Thomas F., *Race: The History of an Idea in America*, Southern Methodist University Press, Dallas, 1963.

Gottlieb, David, and Warren O. TenHouten, "Racial Composition and the Social Systems of Three High Schools," *Journal of Marriage and the Family*, 1965, **27**, 2, May, pp. 204–212.

Grebler, Leo, "The Naturalization of Mexican Immigrants in the United States," *International Migration Review*, 1966, **1**, 1, Fall, pp. 17–32.

———, et al., *The Mexican-American People: The Nation's Second Largest Minority*, Free Press, New York, 1970.

Gregor, A. James, "Black Nationalism," *Science and Society*, 1963, **27**, 4, Fall, pp. 415–432.

Gregor, A. L., "Race Relations, Frustration and Aggression," *Revue Internationale de Sociologie*, 1965, **2**, 2, December, pp. 90–112.

Greenberg, Jack, *Race Relations and American Law*, Columbia University Press, New York, 1959.

Greer, Scott A., *Last Man In: Racial Access to Union Power*, Free Press, Glencoe, Ill., 1959.

Grier, W. H., and P. M. Cobbs, *Black Rage*, Bantam Books, New York, 1968, chap. 6.

Griggs, Sutton E., *Wisdom's Call*, Orion Publishing, Nashville, Tenn., 1969.

Grimshaw, Allen D., "Lawlessness and Violence in America and Their Special Manifestations in Changing Negro-White Relationships," *Journal of Negro History*, 1959, **54**, 1, January, pp. 52–72.

———, "Relationships among Prejudice, Discrimination, Social Tension and Social Violence," *Journal of Intergroup Relations,* 1961, **2,** 4, August, pp. 302–310.

———, "Police Agencies and the Prevention of Racial Violence," *Journal of Criminal Law, Criminology, and Police Science,* 1963, **54,** 1, March, pp. 110–113.

——— (ed.), *Racial Violence in the United States,* Aldine, Chicago, 1969.

Grodzins, Morton, *Americans Betrayed: Politics and the Japanese Evacuation,* University of Chicago Press, Chicago, 1949.

Gross, Feliks, *World Politics and Tension Areas,* New York University Press, New York, 1966.

Guttman, Louis, "A Structural Theory for Intergroup Beliefs and Action," *American Sociological Review,* 1959, **24,** 3, June, pp. 318–328.

Hagan, William T., *American Indians,* University of Chicago Press, Chicago, 1961.

Haller, John S., Jr., *Outcasts from Evolution: Scientific Attitudes of Racial Inferiority, 1859–1900,* University of Illinois Press, Chicago, 1971.

Halpern, Ben, *Jews and Blacks: The Classic American Minorities,* Herder and Herder, New York, 1971.

Halstead, Michael, "Race, Class and Power: A Paradigm of the Means of Power for the Negro American," *Human Mosaic,* 1968, **2,** 2, Spring, pp. 133–146.

Hamblin, Robert L., "The Dynamics of Racial Discrimination," *Social Problems,* 1962, **10,** 2, Fall, pp. 103–121.

Hammond, Harley Ross, "Race, Social Mobility and Politics in Brazil," *Race,* 1963, **4,** 2, May, pp. 3–13.

Hamnett, Ian, "The Maseru Stockfell Club: A Multi-Racial Experiment in Southern Africa," *Race,* 1966, **8,** 2, October, pp. 175–184.

Handlin, Oscar, *Race and Nationality in American Life,* 1st ed., Little, Brown, Boston, 1957.

Harding, John, and Russell Hogrefe, "Attitudes of White Department Store Employees toward Negro Co-Workers," *Journal of Social Issues,* 1952, **8,** pp. 18–28.

Harlan, Louis R., *Separate and Unequal: Public School Campaigns and Racism in the Southern Seaboard States 1901–1915,* The University of North Carolina, Chapel Hill, 1958.

Harmon, George D., *Sixty Years of Indian Affairs, Political, Economic, and Diplomatic, 1789–1850,* University of North Carolina Press, Chapel Hill, 1941.

Harris, Edward E., "Family and Student Identities: An Exploratory Study in Self and 'We-Group' Attitudes," *Journal of Negro Education,* 1965, **34,** 1, Winter, pp. 17–22.

———, "Racial and National Identities: An Exploratory Study in Self and 'We-Group' Attitudes," *Journal of Negro Education,* 1965, **34,** 4, Fall, pp. 425–430.

Harris, Louis, and Bert E. Swanson, *Black-Jewish Relations in New York City,* Praeger, New York, 1970.

Harris, Marvin, and Conrad Kottak, "The Structural Significance of Brazilian Racial Categories," *Sociologia,* 1963, **25,** 3, September, pp. 203–208.

Harris, Richard E., *Delinquency in Our Democracy,* Wetzel, Los Angeles, 1954.

Hart, Albert B., *The Southern South,* Association Press, New York, 1911.

Haselden, Kyle, *The Racial Problem in Christian Perspective,* 1st ed., Harper, New York, 1959.

———, and Elizabeth Haselden, "Racial Tension: Enemy and Ally," *Dialog,* 1964, **3,** pp. 107–111.

Hayashi, W., "Countering Our Pearl Harbor Mentality," *Hawaii Pono Journal,* 1971, **1,** pp. 46–58.

Hayden, Thomas, *Rebellion in Newark: Official Violence and Ghetto Response,* Random House, New York, 1967.

Haynes, George E., *The Trend of the Races,* Council of Women for Home Missions and Missionary Education Movement of the U.S. and Canada, New York, 1922.

Hays, Brooks, *A Southern Moderate Speaks,* University of North Carolina Press, Chapel Hill, 1959.

Height, Dorothy I., *Step by Step with Interracial Groups,* Woman's Press, New York, 1948.

Heller, Celia S., and Alphonso Pinkney, "The Attitudes of Negroes toward Jews," *Social Forces,* 1965, **43,** 3, March, pp. 364–369.

Helper, Hinton R., *Miscegenation: The Theory of the Blending of the Races, Applied to the American White Man and Negro,* H. Dexter, Hamilton, New York, 1864.

Herbers, John, *The Lost Priority: What Happened to the Civil Rights Movement in America?* Funk & Wagnalls, New York, 1970.

Herman, Reg, "Power and Prejudice: A Survey and A Hypothesis," *Journal of Human Relations,* 1969, **17,** 1, pp. 1–11.

Herman, Simon N., and Erling Schild, "Ethnic Role Conflict in A Cross-Cultural Situation," *Human Relations,* 1960, **13,** 3, August, pp. 215–228.

Hernton, Calvin C., *Sex and Racism in America: An Analysis of the Influence of Sex on the Race Problem*, Doubleday, Garden City, N.Y., 1965.

———, *Coming Together: Black Power, White Hatred, and Sexual Hang-ups*, Random House, New York, 1971.

Hesslink, George K., *Black Neighbors: Negroes in a Northern Rural Community*, Bobbs-Merrill, Indianapolis, 1968.

Higbee, Jay A., *Development and Administration of the New York State Law against Discrimination*, University of Alabama Press, University, 1966.

Higginson, Thomas W., *Black Rebellion: A Selection from Travellers and Outlaws*, Arno, New York, 1969.

Hill, John L., *Negro: National Asset or Liability?* Literary Associates, New York, 1930.

Hill, Roy L., *Rhetoric of Racial Revolt*, Golden Bell Press, Denver, 1964.

Hills, Stuart L., "Are Negroes Just Another Immigrant Group?" *Discourse*, 1968, **11**, 4, Autumn, pp. 450–459.

Himes, Joseph S., "Negro Teen-Age Culture," *AAAPSS*, 1962, **338**, November, pp. 91–101.

Hiro, Dilip, *Black British, White British*, Eyre and Spottiswoode, London, 1971.

Hirshson, Stanley P., *Farewell to the Bloody Shirt: Northern Republicans and the Southern Negro, 1877–1893*, Indiana University Press, Bloomington, 1962.

Hooker, Robert W., *Displacement of Black Teachers in the Eleven Southern States*, Race Relations Information Center, Nashville, Tenn., 1970.

Hoopes, A. W., *Indian Affairs and Their Administration: With Special Reference to the Far West, 1849–1880*, University of Pennsylvania Press, Philadelphia, 1932.

Hormann, Bernhard L., *Community Forces in Hawaii*, University of Hawaii, Honolulu, 1956.

Horowitz, I. L., *Revolution in Brazil: Politics and Society in a Developing Nation*, Dutton, New York, 1964.

Horsman, Reginald, *Expansion and American Indian Policy, 1783–1812*, Michigan State University Press, East Lansing, 1967.

Horton, James A. B. (ed.), *Black Nationalism in Africa, 1867*, Africana Publishing, New York, 1969.

Hotopf, W. H. N., "Psychological Studies of Race Prejudice," *Political Quarterly*, 1961, **32**, 4, October–December, pp. 328–340.

Hourani, A., "The Concept of Race Relations: Thoughts after a Conference," *International Social Science Bulletin,* 1955, **7**, 2, pp. 335–340.

Howard, Alan, and Ronald Gallimore (eds.), "Adoption and the Significance of Children to Hawaiian Families," in *Studies in a Hawaiian Community: Na Makamaka o Nanakuli,* Pacific Anthropological Records No. 1, Honolulu, 1968, pp. 87–101.

Howe, Russell W., "Prejudice, Superstition and Economics," *Phylon,* 1956, **17**, 3, October, pp. 215–226.

Hughes, Everett C., and Helen MacGill Hughes, *Where Peoples Meet: Racial and Ethnic Frontiers,* Free Press, Glencoe, Ill., 1952.

Hughes, Everett C., "Race Relations and the Sociological Imagination," *American Sociological Review,* 1963, **28**, 6, December, pp. 879–890.

Humphrey, Seth K., *The Racial Prospect: A Re-Writing and Expansion of the Author's Book 'Mankind,'* Scribner, New York, 1920.

Hunter, Guy, *Industrialisation and Race Relations: A Symposium,* Oxford University Press, New York, 1965.

Huszar, George B., *Anatomy of Racial Intolerance,* H. W. Wilson, New York, 1946.

Hutchinson, Harry W., *Village and Plantation Life in Northeastern Brazil,* University of Washington Press, Seattle, 1957.

Hutt, William H., *The Economics of the Colour Bar: A Study of the Economic Origins and Consequences of Racial Segregation in South Africa,* A. Deutsch, London, 1964.

Ianni, Octavio, "A Ideologia Racial Do Negro E Do Mulato Em Florianopolis," *Sociologia,* 1958, **20**, 3, August, pp. 352–365.

Ichihashi, Yamato, *Japanese in the United States: A Critical Study of the Problems of the Japanese Immigrants and Their Children,* Stanford University Press, Stanford, Calif., 1932.

Ingle, Dwight J., "Racial Differences and the Future," *Science,* 1964, **146**, 3642, October 16, pp. 375–379.

Insko, Chester A., and James E. Robinson, "Belief Similarity versus Race as Determinants of Reactions to Negroes by Southern White Adolescents: A Further Test of Rokeach's Theory," *Journal of Personality and Social Psychology,* 1967, **7**, 2, October, pp. 216–221.

Ireland, Ralph R., "The Role of Economic Motivation in Ethnic Relations," *Sociology and Social Research,* 1958, **43**, 2, November–December, pp. 119–126.

Irish, Donald P., "Reactions of Caucasian Residents to Japanese-American Neighbors," *Journal of Social Issues,* 1952, **8**, pp. 10–17.

Irvine, Keith, *The Rise of the Colored Races,* Norton, New York, 1970.

Issacs, Harold R., "World Affairs and U.S. Race Relations: A Note on Little Rock," *Public Opinion Quarterly,* 1958, **22,** 3, Fall, pp. 364–370.

Jacobs, Paul, Saul Landau, and Eve Pell, *To Serve the Devil,* Random House, New York, 1971.

Jacobs, Wilbur R., *Diplomacy and Indian Gifts: Anglo-French Rivalry Along the Ohio and Northwest Frontiers, 1748–1763,* Stanford University Press, Stanford, Calif., 1950.

———, *Wilderness Politics and Indian Gifts: The Northern Colonial Frontier, 1748–1763,* University of Nebraska Press, Lincoln, 1966.

Jamal, Hakim A., *From the Dead Level: Malcom X and Me,* A. Deutsch, London, 1971.

Janis, Irving L., and Daniel Katz, "The Reduction of Intergroup Hostility: Research Problems and Hypothesis," *Journal of Conflict Resolution,* 1959, **3,** 1, March, pp. 85–100.

Janowitz, Morris, *Social Control of Escalated Riots,* Center for Policy Study, University of Chicago, Chicago, 1968.

Janowsky, Oscar I. (ed.), *The American Jew: A Reappraisal,* 1st ed., Jewish Publication Society of America, Philadelphia, 1964.

Javits, Jacob K., *Discrimination: U.S.A.,* 1st ed., Harcourt, Brace, New York, 1960.

Jeffries, Vincent, and H. Edward Ransford, "Interracial Social Contact and Middle-Class White Reactions to the Watts Riot," *Social Problems,* 1969, **16,** 3, Winter, pp. 312–324.

Jensen, A. R., "How Much Can We Boost I.Q. and Scholastic Achievement?" *Harvard Educational Review,* **39,** 1969.

Jiobu, R. M., and H. H. Marshall, "Urban Structure and the Differentiation between Blacks and Whites," *American Sociological Review,* 1971, **36,** pp. 638–649.

Johnson, Charles R., *Black Humor,* Johnson Publishing, Chicago, 1970.

Johnson, Charles Spurgeon, *The Negro in American Civilization: A Study of Negro Life and Race Relations in the Light of Social Research,* Henry Holt and Company, New York, 1930.

———, *Patterns of Negro Segregation,* Harper, New York, 1943.

Johnson, David C., "White Resistance to Racial Integration," *Dialog,* 1964, **3,** pp. 112–117.

Johnson, Guy B., "Racial Integration in Southern Higher Education," *Social Forces,* 1956, **34,** 4, May, pp. 309–312.

Jones, LeRoi, *Raise, Race, Rays, Raze: Essays Since 1965,* Random House, New York, 1971.

Jones, M. H., and A. Willingham, "The White Custodians of the Black Experience," *Social Science Quarterly,* 1970, **51,** 1, pp. 31–36.

Joseph, Samuel, *Jewish Immigration to the United States from 1881 to 1910,* Arno, New York, 1914.

Josey, Charles C., *Race and National Solidarity,* Scribner, New York, 1923.

Kahane, Meir, *Never Again! A Program for Survival,* Nashville Publishers, Nashville, Tenn., 1971.

Kain, John F. (ed.), *Race and Poverty: The Economics of Discrimination,* Prentice-Hall, Englewood Cliffs, N.J., 1969.

Katz, Daniel: "Consistent Reactive Participation of Group Members and Reduction of Intergroup Conflict," *Journal of Conflict Resolution,* 1959, **3,** 1, March, pp. 28–40.

Katz, Irwin, *Conflict and Harmony in an Adolescent Interracial Group,* New York University Press, New York, 1955.

———, and Patricia Gurin (eds.), *Race and the Social Sciences,* Basic Books, New York, 1969.

Katzman, Martin T., "Opportunity, Subculture, and the Economic Performance of Urban Ethnic Groups," *American Journal of Economics and Sociology,* 1969, **28,** 4, October, pp. 351–366.

Kelly, Arthur R., *Physical Anthropology of a Mexican Population in Texas: A Study in Race-Mixture,* New Orleans Middle American Research Institute, Tulane University of Louisiana, New Orleans, 1947.

Kertzer, Morris N., *Today's American Jew,* 1st ed., McGraw-Hill, New York, 1967.

Kennedy, Robert E., *Black Cameos,* Boni, New York, 1924.

Kennedy, S., *Southern Exposure,* Doubleday, Garden City, N.Y., 1946.

———, *Jim Crow Guide to the U.S.A.: The Laws, Customs and Etiquette Governing the Conduct of Nonwhites and Other Minorities as Second-Class Citizens,* Lawrence and Wishart, London, 1959.

Kerlin, Robert T., *The Voice of the Negro, 1919,* Dutton, New York, 1920.

Kidd, J. S., and Donald T. Campbell, "Conformity to Groups as a Function of Group Success," *Journal of Abnormal Social Psychology,* 1955, **51,** 3, November, pp. 390–393.

Kiell, Norman, *The Psychodynamics of American Jewish Life: An Anthology,* Twayne, New York, 1967.

Killian, Lewis M., and Charles Grigg, *Racial Crisis in America: Leadership in Conflict,* Prentice-Hall, Englewood Cliffs, N.J., 1964.

———, *White Southerners,* Random House, New York, 1970.

King, Larry L., *Confessions of a White Racist,* Viking, New York, 1971.

Kinloch, G. C., "Social Types and Race Relations in the Colonial Setting: A Case Study of Rhodesia," *Phylon,* 1972, third quarter, pp. 276–289.

———, *The Sociological Study of South Africa: An Introduction,* Macmillan, Johannesburg, So. Africa, 1972.

———, and J. Borders, "Racial Stereotypes and Social Distance among Elementary School Children in Hawaii," *Sociology and Social Research,* 1972, **56,** pp. 368–377.

———, "Race, Socioeconomic Status, and Social Distance in Hawaii," *Sociology and Social Research,* 1973, **57.**

Kinney, Jay P., *A Continent Lost—A Civilization Won: Indian Land Tenure in America,* Johns Hopkins, Baltimore, 1937.

Kitagawa, Daisuke, *Issei and Niesi: The Internment Years,* Seabury, New York, 1967.

Kitano, Harry L., *Japanese Americans: The Evolution of a Subculture,* Prentice-Hall, Englewood Cliffs, N.J., 1969.

Klineberg, Otto, "The Multi-National Society: Some Research Problems," *Social Science Information,* 1967, **6,** 6, December, pp. 81–99.

Kneale, Albert H., *Indian Agent,* Caxton, Caldwell, Idaho, 1950.

Knox, Robert, *The Races of Men: A Fragment,* Lea and Blanchard, Philadelphia, Penn., 1850; reprinted by Mnemosyne, Miami, 1969.

Kogan, Lawrence A., "The Jewish Conception of Negroes in the North: An Historical Approach," *Phylon,* 1967, **28,** 4, Winter, pp. 376–385.

Kohn, Melvin L., and Robin M. Williams, Jr., "Situational Patterning in Intergroup Relations," *American Sociological Review,* 1956, **21,** 2, April, pp. 164–174.

Kovarsky, Irving, and William Albrecht, *Black Employment: The Impact of Religion, Economic Theory, Politics, and Law,* Iowa State University Press, Ames, 1970.

Kovel, Joel, *White Racism: A Psychohistory,* Pantheon, New York, 1970.

Kramer, Judith R., and Seymour Leventman, *Children of the Gilded Ghetto: Conflict Resolutions of Three Generations of American Jews,* Yale University Press, New Haven, Conn., 1961.

Kren, George M., "Race and Ideology," *Phylon,* 1962, **23,** 2, Summer, pp. 167–176.

Kronus, Sidney, *The Black Middle Class,* Merrill, Columbus, Ohio, 1971.

Kuper, Leo, Hilstan Watts, and Ronald Davies, *Durban: A Study in Racial Ecology,* Columbia University Press, New York, 1958.

———, "Racialism and Integration in South African Society," *Race,* 1963, **4,** 2, May, pp. 26–31.

————, "The Problem of Violence in South Africa," *Inquiry,* 1964, **7**, 3, Autumn, pp. 295–303.

Kuttner, Robert E. (ed.), *Race,* Social Science Press, New York, 1967.

Lacy, Leslie A., *The Rise and Fall of a Proper Negro: An Autobiography,* Macmillan, New York, 1970.

LaFarge, Oliver, *As Long as The Grass Shall Grow,* Alliance Book Corporation, New York, 1940.

Lai, Kum Pui, "Fifty Aged Puerto Ricans," *Social Process in Hawaii,* 1936, **2**, pp. 24–27.

Land, K. C., "Formal Theory," in H. L. Costner (ed.), *Sociological Methodology, 1971,* Jossey-Bass, San Francisco, 1971, pp. 175–220.

Landes, Ruth, "Biracialism in American Society: A Comparative View," *American Anthropology,* 1955, **57**, 6, December, pp. 1253–1263.

Lapides, Frederick R., and David J. Burrows (eds.), *Racism: A Casebook,* Thomas Y. Crowell, New York, 1971.

Larsson, Clotye Murdock (ed.), *Marriage across the Color Line,* Johnson Publishing, Chicago, 1965.

Latham, Henry, *Black and White: A Journal of a Three Months' Tour in the United States,* Lippincott, Philadelphia, 1867.

Laue, James H., and Leon M. McCorkle, Jr., "The Association of Southern Women for the Prevention of Lynching: A Commentary on the Role of the 'Moderate,' " *Sociological Inquiry,* 1965, **35**, 1, Winter, pp. 80–93.

Laurence, J. E., "White Socialization—Black Reality," *Psychiatry,* 1970, **33**, 2, May, 174–194.

Lawinson, Paul, *Race, Class, and Party: A History of Negro Suffrage and White Politics in the South,* Oxford University Press, New York, 1932.

Le Conte, Joseph, *The Race Problem in the South,* Mnemosyne, Miami, 1969.

Lee, Frank, "A Cross-Institutional Comparison of Northern and Southern Race Relations," *Sociology and Social Research,* 1958, **42**, 3, January–February, pp. 185–191.

————, "Social Controls in British Race Relations," *Sociology and Social Research,* 1960, **44**, 5, May–June, pp. 326–334.

————, *Negro and White in Connecticut Town,* Bookman Associates, New York, 1961.

Lefton, Mark, "Race, Expectations and Anomia," *Social Forces,* 1968, **46**, 3, March, pp. 347–352.

Leighton, Alexander H., *The Governing of Men: General Principles and Recommendations Based on Experience at a Japanese Relocation Camp,* Princeton University Press, Princeton, N.J., 1945.

Le Melle, Tilden J., and Wilbert J. Le Melle, *The Black College: A Strategy for Achieving Relevancy,* Praeger, New York, 1969.

Lester, Julius, *Look Out, Whitey! Black Power's Gon' Get Your Mama!* Dial, New York, 1968.

Lever, Henry, "An Experimental Modification of Social Distance in South Africa," *Human Relations,* 1965, **18,** 2, May, pp. 149–154.

Lewin, J., "Power, Law, and Race Relations in South Africa," *Political Quarterly,* 1959, **30,** 4, October–December, pp. 389–399.

Lieberman, L., "The Debate over Race: A Study in the Sociology of Knowledge," *Phylon,* 1968, **29,** 127–142.

Lieberson, Stanley, "The Impact of Residential Segregation on Ethnic Assimilation," *Social Forces,* 1961, **40,** 1, October, pp. 52–58.

———, "A Societal Theory of Race and Ethnic Relations," *American Sociological Review,* 1961, **26,** pp. 902–910.

———, and A. R. Silverman, "The Precipitants and Underlying Conditions of Race Riots," *American Sociological Review,* 1965, **30,** pp. 887–898.

Lightfoot, Claude M., *Ghetto Rebellion to Black Liberation,* 1st ed., International Publishers, New York, 1968.

Lincoln, Charles E., *The Black Muslims in America,* Beacon Press, Boston, 1961.

———, *My Face Is Black,* Beacon Press, Boston, 1864.

Lind, Andrew W., *Hawaii's Japanese: An Experiment in Democracy,* Princeton University Press, Princeton, N.J., 1946.

———, *Hawaii's People,* University of Hawaii Press, Honolulu, 1955.

———, "Interracial Marriage as Affecting Divorce in Hawaii," *Sociology and Social Research,* 1964, **49,** pp. 17–26.

———, "Race Relations in the Islands of the Pacific," in *Research on Racial Relations,* UNESCO, Paris, 1966, pp. 229–248.

———, "Towards a Theory of Race Relations," paper presented to the Social Science Seminar, University of Singapore, September 23, 1969 (mimeographed).

———, *Hawaii: The Last of the Magic Isles,* Oxford University Press, London, 1969.

Lindquist, Gustavus E. E., *The Indian in American Life,* Friendship Press, New York, 1944.

Lippitt, Ronald, *Training in Community Relations: A Research Exploration toward New Group Skills,* Harper, New York, 1949.

Little, Malcolm, and George Breitman (eds.), *Malcolm X Speaks: Selected Speeches and Statements,* Grove Press, New York, 1966.

———, and Archie Epps (eds.), *The Speeches of Malcolm X at Harvard,* Morrow, New York, 1968.

————, and George Breitman (eds.), *By Any Means Necessary: Speeches, Interviews, and a Letter,* Pathfinder Press, New York, 1970.

Liu, William T., "The Community Reference System Religiosity, and Race Attitudes," *Social Forces,* 1961, **39**, 4, May, pp. 324–328.

Locke, Alain L, and Bernhard J. Stern, *When Peoples Meet: A Study in Race and Culture Contacts,* Committee on Workshops, Progressive Education Association, New York, 1942.

Locke, Hubert G., *The Care and Feeding of White Liberals: The American Tragedy and the Liberal Dilemma,* Newman Press, New York, 1970.

Lohman, Joseph D., and Dietrich C. Reitzes, "Note on Race Relations in Mass Society," *American Journal Sociology,* 1952, **58**, pp. 240–246.

Lomax, Louie E., *The Negro Revolt,* Harper, New York, 1962.

Loomis, Charles, P., and Julian Samora, "Prejudice and Religious Activity in Mexico and the United States," *Sociology Analyses,* 1965, **26**, 4, Winter, pp. 212–216.

Lopreato, Joseph, *Italian Americans,* Random House, New York, 1970.

Lotz, Philip H., *Distinguished American Jews,* Association Press, New York, 1945.

Lowinger, Paul, "Sex, Selma and Segregation: A Psychiatrist's Reaction," *International Journal of Social Psychiatry,* 1968, **14**, 2, Spring, pp. 119–124.

Loye, David, *The Healing of a Nation,* Norton, New York, 1971.

Lubell, Samuel, *White and Black: Test of a Nation,* 1st ed., Harper & Row, New York, 1964.

Lummis, Charles F., and Robert Easton (eds.), *Bullying the Moqui,* Prescott College Press, Prescott, Ariz., 1968.

Lyman, Stanford M., "The Race Relations Cycle of Robert E. Park," *Pacific Sociological Review,* 1968, **11**, 1, Spring, pp. 16–22.

McCandless, B. R., and H. D. Holloway, "Race Prejudice and Intolerance of Ambiguity in Children," *Journal of Abnormal Social Psychology,* 1955, **51**.

MacCrone, Ian Douglas, *Race Attitudes in South Africa: Historical Experimental, and Psychological Studies,* Witwatersrand University Press, Johannesburg, 1957.

McDaniel, Paul A., and Nicholas Babchuk, "Negro Conceptions of White People in a Northeastern City," *Phylon,* 1960, **21**, 1, Spring, pp. 7–19.

McDill, E. L., "Anomie, Authoritarianism, Prejudice, and Socioeconomic Status: An Attempt at Clarification," *Social Forces,* 1961, **39,** pp. 239–245.

McGill, Ralph Emerson, *The South and the Southerner,* Little, Brown, Boston, 1963.

MacIver, Robert M., *The More Perfect Union: A Program for the Control of Intergroup Discrimination in the United States,* Macmillan, New York, 1948.

McKee, James B., "Community Power and Strategies in Race Relations: Some Critical Observations," *Social Problems,* 1958, **59,** 6, 3, Winter, pp. 195–203.

McLean, H. V., "Psychodynamic Factors in Racial Relations," *Annals of American Academy of Political and Social Science,* 1946, **244.**

McNeil, Elaine O., "Dynamics of Negro-White Relations in the South, *Kansas Journal of Sociology,* 1964, **1,** 1, Winter, pp. 36–41.

Mack, Raymond W., "Desegregation and the Frustrated White Rats," *New Society,* 1963, **1,** 37, June 13, pp. 6–8.

———, *Race, Class, and Power,* American Book, New York, 1963.

———, *Race, Class, and Power,* 2nd ed., Van Nostrand Reinhold, New York, 1968.

———, "Riot, Revolt, or Responsible Revolution: Or Reference Groups and Racism," *Sociological Quarterly,* 1969, **10,** 2, Spring, pp. 147–156.

——— (ed.), *Prejudice and Race Relations,* Quadrangle, Chicago, 1970.

MacRae, D. C., "Race and Sociology in History and Theory," in P. Mason (ed.), *Man, Race, and Darwin,* Oxford University Press, London, 1960.

McWilliams, Carey, *Prejudice: Japanese-Americans: Symbol of Racial Intolerance,* Little, Brown, Boston, 1944.

Madsen, William, *Mexican-Americans of South Texas,* Holt, New York, 1966.

Maldonado-Denis, Manuel, "The Puerto Ricans: Protest or Submission?" *Annals of the American Academy of Political and Social Science,* 1969, **382,** March, pp. 26–31.

Manchester, A. K., *British Preeminence in Brazil, Its Rise and Decline: A Study in European Expansion,* University of North Carolina Press, Chapel Hill, 1933.

Manheim, Henry L., "Intergroup Interaction as Related to Status and Leadership Differences between Groups," *Sociometry,* 1960, **23,** 4, December, pp. 415–427.

Manners, Ande, *Poor Cousins,* Coward-McCann & Geoghegan, New York, 1972.

Mannix, Daniel Pratt, *Black Cargoes: A History of the Atlantic Slave Trade, 1518–1865,* Viking, New York, 1962.

Manypenny, George Washington, *Our Indian Wards,* R. Clarke and Co., Cincinnati, 1880.

Marchionne, A. M., and F. L. Marcuse, "Sensitization and Prejudice," *Journal of Abnormal Social Psychology,* 1955, **51,** 3, November, pp. 637–640.

Marcus, Jacob Rader, *Memoirs of American Jews, 1775–1865,* Jewish Publication Society of America, Philadelphia, 1955.

———, *Studies in American Jewish History: Studies and Addresses,* Hebrew Union College Press, Cincinnati, 1969.

———, *The Colonial American Jew, 1492–1776,* Wayne State University Press, Detroit, 1970.

Marrow, Alfred Jay, *Living without Hate: Scientific Approaches to Human Relations,* 1st ed., Harper, New York, 1951.

Martin, John Bartlow, *The Deep South Says "Never,"* Ballantine Books, New York, 1957.

Martin, James G., "Group Discrimination in Organizational Membership Selection," *Phylon,* 1959, **20,** 2, Summer, pp. 186–192.

———, "Intergroup Tolerance-Prejudice," *Journal of Human Relations,* 1962, **10,** 2, and 3, Winter and Spring, pp. 197–204.

Marvin, Francis S. (ed.), *Western Races and the World,* Books for Libraries Press, New York, 1968.

Mason, Philip, "An Approach to Race Relations," *Race,* 1959, **1,** 1, November, pp. 41–52.

———, *Prospero's Magic: Some Thoughts on Class and Race,* Oxford University Press, New York, 1962.

———, "Race, Intelligence and Professor Jensen," *Race Today,* July, 1969, pp. 76–77.

———, *Patterns of Dominance,* Oxford University Press, New York, 1970.

———, *Race Relations,* Oxford University Press, New York, 1970.

Masotti, Louis H., John R. Krause, Jr., and Sheldon R. Gawiser, *Race and Representation in Detroit and the Six County Metropolitan Region,* Metropolitan Fund, Detroit, 1968.

———, et al.: *A Time to Burn?* Rand McNally, Chicago, 1969.

Masuoka, Jitsuichi, "Conflicting Role Obligations and Role Types: With Special Reference to Race Relations," *Japanese Sociological Review,* 1960, **11,** 1, July, pp. 76–108.

———, and Preston Valien (eds.), *Race Relations: Problems and Theory: Essays in Honor of Robert E. Park,* University of North Carolina Press, Chapel Hill, 1961.

Matthews, Donald R., and James W. Prothro, "Southern Racial Attitudes: Conflict, Awareness, and Political Change," *American Academy of Political and Social Science,* 1962, **344,** November, pp. 108–121.

Maunier, Rene, and E. O. Lorimer (ed. and trans.), *The Sociology of Colonies,* Routledge, London, 1949.

Mead, Margaret, "The Student of Race Problems Can Say . . . ," *Race,* 1961, **3,** 1, November, pp. 3–9.

———, *Science and the Concept of Race,* Columbia University Press, New York, 1968.

———, and James Baldwin, *A Rap on Race,* Lippincott, Philadelphia, 1971.

Mecklin, J. M., *Democracy and Race Friction: A Study in Social Ethics,* Macmillan, New York, 1914.

Melden, Charles Manly, *From Slave to Citizen,* Methodist Book Concern, New York, 1921.

Mercer, Charles V., "Interrelations among Family Stability, Family Composition, Residence, and Race," *Journal of Marriage and the Family,* 1967, **29,** 3, August, pp. 456–460.

Messner, Gerald, *Another View: To Be Black in America,* Harcourt Brace Jovanovich, New York, 1970.

Middleton, Russell, and John Moland, "Humor in Negro and White Subcultures: A Study of Jokes among University Students," *American Sociological Review,* 1959, **24,** 1, February, pp. 61–69.

———, "Negro and White Reactions to Racism," *Sociometry,* 1959, **22,** 2, June, pp. 175–183.

Miller, Herbert A., *Races, Nations and Classes: The Psychology of Domination and Freedom,* Lippincott, Philadelphia, 1924.

Miller, Kelly, *Race Adjustment: Essays on the Negro in America,* Neale, New York, 1908.

———, *Out of the House of Bondage,* Arno, New York, 1969.

Miller, Roger R. (ed.), *Race, Research, and Reason: Social Work Perspectives: Report,* National Association of Social Workers, New York, 1969.

Minard, Ralph D., "Race Relationships in the Pocahontas Coal Field," *Journal of Social Issues,* 1952, **8,** pp. 29–44.

Mitchell, Glenford E., and William H. Peace (eds.), *The Angry Black South,* Corinth Books, New York, 1962.

Mitchell, J. (ed.), *Race Riots in Black and White,* Prentice-Hall, Englewood Cliffs, N.J., 1970.

Mittlebeeler, Emmet V., "Race and Jury in South Africa," *Howard Law Journal,* 1968, **14,** 1, Winter, pp. 90–104.

Miyamoto, S. Frank, "The Process of Intergroup Tension and Conflict," in E. W. Burgess and D. J. Bogue (eds.), *Contributions to Urban Sociology,* University of Chicago Press, Chicago, 1964, pp. 389–403.

Mkele, Nimrod, "The Effects of Apartheid," *New Society,* 1963, **2,** 46, August, pp. 6–7.

Mohr, Walter H., *Federal Indian Relations, 1774–1788,* University of Pennsylvania Press, Philadelphia, 1933.

Molotch, Harvey, "Racial Integration in a Transition Community," *American Sociological Review,* 1969, **34,** 4, December, pp. 878–893.

Monahan, Thomas P., "Interracial Marriage and Divorce in the State of Hawaii," *Eugenics Quarterly,* 1966, **13,** pp. 40–47.

Montagu, Ashley, "The Concept of Race," *American Anthropology,* 1962, **64,** 5, 1, October, pp. 919–928.

———, *Man's Most Dangerous Myth: The Fallacy of Race,* 4th ed., Cleveland World Publishing, Cleveland, 1964.

——— (ed.), *The Concept of Race,* Free Press of Glencoe, New York, 1964.

Moon, Bucklin, *The High Cost of Prejudice,* Messner, New York, 1947.

Moore, J. W., "Racial Recognition by Nursery School Children in Lynchburg, Virginia," *Social Forces,* 1958, **37,** 2, December, pp. 133–137.

———, *Mexican-Americans,* Prentice-Hall, Englewood Cliffs, N. J., 1970.

Morland, Kenneth J., "Racial Acceptance and Preference of Nursery School Children in a Southern City," *Merrill-Palmer Quarterly,* 1962, **8,** 4, October, pp. 271–280.

———, "The Development of Racial Bias in Young Children," *Theory into Practice,* 1963, **2,** 3, June, pp. 120–127.

———, "Racial Self-Identification: A Study of Nursery School Children," *American Catholic Sociological Review,* 1963, **24,** 3, Fall, pp. 231–242.

———, "A Comparison of Race Awareness in Northern and Southern Children," *American Journal of Orthopsychiatry,* 1966, **36,** January, pp. 22–21.

———, and John E. Williams, "Cross-Cultural Measurement of Racial and Ethnic Attitudes by the Semantic Differential," *Social Forces,* 1969, **69,** 1, September, pp. 107–112.

Morner, Magnus (ed.), *Race and Class in Latin America,* Columbia University Press, New York, 1970.

Morris, Willie (ed.), *The South Today: 100 Years after Appomattox,* Harper & Row, New York, 1965.

Morse, Jedidiah, *A Report to the Secretary of War of the United States on Indian Affairs*, S. Converse, New Haven, Conn., 1822.

Morsell, John A., "Schools, Courts, and the Negro's Future," *Harvard Educational Review*, 1960, **30**, 3, Summer, pp. 179–194.

Moss, James Allen, "Currents of Change in American Race Relations," *British Journal of Sociology*, 1960, **11**, 3, September, pp. 232–243.

Moton, Robert Russa, *What the Negro Thinks*, Doubleday, Doran, Garden City, N.Y., 1929.

Muir, Donal E., and Donald McGlamery, "The Evolution of Desegregation Attitudes of Southern University Students," *Phylon*, 1968, **29**, 2, Summer, pp. 105–118.

Murphy, Edgar G., *The Basis of Ascendancy*, Longmans, New York, 1909.

Murphy, Raymond J., and Howard Elinson (eds.), *Problems and Prospects of the Negro Movement*, Wadsworth, Belmont, Calif., 1966.

Murray, Pauli (ed.), *State's Laws on Race and Color*, Board of Missions and Church Extension, Methodist Church, Cincinnati, 1950.

Musmanno, Michael Angelo, *The Story of the Italians in America*, 1st ed., Doubleday, Garden City, N.Y., 1965.

Myer, Dillon S., *Uprooted Americans: The Japanese Americans and the War Relocation Authority during World War II*, University of Arizona Press, Tucson, 1971.

Myrdal, Gunnar, *An American Dilemma: The Negro Problem and Modern Democracy*, Harper, New York, 1944.

Nam, Charles B., and Mary G. Powers, "Variations in Socioeconomic Structure by Race, Residence, and the Life Cycle," *American Sociological Review*, 1965, **30**, pp. 907–1102.

Nammack, Georgiana C., *Fraud, Politics, and the Dispossession of the Indians: The Iroquois Land Frontier in the Colonial Period*, University of Oklahoma Press, Norman, 1969.

Nash, Gary B., and Richard Weiss (eds.), *The Great Fear: Race in the Mind of America*, Holt, New York, 1970.

Nearing, Scott, *Black America*, Vanguard, New York, 1929.

Nelson, Harold A., "On Liberals and the Current Racial Situation," *Phylon*, 1964, **25**, 4, Winter, pp. 389–398.

Newby, Idus A., *Jim Crow's Defense: Anti-Negro Thought in America, 1900–1930*, Louisiana State University Press, Baton Rouge, 1965.

———, *Challenge to the Court: Social Scientists and the Defense of Segregation, 1954–1966*, Louisiana State University Press, Baton Rouge, 1967.

Nicholls, William Hord, *Southern Tradition and Regional Progress*, University of North Carolina Press, Chapel Hill, 1960.

Noel, Donald L., and Alphonso Pinkney, "Correlates of Prejudice: Some Racial Differences and Similarities," *American Journal of Sociology*, 1964, **69**, 6, May, pp. 609–622.

Noel, S. L., "A Theory of the Origin of Ethnic Stratification," *Social Problems*, 1968, **16**, pp. 157–172.

Nolen, Claude H., *The Negro's Image in the South: The Anatomy of White Supremacy*, University of Kentucky Press, Lexington, 1967.

Norris, Hoke (ed.), *We Dissent*, St. Martin's Press, New York, 1962.

Northwood, L. K., "The Threat and Potential of Urban Renewal: A 'Workable Program' for Better Race Relations," *Journal of Intergroup Relations*, 1961, **2**, 2, Spring, pp. 101–114.

Odum, Howard W., *Race and Rumors of Race: Challenge to American Crisis*, University of North Carolina Press, Chapel Hill, 1943.

Orbell, John, and Eugene K. Sherrill, "Racial Attitudes and the Social Context," *Public Opinion Quarterly*, 1969, **33**, 1, Spring, pp. 46–54.

Orleans, Peter, and William Russell Ellis (eds.), *Race, Change, and Urban Society*, Sage Publications, Beverly Hills, Calif., 1971.

Osofsky, Gilbert, *Harlem: The Making of a Ghetto: Negro New York, 1890–1930*, Harper & Row, New York, 1966.

———, *The Burden of Race: A Documentary History of Negro-White Relations in America*, 1st ed., Harper & Row, New York, 1967.

———, "The Enduring Ghetto," *Journal of American History*, 1968, **55**, 2, September, pp. 243–255.

Page, Thomas Nelson, *The Negro: The Southerner's Problem*, Scribner, New York, 1904.

Palmer, A. W., *The Human Side of Hawaii: Race Problems in the Mid-Pacific*, Pilgrim, Boston, 1924.

Paredes, Americo, "Texas' Third Man: The Texas-Mexican," *Race*, 1963, **4**, 2, May, pp. 49–58.

Park, Robert Ezra, *Race and Culture*, Free Press, Glencoe, Ill., 1950.

Parker, Thomas V., *The Cherokee Indians*, Grafton Press, New York, 1907.

Parkman, Margaret A., and Jack Sawyer, "Dimensions of Ethnic Intermarriage in Hawaii," *American Sociological Review*, 1966, **32**, pp. 593–607.

Parsons, T., *The Social System*, Free Press, Glencoe, Ill., 1951.

Pastalan, Leon A., "An Experiment in Structured Assimilation," *Phylon*, 1964, **25**, 4, Winter, pp. 331–336.

Peake, Ora Brooks, *A History of the United States Indian Factory System, 1795–1822*, Sage Books, Denver, Colo., 1954.

Pease, Jane H., and William H. Pease, "Black Power: The Debate in 1840," *Phylon*, 1968, **29**, 1, Spring, pp. 19–26.

Peithmann, Irvin M., *Broken Peace Pipes: A Four-Hundred-Year History of the American Indian,* Charles C Thomas, Springfield, Ill., 1964.

Penalosa, Fernando, "The Changing Mexican-American in Southern California," *Sociology and Social Research,* 1967, **51,** 4, July, pp. 405–417.

Peters, William, *The Southern Temper,* Doubleday, Garden City, N.Y., 1959.

Petersen, William, "The Classification of Subnations in Hawaii: An Essay in the Sociology of Knowledge," *American Sociological Review,* 1969, **34,** 6, December, pp. 863–877.

———, *Japanese-Americans: Oppression and Success,* Random House, New York, 1971.

Pettigrew, Thomas F., "Personality and Sociocultural Factors in Intergroup Attitudes: A Cross-National Comparison," *Journal of Conflict Resolution,* 1958, **2,** 1, March, pp. 29–42.

———, "Regional Differences in Anti-Negro Prejudice," *Journal of Abnormal Social Psychology,* 1959, **59,** 1, July, pp. 28–36.

———, "Social Psychology and Desegregation Research," *American Psychology,* 1961, **16,** 3, March, pp. 105–112.

———, *A Profile of the Negro American,* Van Nostrand, Princeton, N.J., 1964.

———, *Racially Separate or Together?* McGraw-Hill, New York, 1971.

Pickett, William Passmore, *The Negro Problem: Abraham Lincoln's Solution,* Putnam, New York, 1909.

Piedmont, Eugene B., "Changing Racial Attitudes at a Southern University: 1947–1964," *Journal of Negro Education,* 1967, **36,** 1, Winter, pp. 32–41.

Pierson, Donald, *Negroes in Brazil,* Southern Illinois University Press, Carbondale, 1942.

Pinkney, Alphonso, "The Quantitative Factor in Prejudice," *Sociology and Social Research,* 1963, **47,** 2, January, pp. 161–168.

———, *Black Americans,* Prentice-Hall, Englewood Cliffs, N.J., 1969.

Pisani, Lawrence Frank, *The Italian in America: A Social Study and History,* 1st ed., Exposition Press, New York, 1957.

Pitt, Leonard, *The Decline of the Californios: A Social History of the Spanish-speaking Californians, 1846–1890,* University of California Press, Berkeley, 1966.

Pittard, Eugene, *Race and History: An Ethnological Introduction to History,* Knopf, New York, 1926.

Pollard, William Robert, *Black Literature,* North Carolina State University, Raleigh, 1969.

Pope, Liston, *The Kingdom beyond Caste,* Friendship Press, New York, 1957.

Powdermaker, Hortense, *Probing Our Prejudices: A Unit for High School Students,* Harper, New York 1944.

Pound, Merritt B., *Benjamin Hawkins, Indian Agent,* University of Georgia Press, Athens, 1951.

Powledge, Fred, *Black Power—White Resistance Notes on the New Civil War,* World Publishing, New York, 1967.

Prager, J., "White Racial Privilege and Social Change: An Examination of Theories of Racism," *Berkeley Journal of Sociology,* 1972-73, **17**, pp. 117–150.

Prado, C., *The Colonial Background of Modern Brazil,* University of California Press, Berkeley, 1967.

Priest, Loring B., *Uncle Sam's Stepchildren: The Reformation of United States Indian Policy, 1865–1887,* Rutgers University Press, New Brunswick, N.J., 1942.

Prucha, Francis P., *American Indian Policy in the Formative Years: The Indian Trade and Intercourse Acts, 1780–1834,* Harvard University Press, Cambridge, Mass., 1962.

Quint, Howard H., *Profile in Black and White: A Frank Portrait of South Carolina,* Public Affairs Press, Washington, D.C., 1958.

Raab, Earl (ed.), *American Race Relations Today,* Doubleday, Garden City, N.Y., 1962.

———, and S. M. Lipset, "The Prejudiced Society," in E. Raab, *American Race Relations,* Doubleday, Garden City, N.Y., 1962.

Rasmussen, Karl R., "The Multi-Ordered Urban Area: A Ghetto," *Phylon,* 1968, **29**, 3, Fall, pp. 282–290.

Record, Wilson, "Changing Patterns of Internal Differentiation among Negroes in the United States," *Sociologus,* 1959, **9**, 2, pp. 115–131.

———, *Race and Radicalism: The NAACP and the Communist Party in Conflict,* Cornell University Press, New York, 1964.

Redding, Jay S., *The Lonesome Road,* Doubleday, Garden City, N.Y., 1958.

Redkey, Edwin S., *Black Exodus: Black Nationalist and Back-to-Africa Movements, 1890–1910,* Yale University Press, New Haven, Conn., 1969.

Reid, Ira De Augustine, *The Negro Immigrant, His Background, Characteristics, and Social Adjustment, 1899–1937,* Columbia University Press, New York, 1939.

Reitzes, Dietrich C., "Institutional Structure and Race Relations," *Phylon,* 1959, **20**, 1, Spring, pp. 48–66.

————, "Behavior in Urban Race Contacts," in E. W. Burgess and D. J. Bogue, *Contributions to Urban Sociology,* University of Chicago Press, Chicago, 1964, pp. 471–486.

Rentoul, Robert R., *Race Culture or Race Suicide? A Plea for the Unborn,* Walter Scott, New York, 1906.

Reuter, Edward B., *The Mulatto in the United States,* Badger, Boston, 1918.

————, *The American Race Problem: A Study of the Negro,* Thomas Y. Crowell, New York, 1927.

————(ed.), *Race and Culture Contacts,* McGraw-Hill, New York, 1934.

————, *The American Race Problem,* 3d ed., Thomas Y. Crowell, New York, 1970.

Rex, John, and Robert Moore, *Race, Community and Conflict: A Study of Sparkbrook,* Oxford University Press, New York, 1967.

————, "Race as a Social Category," *Journal of Biosocial Science,* 1969, Supplement, 1, July, pp. 145–152.

————, *Race Relations in Sociological Theory,* Schocken Books, New York, 1970.

Rhyne, Edwin Hoffman, "Racial Prejudice and Personality Scales: An Alternative Approach," *Social Forces,* 1962, **41**, 1, October, pp. 44–53.

Richardson, R. N., *The Comanche Barrier to South Plains Settlement: A Century and a Half of Savage Resistance to the Advancing White Frontier,* Clark, Glendale, Calif., 1933.

Richmond, Anthony H., "Immigration as a Social Process: The Case of Colored Colonials in the United Kingdom," *Social and Economic Studies,* 1956, **5**, 1, pp. 185–201.

————, "Teaching Race Questions," *Phylon,* 1956, **17**, 3, October, pp. 239–249.

————, "Sociological and Psychological Explanations of Racial Prejudice: Some Light on the Controversy from Recent Researchers in Britain," *Pacific Sociological Review,* 1962, **4**, 2, Fall.

Riesman, D., N. Glazer, et al., *The Lonely Crowd,* Yale University Press, New Haven, Conn., 1950.

Riley, Benjamin F., *The White Man's Burden,* B. F. Riley, Birmingham, Ala., 1910.

Rinder, I. D., "Minority Orientations: An Approach to Intergroup Relations Theory through Social Psychology," *Phylon,* 1965, **26**, pp. 5–17.

Ringer, Benjamin B., *The Edge of Friendliness: A Study of Jewish-Gentile Relations,* Basic Books, New York, 1967.

Rodrigues, J. H., *Brazil and Africa,* University of California Press, Berkeley, 1965.

——, *The Brazilians: Their Character and Aspirations,* University of Texas Press, Austin, 1967.

Rogler, Lloyd H., "The Growth of an Action Group: The Case of a Puerto Rican Migrant Voluntary Association," *International Journal of Comparative Sociology,* 1968, **9,** 3–4, September–December, pp. 223–234.

Rolle, Andrew F., *The Immigrant Upraised: Italian Adventures and Colonists in an Expanding America,* 1st ed., University of Oklahoma Press, Norman, 1968.

Rose, Arnold M., and Caroline Rose, *America Divided: Minority Group Relations in the United States,* 1st ed., Knopf, New York, 1948.

——, *The Negro in America,* Harper, New York, 1948.

—— (ed.), *Race Prejudice and Discrimination: Readings in Intergroup Relations in the United States,* Knopf, New York, 1951.

——, "Inconsistencies in Attitudes toward Negro Housing," *Social Problems,* 1961, **8,** 4, Spring, pp. 286–292.

—— (ed.), *Assuring Freedom to the Free: A Century of Emancipation in the USA,* Wayne State University Press, Detroit, 1964.

Rose, Peter I., *They and We,* Random House, New York, 1964.

——, "Outsiders in Britain," *Trans-Action,* 1967, **4,** 4, March, pp. 18–23.

——, *The Subject is Race: Traditional Ideologies and the Teaching of Race Relations,* Oxford University Press, New York, 1968.

Rosenau, James N., *Race in International Politics: A Dialogue in Five Parts,* University of Denver Press, Denver, Colo., 1970.

Rosenberg, Alfred, *Race and Race History and Other Essays,* Harper & Row, New York, 1970.

Rosenthal, Gilbert S. (ed.), *The Jewish Family in a Changing World,* Yoseloff, New York, 1970.

Roucek, Joseph S., "The Sociological Aspects of the Progress of Integration of American Minorities," *Sociological International,* 1964, **2,** 2, pp. 143–156.

Rothman, Jack, *Minority Group Identification and Intergroup Relations: An Examination of Kurt Lewin's Theory of Jewish Group Identity,* Research Institute for Group Work in Jewish Agencies, New York, 1965.

Rowan, Carl T., *South of Freedom,* 1st ed., Knopf, New York, 1952.

——, *The Pitiful and the Proud,* Random House, New York, 1956.

Royce, Josiah, *Race Questions, Provincialism, and Other American Problems,* Books for Libraries Press, Freeport, N.Y., 1967.

Rubano, J., *Culture and Behavior in Hawaii: An Annotated Bibliography,* University of Hawaii, Social Science Research Institute, Honolulu, 1971.

Rubin, Irwin M., "Increased Self-Acceptance: A Means of Reducing Prejudice," *Journal of Personality and Social Psychology,* 1967, **5,** 2, February, pp. 233–238.

Ruchames, Louis, *Race, Jobs and Politics: The Story of FEPC,* Columbia University Press, New York, 1953.

Rudwick, Elliott M., *Race Riot at East St. Louis, July 2, 1917,* Southern Illinois University Press, Carbondale, 1964.

Russell-Wood, A. J. R., "Race and Class in Brazil 1937–1967: A Re-Assessment: A Review," *Race,* 1963, **10,** 2, October, pp. 185–192.

Ryan, W., *Blaming the Victim,* Pantheon, New York, 1971.

Sachs, Wulf, *Black Anger,* Greenwood Press, New York, 1947.

Safa, Helen I., "The Case for Negro Separatism: The Crisis of Identity in the Black Community," *Urban Affairs Quarterly,* 1968, **4,** 1, September, pp. 45–64.

Saldaha, P. H., "Race Mixture among Northeastern Brazilian Populations," *American Anthropology,* 1962, **64,** 4, August, pp. 751–759.

St. John, Robert, *Jews, Justice, and Judaism,* Doubleday, Garden City, N.Y., 1969.

Salzano, Francisco M., "Race Mixture," *International Social Science Journal,* 1965, **17,** pp. 135–138.

Saunders, Lyle, *A Guide to Materials Bearing on Cultural Relations in New Mexico,* University of New Mexico Press, Albuquerque, 1944.

Scanzoni, John H., *The Black Family in Modern Society,* Allyn and Bacon, Boston, 1971.

Schappes, Morris U., *A Documentary History of the Jews in the United States, 1654–1875,* 3rd ed., Schocken Books, New York, 1971.

Schatz, Walter (ed.), *Directory of Afro-American Resources,* Bowker, New York, 1970.

Schermerhorn, Richard A., "Minorities: European and American," *Phylon,* 1959, **20,** 2, Summer, pp. 178–185.

———, "Toward a General Theory of Minority Groups," *Phylon,* 1964, **25,** pp. 238–246.

———, *Comparative Ethnic Relations: A Framework for Theory and Research,* Random House, New York, 1970.

Schmeckebier, Laurence F., *The Office of Indian Affairs: Its History, Activities and Organization,* Johns Hopkins, Baltimore, 1927.

Schmid, Calvin F., and Charles E. Nobble, "Socioeconomic Differentials among Nonwhite Races," *American Sociological Review,* 1965, **30,** 6, December, pp. 909–922.

Schmitt, Robert C., *Demographic Statistics of Hawaii: 1776–1965,* University of Hawaii Press, Honolulu, 1968.

Schnieder, Louis, and Arthur J. Brodbeck, "Some Notes on Moral Paradoxes in Race Relations," *Phylon,* 1955, **16,** 2, June, pp. 149–158.

———, "Race, Reason, and Rubbish Again," *Phylon,* 1962, **23,** 2, Summer, pp. 149–155.

Schonfield, Jacob, "Differences in Smoking, Drinking, and Social Behavior by Race and Delinquency Status in Adolescent Males," *Adolescence,* 1966–67, **1,** 4, Winter, pp. 367–380.

Schrieke, Bertram J., *Alien Americans: A Study of Race Relations,* Viking, New York, 1936.

Schrag, Peter, *The Decline of the WASP,* Simon and Schuster, New York, 1971.

Schuchter, Arnold, *Reparations: The Black Manisfesto and Its Challenge to White America,* Lippincott, Philadelphia, 1970.

Schuman, Howard, and John Harding, "Prejudice and the Norm of Rationality," *Sociometry,* 1964, **27,** 3, September, pp. 353–371.

Scott, Benjamin, *The Coming of the Black Man,* Beacon Press, Boston, 1969.

Seabrook, Issac DuBose, *Before and After: The Relations of the Races at the South,* Louisiana State University Press, Baton Rouge, 1967.

Searles, Ruth, and J. Allen Williams, "Negro College Students' Participation in Sit-ins," *Social Forces,* 1962, **40,** 3, March, pp. 215–220.

Segal, Bernard E., "Contact, Compliance, and Distance among Jewish and Non-Jewish Undergraduates," *Social Problems,* 1965, **13,** 1, Summer, pp. 66–74.

——— (ed.), *Racial and Ethnic Relations: Selected Readings,* Thomas Y. Crowell, New York, 1966.

Segal, David R., "Status Inconsistency, Cross Pressures, and American Political Behavior," *American Sociological Review,* 1969, **34,** 3, June, pp. 352–385.

Segal, Ronald, *The Race War,* Viking, New York, 1967.

Seligmann, Herbert J., *The Negro Faces America,* Harper, New York, 1920.

Selznick, G. J., and S. Steinberg, *The Tenacity of Prejudice: Anti-Semitism in Contemporary America,* Harper & Row, New York, 1969.

Senior, Clarence O., *The Puerto Ricans: Strangers—Then Neighbors,* Quadrangle, Chicago, 1965.

Service, Elman R., "Indian-European Relations in Colonial Latin America," *American Anthropology,* 1955, **57**, 3, June, pp. 411–425.

Shannon, Alexander H., *Racial Integrity and Other Features of the Negro Problem,* Publishing House of the M. E. Church, Nashville, Tenn., 1907.

———, *The Racial Integrity of the American Negro,* Parthenon Press, Nashville, Tenn., 1951.

Shapiro, Theresa R., *Black Construction Contractors in New Orleans,* Division of Business and Economic Research, Louisiana State University, New Orleans, 1970.

Shepherd, George W., *Racial Influences on American Foreign Policy,* Basic Books, New York, 1970.

———, Tilden J. LeMelle, et al. (eds.), *Race among Nations: A Conceptual Approach,* Lexington Books, Lexington, Mass., 1970.

Sherman, Charles B., *The Jew within American Society: A Study in Ethnic Individuality,* Wayne State University Press, Detroit, 1961.

Sherwin-White, Adrian N., *Racial Prejudice in Imperial Rome,* Cambridge University Press, London, 1967.

Shibutani, T., and K. M. Kwan, *Ethnic Stratification,* Macmillan, New York, 1965.

Shogan, Robert, and Tom Craig, *The Detroit Race Riot: A Study in Violence,* Chilton, Philadelphia, 1964.

Siegel, Paul M., "On the Cost of Being a Negro," *Sociological Inquiry,* 1965, **35**, 1, April, pp. 41–57.

Silberman, Charles E., *Crisis in Black and White,* Random House, New York, 1964.

Silberman, Leo, and Betty Spice, *Colour and Class in Six Liverpool Schools,* University Press of Liverpool, Liverpool, 1950.

Silverman, Corinne, *The Little Rock Story,* University of Alabama Press, University, 1958.

Silverman, Sondra (ed.), *The Black Revolt and Democratic Politics,* Heath, Lexington, Mass., 1970.

Simonhoff, Harry, *Jewish Notables in America, 1776–1865: Links of an Endless Chain,* Greenberg, New York, 1956.

Simpich, F., *Anatomy of Hawaii,* Coward, McCann & Geohegan, New York, 1971.

Simpson, George E., and J. Milton Yinger, *Racial and Cultural Minorities: An Analysis of Prejudice and Discrimination,* 3rd ed., Harper & Row, New York, 1965.

Singer, Dorothy G., "Reading, Writing, and Race Relations," *Trans-Action,* 1967, **4**, 7, June, pp. 27–31.

Singer, L., "Ethnogenesis and Negro-Americans Today," *Social Research*, 1962, **29**, 4, Winter, pp. 419–432.

Skipper, James, W. J. Powhatan, and Robert C. Leonard, "Race, Status, and Interaction between Patients and Hospital Personnel," *Sociological Quarterly*, 1968, **9**, 1, Winter, pp. 35–46.

Sklare, Marshall, and Joseph Greenblum, *Jewish Identity on the Suburban Frontier: A Study of Group Survival in the Open Society*, Basic Books, New York, 1967.

————, *America's Jews*, Random House, New York, 1971.

Skolnick, J., *Politics of Protest*, Simon and Schuster, New York, 1969.

Slotkin, James S., *The Peyote Religion: A Study in Indian-White Relations*, Free Press, Glencoe, Ill., 1956.

Smith, Bradford, *Americans from Japan*, 1st ed., Lippincott, Philadelphia, 1948.

Smith, Carole R., Lev Williams, and Richard H. Willis, "Race, Sex, and Belief as Determinants of Friendship Acceptance," *Journal of Personality and Social Psychology*, 1967, **5**, 2, February, pp. 127–137.

Smith, Frank E., *Look Away from Dixie*, Louisiana State University Press, Baton Rouge, 1965.

Smith, T. L., *Brazil: People and Institutions*, Louisiana University Press, Baton Rouge, 1963.

Smith, William C., *Americans in Process: A Study of Our Citizens of Oriental Ancestry*, Edwards Brothers, Ann Arbor, Mich., 1937.

Smythe, H. H., and Myrna Siedman, "Name Calling: Significant Factor in Human Relations," *Human Relations*, 1958, **6**, 1, Autumn, pp. 71–77.

————, and L. Chase, "Current Research on the Negro: A Critique," *Sociology and Social Research*, 1958, **42**, 3, January–February, pp. 199–202.

Sone, Monica, *Nisei Daughter*, 1st ed., Little, Brown, Boston, 1953.

Soper, Edmund D., *Racism: A World Issue*, Abingdon-Cokesbury, New York, 1947.

Sorkin, Alan L., *American Indians and Federal Aid*, Brookings Institution, Washington, D.C., 1971.

Spear, Allan H., *Black Chicago: The Making of a Negro Ghetto, 1890–1920*, University of Chicago Press, Chicago, 1967.

Spero, Sterling D., and Abram L. Harris, *The Black Worker: A Study of the Negro and the Labor Movement*, Columbia University Press, New York, 1931.

Spilerman, S., "The Causes of Racial Disturbances: A Comparison of

Alternative Explanations," *American Sociological Review,* 1970, **35,** pp. 627–650.

———, "The Causes of Racial Disturbances: Tests of an Explanation," *American Sociological Review,* 1971, **36,** pp. 427–442.

Stalvey, Lois M., *The Education of a WASP,* Morrow, New York, 1970.

Staples, Robert, *The Black Family: Essays and Studies,* Wadsworth, Belmont, Calif., 1971.

Stearns, Charles, *The Black Man of the South, and the Rebels,* Kraus Reprint Company, New York, 1969.

Stein, David D., Jane Allyn Hardyck, and M. Brewster Smith, "Race and Belief: An Open and Shut Case," *Journal of Personality and Social Psychology,* 1965, **1,** 4, April, pp. 281–289.

Steiner, Jesse F., *The Japanese Invasion: A Study in the Psychology of Inter-racial Contacts,* A. C. McClurg, Chicago, 1917.

Steiner, Stanley, *The New Indians,* 1st ed., Harper & Row, New York, 1968.

Stemons, James S., *As Victim to Victims: An American Negro Laments with Jews,* Fortuny's, New York, 1941.

Sterling, Dorothy, and Donald Gross, *Tender Warriors,* Hill and Wang, New York, 1958.

Stinchcombe, Arthur L., Mary McDill, and W. Dollie, "Is There a Racial Tipping Point in Changing Schools?" *Journal of Social Issues,* 1969, **25,** 1, January, pp. 127–134.

Stocking, George W., *Race, Culture, and Evolution: Essays in the History of Anthropology,* Free Press, New York, 1968.

Stoddard, Theodore L., *The Rising Tide of Color Against White World-Supremacy,* Scribner, New York, 1920.

Stone, Alfred H., *Studies in the American Race Problem,* Doubleday, New York, 1908.

Stonequist, Everett V., "The Marginal Man: A Study in Personality and Culture Conflict," in E. W. Burges and D. J. Bogue, *Contributions to Urban Sociology,* University of Chicago Press, Chicago, 1964, pp. 327–345.

Strong, Donald S., *Organized Anti-Semitism in America: The Rise of Group Prejudice during the Decade 1930–40,* Council on Public Affairs, Washington, D.C., 1941.

Stroup, Atlee L., and Joseph Landis, "Change in Race-Prejudice Attitudes as Related to Changes in Authoritarianism and Conservatism in a College Population," *Southwestern Social Science Quarterly,* 1965, **46,** 3, December, pp. 255–263.

Stryker, Sheldon, "Social Structure and Prejudice," *Social Problems,* 1958–59, **6**, 4, Winter, pp. 340–354.

Tait, Joseph W., *Some Aspects of the Effect of the Dominant American Culture upon Children of Italian-Born Parents,* Columbia University Press, New York, 1942.

Tajfel, Henri, "Stereotypes," *Race,* 1963, **5**, 2, October, pp. 3–14.

———, and John L. Dawson (eds.), *Disappointed Guests: Essays by African, Asian, and West Indian Students,* Oxford University Press, New York, 1965.

Talmadge, Herman E., *You and Segregation,* Vulcan Press, Birmingham, Ala., 1955.

Tatum, Lawrie, *Our Red Brothers and the Peace Policy of President Ulysses S. Grant,* University of Nebraska Press, Lincoln, 1970.

Taueber, Karl E., "The Effects of Income Redistribution on Racial Residential Segregation," *Urban Affairs Quarterly,* 1963, **4**, 1, September, pp. 5–14.

Taylor, Thomas G., *Environment and Race: A Study of the Evolution Migration Settlement and Status of the Races of Man,* Oxford University Press, London, 1927.

Teller, Judd L., *Strangers and Natives,* Delacorte Press, New York, 1968.

Terry, Robert W., *For Whites Only,* Eerdmans, Grand Rapids, Iowa, 1970.

Theobald, Robert (ed.), *An Alternative Future for America: Essays and Speeches,* Swallow Press, Chicago, 1968.

Thompson, Edgar T., and Alma M. Thompson, *Race and Region,* University of North Carolina, Chapel Hill, 1949.

———, and Everett C. Hughes (eds.), *Race, Individual and Collective Behavior,* Free Press, Glencoe, Ill., 1958.

Thurow, Lester C., *Poverty and Discrimination,* Brookings, Washington, 1969.

Tillman, James A., "The Quest for Identity and Status: Facets of the Desegregation Process in the Upper Midwest," *Phylon,* 1961, **22**, 4, Winter, pp. 329–339.

Tilly, Charles, Wagner D. Jackson, and Barry Kay, *Race and Residence in Wilmington, Delaware,* Bureau of Publication, Teachers, Columbia University, New York, 1965.

Tomlinson, T. M., "The Development of a Riot Ideology among Urban Negroes," *American Behavior Scientist,* 1968, **11**, 4, March–April, pp. 27–31.

Tougee, Albion W., *An Appeal to Caesar,* Fords, Howard, and Hulbert, New York, 1884.

Towler, Judy E., *The Police Role in Racial Conflicts,* Charles C Thomas, Springfield, Ill., 1964.

Trevor, Jack C., *Race Crossing in Man: The Analysis of Metrical Characters,* Cambridge University Press, New York, 1953.

Triandis, C. Harry, and Leight Minturn Triandis, "Race, Social Class, Religion, and Nationality as Determinants of Social Distance," *Journal of Abnormal Social Psychology,* 1960, **61,** 1, July, pp. 110–118.

———, and Vasso Vassiliou, "Frequency of Contact and Stereotyping," *Journal of Personality and Social Psychology,* 1967, **7,** 3, November, pp. 316–328.

Tiryakian, Edward A., "Sociological Realism: Partition for South Africa?" *Social Forces,* 1976, **46,** 2, December, pp. 208–220.

Tuck, Ruth D., *Not with the First: Mexican-Americans in a Southwest City,* Harcourt, Brace, New York, 1946.

Tucker, Frank H., *The White Conscience,* Ungar, New York, 1969.

Tucker, Sterling, *Black Reflection on White Power,* Eerdmans, Grand Rapids, Iowa, 1969.

Tumin, Melvin M., (ed.), *Comparative Perspectives on Race Relations,* Little, Brown, Boston, 1969.

Turner, Katherine C., *Red Men Calling on the Great White Father,* University of Oklahoma Press, Norman, 1951.

Tuttle, William M., *Race Riot: Chicago in the Red Summer of 1919,* Atheneum, New York, 1970.

Tyler, Samuel L., *Indian Affairs: A Study of the Changes in Policy of the United States toward Indians,* Brigham Young University, Provo, Utah, 1964.

U.S. Congress, House, Committee on Indian Affairs, *Remove Indians Westward,* Gales and Seaton, Washington, D.C., 1829.

Van den Berghe, P. L., "Race Attitudes in Durban, South Africa," *Journal of Social Psychology,* 1962, **57,** p. 55–72.

———, "Dialectic and Functionalism: Toward a Theoretical Synthesis," *American Sociological Review,* 1963, pp. 695–705.

———, *South Africa: A Study in Conflict,* Wesleyan University Press, Middletown, Conn., 1965.

———, *Race and Racism: A Comparative Perspective,* Wiley, New York, 1967.

———, *Race and Ethnicity: Essays in Comparative Sociology,* Basic Books, New York, 1970.

Van den Haag, Ernest, *The Jewish Mystique,* Stein and Day, New York, 1969.

Van Der Slik, Jack R. (ed.), *Black Conflict with White America: A Reader in Social and Political Analysis,* Merrill, Columbus, Ohio, 1970.

Vander Zanden, James W., "Desegregation and Social Strains in the South," *Journal of Social Issues,* 1959, **15**, 4, pp. 53–60.

———, "Voting on Segregationist Referenda," *Public Opinion Quarterly,* 1961, **25**, 1, Spring, pp. 92–105.

———, "The Non-Violent Resistance Movement against Segregation," *American Journal of Sociology,* 1963, **68**, 5, March, pp. 544–559.

———, *American Minority Relations: The Sociology of Race and Ethnic Groups,* Ronald Press, New York, 1963.

———, *Race Relations in Transition: The Segregation Crisis in the South,* Random House, New York, 1965.

Van Elvery, Dale, *Disinherited: The Lost Birthright of the American Indian,* Morrow, New York, 1966.

Vincent, John J., *The Race Race,* S.C.M. Press, London, 1970.

Vivian, C. T., *Black Power and the American Myth,* Fortress Press, Philadelphia, 1970.

Wagerly, C. W., and M. Harris, "The Situation of the Negro in the United States, *International Social Science Bulletin,* 1957, **9**, 4, pp. 427–438.

Wagley, C., *An Introduction to Brazil,* Columbia University Press, New York, 1963.

———, *Race and Class in Rural Brazil,* Columbia University Press, New York, 1963.

Wainwright, David, *Race and Employment: Managing a Multi-racial Labour Force,* Institute of Personnel Management, London, 1970.

Walden, Daniel, "Race and Imperialism: The Achilles Heel of the Progressives," *Science and Society,* 1967, **31**, 2, Spring, p. 222–232.

Walker, H. J., "Changes in the Status of the Negro in American Society," *International Social Bulletin,* 1957, **9**, 4, pp. 438–474.

Washington, Joseph R., *Black and White Power Subreption,* Beacon Press, Boston, 1969.

———, *Marriage in Black and White,* Beacon Press, Boston, 1970.

Waskow, Arthur I., *Running Riot: A Journey through the Official Disasters and Creative Disorder in American Society,* Herder and Herder, New York, 1970.

Watson, Goodwin B., *Action for Unity,* Harper & Brothers, New York, 1947.

Watson, S. G. S., and H. Lampkin, "Race and Socioeconomic Status as Factors in the Friendship Choices of Pupils in a Racially Heterogeneous South African School," *Race,* 1968, **10,** 2, October, pp. 181–184.

Watts, Lewis G., "Social Integration and the Use of Minority Leadership in Seattle, Washington," *Phylon,* 1960, **21,** 2, pp. 136–143.

Wax, M. L., *Indian Americans: Unity and Diversity,* Prentice-Hall, Englewood Cliffs, N.J., 1971.

Wax, Rosalie H., and Robert K. T., "American Indians and White People," *Phylon,* 1961, **22,** 4, Winter, pp. 305–314.

Weatherford, Willis D., and Charles S. Johnson, *Race Relations: Adjustment of Whites and Negroes in the United States,* Heath, Boston, 1934.

Weaver, E. K., "Racial Sensitivity among Negro Children," *Phylon,* 1956, **17,** 1, March, pp. 52–60.

Weaver, Robert C., "The Changing Status of Racial Groups," *Journal of Intergroup Relations,* 1961, **2,** 1, Spring, pp. 6–17.

Weaver, S. P., *Hawaii, U.S.A.: A Unique National Heritage,* Pageant Press, New York, 1959.

Webster, Edgar H., *Chums and Brothers: An Interpretation of a Social Group of Our American Citizenry Who Are in the First and Last Analysis "Just Folks,"* R. C. Badger, Boston, 1920.

Weltner, Charles L., *Southerner,* Lippincott, Philadelphia, 1966.

Werner, Emmy E., Kenneth Simonian, and Ruth S. Smith, "Ethnic and Socioeconomic Status Differences in Abilities and Achievement Among Preschool Children in Hawaii," *Journal of Social Psychology,* **75,** 1968, pp. 43–59.

Westie, F. R., "Race and Ethnic Relations," in R. E. L. Faris (ed.), *Handbook of Modern Sociology,* Rand McNally, Chicago, 1964.

Weston, R. F., *Racism in U.S. Imperialism: The Influence of Racial Assumptions on American Foreign Policy, 1893–1946,* University of South Carolina Press, Columbia, 1972.

Weyl, Nathaniel, *The Creative Elite in America,* Public Affairs Press, Washington, D.C., 1966.

White, Walter F., *Rope and Faggot,* Arno, New York, 1969.

Whitman, Frederick L., "Subdimensions of Religiosity and Race Prejudice," *Review of Religious Research,* 1962, **3,** pp. 166–174.

Whyte, William F., *Street Corner Society: The Social Structure of an Italian Slum,* University of Chicago Press, Chicago, 1943.

Williams, John, *This is My Country Too,* New American Library, New York, 1965.

Williams, J. Allen, "Reduction of Tension through Intergroup Contact: A Social Psychological Interpretation," *Pacific Sociological Review,* 1964, **7,** 2, Fall, pp. 81–88.

Williams, John E., "Connotations of Racial Concepts and Color Names," *Journal of Personality and Social Psychology,* 1966, **2,** 6, May, pp. 531–540.

Williams, Robin M., *The Reduction of Intergroup Tensions: A Survey of Research on Problems of Ethnic, Racial, and Religious Group Relations,* Social Science Research Council, New York, 1947.

———, *Strangers Next Door: Ethnic Relations in American Communities,* Prentice-Hall, Englewood Cliffs, N.J., 1964.

———, "Social Change and Social Conflict: Race Relations in the United States, 1944–1964," *Sociological Inquiry,* 1965, **31,** 1, April, pp. 8–25.

Williamson, Robert C., "Race Relations in South Africa," *Sociology and Social Research,* 1955, **39,** 3, January–February, pp. 165–170.

———, "Crime in South Africa: Some Aspects of Causes and Treatment," *Journal of Crime and Law Criminology,* 1957, **48,** 2, July–August, pp. 185–192.

Wilson, Robert L., and James H. Davis, *The Church in the Racially Changing Community,* Abingdon, New York, 1966.

Wilson, Theodore B., *The Black Codes of the South,* University of Alabama Press, University, 1965.

Winter, Gibson, *Being Free: Reflections on America's Cultural Revolution,* Macmillan, New York, 1970.

Winter, Nathan, *Jewish Education in a Pluralist Society: Samson Benderly and Jewish Education in the United States,* New York University Press, New York, 1966.

Wirth, L., "The Problem of Minority Groups," in R. Linton (ed.), *The Science of Man in the World Crisis,* Columbia University Press, New York, 1945,

Wish, Harvey (ed.), *The Negro since Emancipation,* Prentice-Hall, Englewood Cliffs, N.J., 1964.

Wollenberg, Charles, *Ethnic Conflict in California History,* Tinnon-Brown, Los Angeles, 1970.

Wood, Forrest G., *Black Scare: The Racist Response to Emancipation and Reconstruction,* University of California Press, Berkeley, 1968.

Woofter, T. J., and Isaac Fisher (eds.), *Cooperation in Southern Communities: Suggested Activities for County and City Inter-racial Committees,* Commission on Inter-racial Cooperation, Atlanta, 1921.

———, *Races and Ethnic Groups in American Life,* McGraw-Hill, New York, 1933.

————, *Southern Race Progress: The Wavering Color Line,* Public Affairs Press, Washington, D.C., 1957.

Workman, William D., *The Case for the South,* Devin-Adair, New York, 1960.

Wright, Nathan, *Let's Work Together,* Hawthorn, New York, 1968.

Wynes, Charles E. (ed.), *Forgotten Voices: Dissenting Southerners in an Age of Conformity,* Louisiana State University Press, Baton Rouge, 1967.

Yaffe, James, *The American Jews,* Random House, New York, 1968.

Yarrow, Marian R., John D. Campbell, and Leon J. Yarrow, "Acquisition of New Norms: A Study of Racial Desegregation," *Journal of Social Issues,* 1958, **14,** 1, pp. 8–28.

Young, Donald R., *American Minority Peoples: A Study in Racial and Cultural Conflicts in the United States,* Harper & Brothers, New York, 1932.

Young, Richard P. (ed.), *Roots of Rebellion: The Evolution of Black Politics and Protest since World War II,* Harper & Row, New York, 1970.

Zetterberg, H. L., *On Theory and Verification in Sociology,* Bedminster Press, Toronto, Canada, 1965.

Name Index

Subject Index